ALLERTON PARK INSTITUTE

Number 27

Papers Presented at the Allerton Park Institute

Sponsored by

University of Illinois
Graduate School of Library and Information Science

held

November 15-18, 1981
Illini Union
Urbana, Illinois

Conserving and Preserving Library Materials

KATHRYN LUTHER HENDERSON
WILLIAM T HENDERSON

Editors

University of Illinois
Graduate School of Library and Information Science
Urbana-Champaign, Illinois

Library of Congress Cataloging in Publication Data

Main entry under title:

Conserving and preserving library materials.

"Papers presented at the Allerton Park Institute,
sponsored by University of Illinois, Graduate School of
Library and Information Science, held November 15-18,
1981, Illini Union, Urbana, Illinois."
    Includes index.
    1. Library materials—Conservation and restoration—
Congresses. 2. Books—Conservation and restoration—
Congresses. 3. Paper—Preservation—Congresses.
I. Henderson, Kathryn Luther. II. University of
Illinois at Urbana-Champaign. Graduate School of Library
and Information Science. IV. Allerton Park Institute
(27th : 1981 : Urbana, Ill.)
Z701.C587 1983   025.8'4   83-3537
    ISBN 0-87845-067-X

CONTENTS

Introduction

One of the chief concerns in library administration and operations for the 1980s is the conservation and preservation of library materials, an area, which for too long, has been neglected. Faced with rapid deterioration of collections from the ravages of time plus increased widespread use and transportation of materials through networking operations coupled with the rising cost of materials, supplies and staff and other problems associated with inflation, librarians and archivists are finding it increasingly difficult to preserve their collections.

A dozen years have passed since a landmark conference at the University of Chicago Graduate Library School brought to the profession's attention the serious problems of deterioration and opened up for the decade of the seventies many solutions which are now being implemented. In choosing the topic for the annual Allerton Park Institute, the faculty of the Graduate School of Library and Information Science at the University of Illinois at Urbana-Champaign thought it appropriate, at this time, to assess the state-of-the-art and to help set the objectives for the 1980s in conserving and preserving library and archival materials. Specifically the objectives of the conference were to make it possible for those in attendance to: note the scope of preservation problems; discover the philosophy of preservation and conservation of library materials; learn new methods and techniques in the field; identify new research needs; discover cooperative approaches and programs; receive current information on developments in paper manufacturing, deacidification, etc.; gather information on preservation of nonpaper materials such as film, recordings, computer records etc.; learn how and when to use the services of binders, restoration specialists and others outside the local library; learn how restoration specialists

1

work; and find ways to implement a conservation/preservation policy in a local library.

From November 15 to 18, 1981, over one hundred librarians, curators, archivists, conservators, binders, and library and information science faculty and students gathered together to attempt to meet these objectives through the messages of speakers, the viewing of exhibits and demonstrations, and discussion with others.

Warning that the 1980s are the "best of times, the worst of times" for library conservation and preservation efforts, the keynote speaker, Robert H. Patterson, deems these areas the biggest challenge of the next two decades for librarians. Since a shortage of trained and educated personnel exists in these areas, librarians must take the responsibility for education about preservation by designing and implementing their own programs. Preservation is expensive and, therefore, is a crucial part of library management requiring critical judgment and cooperative efforts. Such efforts call for high quality information on preservation including information about clearinghouses and regional treatment centers as well as judicious appraisal of newly developed commercial products. Urging that almost all libraries establish a preservation committee, Patterson outlines the responsibilities for such committees. Many of Patterson's points are elaborated by other speakers.

Reiterating a theme broached by Patterson, Pamela W. Darling notes that preservation is not solely the domain of a few persons who are specialists in the field, but is the responsibility of all librarians. To help librarians utilize information that is emerging on preservation, research efforts are underway by a number of individuals and organizations. With her charge being to describe some of these efforts, Darling notes the Collection Analysis Project (CAP) of the Association of Research Libraries (ARL)/Office of Management Studies (OMS) which called upon many libraries, for the first time, to take a serious look at preservation needs and possibilities as well as other projects of OMS and the Basic Archival Conservation Program of the Society of American Archivists (SAA). She also discusses professional education programs in conservation/preservation now being developed by library schools as well as other research activities in professional organizations and "invisible colleges." In concluding, she notes that only a coordination of all efforts, a sharing of developments, and a dissemination of information will result in solutions to the problems of preservation.

Some such coordinating and sharing efforts are chronicled by Carolyn Clark Morrow. She cites the ARL reports of 1964 and 1972 and the 1969 University of Chicago Graduate Library School's conference as "early warnings" to librarians about the realities of preservation needs. Between the two ARL reports, the Florence flood brought together conservation experts from around the world to aid in recovery and reclamation efforts and to experience, for the first time, the synergism of working together. Other events of particular importance to the growing efforts at cooperation have been the formation of the National Conservation Advisory Council; the Research Libraries Group (RLG) which, for the first time, united an integrated preservation program with dissemination and access; the National Preservation Planning Conference held at the Library of Congress (LC) and the recent establishment of the Preservation of Library Materials Section (PLMS) within the American Library Association's (ALA) Resources and Technical Services Division (RTSD). The best known regional conservation effort has been that of the Northeast Document Conservation Center (NEDCC) which serves several hundred clients and provides professional treatment for a wide variety of materials. Other cooperative efforts which Morrow discusses are the Book Preservation Center, serving the New York metropolitan area; the Western States Materials Conservation Project; the statewide preservation plan developed for Colorado; and the Illinois Cooperative Conservation Program growing out of a plan developed at Southern Illinois University at Carbondale. Areas which Morrow feels are feasible on a cooperative basis for conservation/preservation activities are information, consulting, surveying, cost sharing, coordination and treatment. She concludes with ways that these can be accomplished cooperatively.

In her paper on "Preservation of Paper Based Materials: Mass Deacidification Methods and Projects," Carolyn Harris notes that the term *deacidification* is actually a misnomer. The acid in the paper is neutralized and is buffered so that new acid formed in the paper through further degradation or introduced through pollution is also neutralized. Mass deacidification of library materials will not return the items to their original condition—brittle items are still brittle—but the process of deacidification does return the items to a neutralized state and buffers them as well. Harris evaluates the four most commonly used forms of deacidification—vapor phase deacidification (VPD), the Barrow morpholine process, Wei T'o, and diethyl zinc (DEZ)—against criteria that have been determined essential for a good mass deacidification process. Despite these efforts, Harris warns that "mass deacidification is not the fountain of youth we're seeking; and can't ever be." The future in this area depends on creation of the awareness of library needs among publishers, the economics of papermaking, the development of information storage techniques such as optical discs and complete preservation programs which may, some day, include mass deacidification.

Gerald W. Lundeen picks up on Harris's comments concerning the paper industry by reporting on research and developments in that industry which are affecting the preservation of paper based materials. He reminds us that the essential nature of paper has changed little since its invention in China in A.D. 105—paper still consists of cellulose fibers suspended in water and formed into a matted sheet on screens; however, while handmade methods have changed little, modern machinemade paper is very complex and a highly capital-intensive mix of craft, science and engineering. Decrease in paper strength can be explained primarily by two synergistic chemical processes which attack the paper over time—(1) acid catalyzed hydrolysis of the cellulose polymer linking bond, and (2) oxidation; but paper is susceptible to many other degradation processes: therefore, the study of chemical reactions in paper is difficult and especially so in trying to attribute the effects in physical properties to specific reactions. On the encouraging side, Lundeen notes a trend toward use of alkaline paper as reported by monitoring tests at the Library of Congress. He attributes this trend to economic reasons rather than concern about the lasting quality of paper. Therefore, librarians must continue to work to influence even more publishers to adopt long-lasting paper. This can be done by insisting that standards for paper quality be used when purchasing library materials and by continued work through professional organizations to enhance the longevity of paper based materials.

Considerably less concern for the longevity of nonpaper based materials has been exhibited by librarians than has been shown for paper based materials, yet the problems of these newer materials may be as great, if not greater, than those of paper based materials. Indeed, the problems of paper based materials are not escaped with nonpaper based materials since the latter frequently carry paper labels. In addition, the newer materials are often composed of a mix of materials and these various combinations may find one substance interacting with another according to Gerald D. Gibson, who reviews the principal preservation problems faced in preserving the nonpaper based materials and cites the storage conditions and preservation procedures recommended today. He does not neglect the containers and labels of these materials, speaking to their preservation when they are particularly important. Gibson sees encouraging signs through the active interest presently being shown in the preservation of nonpaper based materials by a number of organizations in the private and public sectors and he reviews the most promising current research and development in this area.

"Preservation and Conservation Decisions in the Local Library" are delineated by William T Henderson. Organizing his decisions around Daniel Boorstin's division of preservation problems into epistemological (or social) questions and technical questions, Henderson cites three broad areas under the first set of questions: Should a library preserve its materials? What should be preserved? and How should things be preserved? Under technical questions, he includes those of preserving the intellectual content versus preserving the original artifact or both. He ends with a description of the treatment of mildew with orthophenylphenol as an illustration of his points.

Probably an area of conservation and preservation about which librarians are least familiar is that relating to the steps taken by the conservator for restoring an item that merits this special kind of conservation because of its intrinsic or artifactual value. Louise Kuflik presents the conservator's decision making process noting that a careful assessment of the problems associated with the item is always made and the principle of reversibility is always applied because a better technique or better material may appear in the future. Kuflik cites the careful physical examination of the item made by the conservator and notes the conditions which are documented before the conservator suggests the proposed treatment and estimates the length of the process. After the decision has been made by the curator of the item to proceed with the conservation, the conservator makes further decisions concerning deacidification, paper mending, washing of the paper, etc. All decisions are based on consideration of use and the stability of materials.

A panel of four representatives from commercial services spoke to their roles in the conservation and preservation of library materials. The first to speak was James Orr, Hertzberg-New Method, Inc., Jacksonville, Illinois. In the commercial binding business for thirty-five years, Orr notes the procedures in the business that have remained essentially the same over that period in time, while emphasizing the changes that have occurred in the binding business as firms attempt to handle current materials as well as semi-rare materials. Orr notes that there are many other new developments which commercial library binders are considering and applying in order to continue to serve their library customers. He emphasizes the development of a new adhesive which, in many cases, is replacing oversewing.

Leedom Kettell, Gaylord Bros., Inc., Syracuse, New York, represented library supply houses. Recognizing that the world is vastly different today from that of eighty-five years ago when the two Gaylord brothers founded the firm and could personally seek the advice of librarians as to new products and could, then, make the products in the Gaylord plant, Kettell finds that today the Gaylord firm is defining itself more as a vendor or distributor of products developed by companies that have large research and development components. He describes a plastic, polypropolene, which is soon to be marketed by Gaylord providing pamphlet binders and boxes for preservation.

Representing hand binders was William Anthony of Kner & Anthony Bookbinders, Chicago, a firm specializing in conservation work and fine bindings. Materials receiving the conservation process generally fall into two categories: those with brittle paper (from the eighteenth through twentieth centuries) and those with flexible paper (from the fifteenth through seventeenth centuries). Anthony explains some of the procedures used in his conservation studio for dealing with brittle paper and rebacking.

Preservation microfilming, an activity which has been going on for over fifty years either to preserve the artifact or the intellectual content (or both), has become increasingly popular in recent years. Anita Werling, University Microfilms International, describes this type of microfilming as well as micropublishing and republishing. She identifies several large microfilming projects which have made important works available to a wider range of libraries and she relates some decisions which an individual library must make when the choice is between saving the object or the intellectual content. Werling gives some advice for librarians faced with the decision of microfilming locally versus sending the material to a commercial microfilmer or micropublisher.

Using Johannes Kepler's conclusion to his *Harmonice mundi*—as a statement of the conservator's cause before the world of scholarship, D.W. Krummel goes on to state what can be expected from scholarly researchers in the way of dialoguing on conservation policy, and handling and using library materials. Admittedly, there are different kinds of scholars resulting in different concepts of library conservation appropriate to each. Krummel concludes that since the classic distinction between physical form and intellectual content will not go away, the medium will continue to be necessary to the scholars of the future; therefore, the scholar must be sensitive to the problems of the conservator and sympathetic to the need for conservation policy.

All of the above considerations are for naught unless the top library administration takes an active and responsible role in conservation and preservation. E. Dale Cluff, Director of Library Services, Southern Illinois University at Carbondale, centers his presentation of that role and responsibility around two challenges: how to cope with present resources and facilities (i.e., curing present ills) and how to insure that steps are taken to prevent the same mistakes from happening again. A library can begin its preservation role by becoming aware of the necessity for a comprehensive policy, and making the library staff at all levels aware of that need. Strong support must come from the top administration. Other activities which must be completed include assessing the needs in some detail; determining the manner in which materials are presently handled; ascertaining the physical condition of materials presently on library shelves; and finally, setting priorities from among the determined needs. Cluff elaborates upon these and other administrative aspects.

In addition to the published papers, the proceedings include the discussion sessions that followed each presentation. These sessions were taped at the conference and transcribed and edited for the proceedings.

Names of the speakers are identified when they were clearly audible from the tapes; otherwise, speakers are unidentified. Impossible to include in the published proceedings is what transpired at the Tuesday evening "Conservation/Preservation Fair" during which time several demonstrations and exhibits were available to the conferees. This proved to be a very popular and well received part of the conference. Carolyn Jane Gammon, Conservator, Library, University of Illinois at Urbana-Champaign, assisted by Daniel Freeman, displayed many tools, techniques and materials that can be used in the local library to foster conservation activities. James Orr, Hertzberg-New Method, Inc., Jacksonville, Illinois, along with Tom Farrell and Jim Fischel explained to the participants the many facets of commercial binding and demonstrated, in person and through audiovisual means, many of the techniques. William Anthony, assisted by Bernie Anthony, answered questions about their exhibit of "before and after" examples illustrating the work done in the Kner & Anthony conservation studio in Chicago. Gerald Gibson, Library of Congress, presented slides illustrating many of the points he made in his presentation earlier that day in addition to making further explanations and comments about the video disc as a future means of storage and preservation of information. During this time, too, each of the speakers was present to answer questions or to comment on his/her presentation.

The anatomy of a conference takes many shapes and involves many persons who should be recognized for their contributions. It is not possible to mention every person who made some contribution to this conference, but there are some who should be singled out for special recognition. First of all, we are grateful to the faculty of the Graduate School of Library and Information Science (GSLIS) for putting aside a previously agreed upon topic until another year in order that this especially timely topic might be given priority. The faculty Planning Committee for the conference included Dean Charles H. Davis and D.W. Krummel, who assisted the co-chairpersons in many ways. As a GSLIS conference proceeds, the staff of the University's Division of Conferences and Institutes of the Office of Continuing Education and Public Services soon becomes involved and we particularly acknowledge the work of Ronald G. Sears, Mary E. Bussert and Mary R. Lewis from that division for their untiring efforts at handling the myriad of logistical and support services which provide for registration, accommodation, transportation, publicity, and so many other important details. Each of the speakers and each participant at the Tuesday evening "Conservation/Preservation Fair" enthusiastically accepted and carried out his/her responsibility. A number of University of Illinois faculty assisted in chairing sessions: Walter C. Allen, Charles H. Davis, Linda C. Smith, and Terry L. Weech, from the GSLIS, and Maynard J. Brichford and Jean Geil from the University of Illinois Library. The following GSLIS students were responsible for taping the sessions so that the discussions and comments to the presentations could be included in the proceedings: Deborah Beckel, Cynthia Fugate, Allen Hoffman, Elaine Huang, Kerry Miller, Deborah Pierce, Kathryn Prichard, Catherine Salika, and Janet Stolp. Kathryn Painter, of the GSLIS staff, carefully transcribed the tapes and cheerfully performed many other responsibilities before and after the conference, while Steve Andrews, Learning Resources Laboratory, served as photographer for the Tuesday evening session.

In the final analysis, this conference does not end with the publication of its proceedings, but in the action of those who have heard and heeded its messages. Long since, we have all become aware of the truth that our worldly library and archival treasures of books, maps, photographs, recordings, films, tapes (even computer tapes) are finite and perishable—they can be "here today" and, perhaps, "gone tomorrow" as books become brittle, maps break at the folds and seams, photographs fade, recordings warp, films ignite, and tapes erase. At the end of the conference, no doubt some attendees found little solace as once again they learned that these problems are persistent and universal—no one has yet performed a miracle in this area. Perhaps, the conference even increased the anxiety for some—dangers that might not even have been suspected are lurking in their libraries and archives—now there is more, not less, to cause worry. If anxieties have increased, so, too, do we hope has resolve toward finding solutions to the problems. We hope that each person has been touched in some way by the messages of the conference and will find some new ways to try out, some new sources and resources in material and people to call upon, and some increased support to persist in the struggles that lie ahead. This seems the time to move from the dire prophecies concerning the doom that the future holds for our collections into the "good news" that a concerted effort is being launched in many ways to conserve and preserve our collections and to move toward action to spread the "gospel" of preservation. We thank each person who attended the conference and who will read the proceedings for the challenges that each takes up and the actions that each brings about to accomplish the goals of "conserving and preserving library materials."

KATHRYN LUTHER HENDERSON
WILLIAM T HENDERSON
Editors

ROBERT H. PATTERSON

Director of Libraries
McFarlin Library
University of Tulsa

Conservation: What We Should Do Until the Conservator and the Twenty-First Century Arrive

Let me begin parenthetically by saying that the keynote speaker—at least in my mind—has both the greatest of handicaps and advantages before him or her. In a conference where a large number of speakers are present, like this one, she/he must avoid being specific about anything, unless she/he duplicates what others plan to say. My remarks, then, must be of the most general nature. And the danger from too broad a generality is that the comments may not be direct enough to be valuable. On the other hand, the advantage that I see is an opportunity to present a broad overview of a complex and challenging subject that has filled my professional life with some of its greatest difficulties and greatest joys.

The Challenge to Conservation in Difficult Times

To paraphrase Dickens, these are the best and the worst of times. We certainly are confronted by a serious economic situation nationally and internationally, and the support libraries enjoyed only a few years ago (relatively speaking) is diminishing. With the exception of a few fortunate institutions, largely in the Sun Belt, funds for staffing, new services and programs, and acquisitions are diminishing. Americans are historically optimistic, I believe, and we all look to things getting better. Perhaps they will, but many of us believe that they will get worse before that occurs. On the other hand, what I believe to be great advances and opportunities are taking place in preservation now and in the future. Conservation must be put in a broad perspective.

I will say that the advent of a heightened preservation awareness, coupled to the development of improved managerial systems to administer

9

programs, plus the revolutionary impact of technology generally on libraries, creates the greatest of ironies. Our resources are smaller, and with all the existing programs libraries are struggling to manage we must—if we are to meet our professional responsibilities—add another expensive program, that of conservation. And, while we attempt to mount this program, we must be increasingly conscious that the emerging information delivery and storage technology will increasingly make printed records obsolete. This is to say, and I will speak to this question later on, that we must not only attempt to develop preservation programs, but that we must also develop stronger critical facilities about what we intend to save, and how we intend to go about it. We have more choices today than we had five years ago, and the number of choices will increase as we move toward the next century.

Preservation as a Library-Wide Concern

One of the most important views I can impart to you is that preservation is a library-wide concern, and that librarians must be the persons who will develop preservation programs. I will say that in my experience, in most libraries, it is the rare book and special collections staff who initially take the leadership of preservation, and who work harder with their administrations to develop programs, competing as they do with other library programs and services. It is, of course, natural for them to do so. They are, by definition, protectors of those materials deemed to be more valuable than those in the general collections. But it has been my observation that since most libraries do not consider their special collections programs to be in the mainstream of their programs, they are not always successful in competing for additional funds. Also, it has been my experience that the needs of special collections librarians (real or imagined) may be treated by general administrators as esoteric, elitist, even precious. The result for an emerging preservation program is that it may take a long time in gaining support. I realize in saying this that this will not parallel the experience in some institutions, but that it has been the experience in many. (But, in fairness, let me also say that special collections librarians often do not see the need for preservation programs in the general collections.) They certainly do so, and if they do work to educate the library staff throughout the library, they will have created a successful strategy that builds a groundswell that will convince administrators of the need for such a program.

Preservation as the Responsibility of the Librarian

My earlier point, the second one, is that librarians must take the responsibility for educating themselves about conservation. They must educate themselves to the point that they can design and implement their own programs. To wait for the conservator, unless one works in an institution blessed with enormous resources and good fortune, is like waiting for Godot, although it is hoped, with a more positive long-term outcome. The reason we must take this responsibility is because we currently lack the corps of conservators we need. In my view, the preservation profession is at the same stage of development that librarianship was in during the last two decades of the nineteenth and first two decades of the twentieth century. With an exponential rate of change characteristic of the last years of this century, we may not expect to wait as long for the preservation profession to develop as we did for the library profession. At this time, conservation does not generally have an accepted curriculum. In a society which has developed highly structured educational paths for careers of all kinds from neurosurgeon to cosmetologist, no clearly defined way yet exists in preservation in which to seek such a career. There are some most hopeful and promising developments taking place right now, but the apprenticeship and internship system which has been the prevailing means of educating conservators is still the rule rather than the exception. I do not mean to suggest that years of hands-on experience still will not be necessary for the conservator, any more than years of experience do not improve the practice of any profession.

But for the time being, there is a shortage of professionals in the preservation world, and while it may be alleviated within the next ten to twenty years, librarians will have to, as I said earlier, educate themselves and develop programs to meet their needs. Actually, I am comfortable about that, because I believe it parallels the way in which librarians have learned to use another technology—automation. Within the past twenty years we have seen librarians educate themselves to the point that, while they were not electrical engineers or computer programmers, they understood the basic principles of data processing and articulated their needs to the computer professionals who designed the systems. Many libraries now have automation officers on their staffs who, in most cases, are librarians with data processing expertise. Within the next few years, we will have preservation officers—again librarians—with the necessary training.

The New Technology and Preservation

The emerging technology—which at this time librarians are not successfully assimilating or interpreting in my view—offers, in the view of some, the prospect of a paperless society. While I personally do not believe that Gutenberg is dead, or that paper will become unknown in the next century, we should try hard to grasp the fact that the new technology adds a complex and challenging factor to preservation. Electronic publishing, alternative forms of electronic transmission (using fiber optics and satellites), new forms of micropublishing (including laser disc with astonishing image storage capacity), mean that we must exercise a greater selectivity and discrimination in decision making. I believe that significant changes in the basic ways in which information is stored and made accessible will change. I do not believe that the library of printed material will go away, but that it may be initially augmented, and then, perhaps, largely supplanted by new forms. We must also recognize that the new means of storing information are unlikely (from the very dim vantage point of today) to retrospectively convert *all* existing printed matter into the new electronic formats.

Preservation in the Context of Collection Development

This leads to the role of the librarian in collection development, of which preservation is a part. My need here, however, is to point out that preservation is a part of the decision-making that librarians are qualified to make (in consort with the scholarly community, to be sure), that deal with the question which is the most basic one: What do we need to keep as objects for their own intrinsic value as objects; and what intellectual content do we need to preserve? In both cases, what means do we use to make our decisions? There are a number of alternatives in both cases, and their number will increase over the next two decades.

You will hear at this conference from a number of speakers who will give you a clear idea of what kinds of choices one has in preservation. Again, I must remind you that they represent parts of the broad continuum of options which exist in a collection development program, which is another way of saying collection management. George Cunha, one of the nation's outspoken champions of conservation has been saying for years that librarians must create and sustain conservation programs and that conservation is, after all, management.

Costs and Implications

A fact of preservation is that it is expensive, whether one is looking at it from a perspective of binding, establishing environmental controls, providing optimum housing conditions, simple repairs, mass deacidification, microform applications, etc. Given that, and the state of resources now or in the immediate future, I will draw several conclusions. The first is that we must exercise the greatest critical judgment in determining in what form we will preserve materials or their intellectual content; and second, that the impulse for cooperation promises enormous short- and long-term benefits. The library profession has a good track record of cooperation almost from the beginning of its development one hundred years ago with its collective programs such as interlibrary loan and now online systems. Given a shortage of professional conservators, short funding, and increased knowledge about the rarity of materials which online bibliographic systems should offer, we can set about to share resources.

Collective Action

The thrust toward cooperative action in preservation is, I believe, its most dynamic characteristic at this time. That impulse to join together has taken shape to meet one of the most pressing goals in preservation today—that of providing education. You will hear considerably more on this subject in the coming days. At this time, let me say only that an explosion of information in preservation is taking place today, and one of the greatest needs we have is for selective, high quality information. To meet that need, a number of institutions and agencies are currently examining the concept of information clearinghouses, as you will hear. I also believe that another collective proposal that ultimately will find support is the regional treatment center. You will hear more of that also as this program continues.

I want to stress that I believe preservation to be the greatest challenge the library and archival professions will face in the next decades. The reason I believe that is the continuing need for good information. Also, preservation is not likely to be supported by commercial applications of technological developments as library automation was bouyed along by computer technology. The potential for enormous technological application, including increased interest from the private sector, is there, but I think it unlikely that the kind of off-the-shelf systems one encounters now will be available soon. This is certainly not to say that the commercial sector does not have (and in some cases has not had), the greatest of interest in preservation. We have seen a large number of new products appear recently, and I feel quite safe in assuring you that there will be more. And, like many of the new automation products, they will promise much. They will often deliver what they promise, but occasionally will not do so. My advice is to look at new products of all kinds with the same caution you should exercise in looking at other products in our profession.

Organizing for Preservation

I would like now to make some very specific suggestions of ways in which you can begin immediately to set up a preservation program in your institution, or to strengthen the program you have now. You will find these suggestions in a large number of places in the literature, and I will try to pull them together for you here. In my experience they represent a way of addressing some basic needs. All but the smallest of libraries can create a preservation committee, or at least charge an individual with developing expertise and responsibility in that area.

Briefly stated, these committee charges, or responsibilities are as follows: (1) examine the library's physical environment, and make recommendations for enhancing environmental factors, including an effective monitoring system; (2) prepare a disaster plan for the library; (3) examine current bindery, handling, processing and repair practices, making recommendations to bring these procedures into conformity with accepted conservation practices; (4) explore avenues which will provide the library with access to professional conservation expertise and facilities; (5) explore and recommend what in-house physical repair and treatment can be undertaken for providing better housing, and minor repair of materials; (6) develop a collection development approach for dealing with materials, developing systematic options for storing and accessing materials; (7) identify possible sources of funding for conservation programs, including national, regional state and local sources; (8) establish an in-house clearinghouse of preservation information for the use of staff; and (9) explore the feasibility of joining cooperative conservation efforts at local, regional and national levels. (These charge responsibilities are outlined in my article appearing in the May 15, 1979 issue of *Library Journal* entitled "Organizing for Conservation.")

In closing, I hope that I have given that broader perspective which I believe conservation badly needs at this point in its development—that it is a library- and profession-wide concern, and that we have many more choices before us than simply how to repair and preserve a valued physical object. We also must face the fact that the emerging information revolution on how information is disseminated and stored will have a significant impact on decision-making in libraries, only a small part of which will include actual physical preservation concerns. Librarians are intelligent and resourceful people, and the profession is recognizing (perhaps belatedly) that higher managerial skills are needed if we are to accomplish our historic mission—that of housing and delivering information to our patrons.

DISCUSSION

Charles H. Davis (Graduate School of Library and Information Science, University of Illinois at Urbana-Champaign): One thing I heard you say pleased me very much. While I'm not a specialist in preserving and conserving things, I am a specialist in automation and think it's a point worth making that we have to conserve things regardless of the medium. I am thinking about magnetic tapes, video discs and the rest of it. Gutenberg, himself, may be dead but the spirit lives on and we'll also have paper for some time I think.

Robert H. Patterson: That's very true.

Louis Jordan (University of Notre Dame Libraries, South Bend, Indiana): What should be the percentage of the total library budget allotted for preservation?

Patterson: That's a very difficult question. I think it depends on the nature of the collection. It depends on where materials come from initially; where they are published. A library, for example, that collects heavily in materials from non-European countries such as Asia, Latin America, Africa, will probably have greater preservation needs than one that collects entirely materials from, let's say, North America because of the nature of the way materials are printed and bound in those particular places. I wouldn't even dare give a percentage.

What we all have to realize is that we spend more money on preservation than we think we do. I think a lot of librarians don't realize that when they pay to have materials bound, they are making a very significant preservation commitment. And while a lot of you won't like this, I would also suggest that one of the ways I have to support preservation programs was to take some money out of the binding budget on the premise that preservation and binding are all part of the same bits and pieces that link this whole thing together.

I think the kind of procedures and practices that we draw to govern our binding practices have to be reviewed as a preservation activity. While class A library binding may be absolutely marvelous for a lot of materials, it is abominable for a lot of other materials. And we have to exercise the judgment that we have as librarians and bibliographers, and as subject specialists, to run our entire binding procedures and specifications through the most careful scrutiny to make sure that we are, in fact, giving the materials the kinds of treatment that they actually need. Very few libraries have done this. There are people here, however, who are taking part in the program, who have and can tell you a great deal about how you go about developing that kind of program.

William DuBois (Northern Illinois University Libraries): How have challenge/match programs for funding aided library preservation efforts?

Patterson: The amount of progress in preservation technology and preservation development, I believe, in the last few years, can be, in at least part, attributed to intelligent use of grant money. I realize that in certain political areas, grant money is under the worse kind of attack, but organizations like NHPRC and the National Endowment for Humanities, just to name two that I think are the most important, have been enormously helpful in developing some important pilot programs that have had a great deal of positive effect and have proven themselves to be very workable, and have helped us learn a lot. Unhappily, the amount of funding available for those programs is not as great as it once was.

Gerald Gibson (Library of Congress, Washington, D.C.): The Library of Congress is very interested in preservation as their paper materials, too, are deteriorating. Nonpaper controls are one method being used for preservation.

Patterson: The directions the Library of Congress seems to be taking in preservation at this point are a very helpful sign. Those of you with preservation problems in the past know that the preservation staff of the Library of Congress has been enormously helpful with any problem. You could simply pick up the phone and call them and they try very hard to help you.

D.W. Krummel (Graduate School of Library and Information Science, University of Illinois at Urbana-Champaign): How much is being done to make conservation less expensive?

Patterson: I think one of the ways that has been tried to address the cost in preservation is to develop collaborative and cooperative ventures. The whole clearinghouse concept which is rapidly emerging is a very important way of getting information into collection development.

Robert J. Adelsperger (University of Illinois at Chicago Circle): What should be the split between conserving and preserving special and general collections? I think we are realizing that special collections and rare books librarians can't carry it alone.

Patterson: I think the only long-term answer to that problem is to educate library administrators and the library world generally, that preservation is not an elitist kind of concern, and that while people in rare books do have an obvious clear vested interest in the process, that it is a problem for the entire general collection. If that kind of information can be imparted and learned, then it will bring, I think, administrators around. Again, I don't want to address specific kinds of things because they will be talked about in much more detail later on, but just the fact that some of the major library organizations, such as the Association of Research Libraries (ARL), have taken a major concern about preservation means that those people who might not ordinarily learn about preservation will have it called to their attention now that their major organizations are examining it. This is important. It's a very important change. I remember talking to several ARL library directors at least ten years ago—"Nothing to worry about." "What problems?" I don't think you could find an ARL director today who would say that. They might think it still in their hearts, but there is enough pressure from within their own national organization to view preservation as a problem. They would have a great deal of difficulty saying that they didn't recognize the problem. That's *enormous* progress.

James C. Dast (University of Wisconsin at Madison): What is the role of library schools in preservation?

Patterson: I'm so glad you asked that question. I think we have seen in library education in the past five years, in particular, a growing interest in preservation. The *Preservation Education Directory,* a publication of the American Library Association, began a few years ago with only one or two pages; now it is thirty pages listing regular courses, workshops and other kinds of programs. I would hope that trend might continue and that the library schools would increasingly offer more and more in this area. Considering the importance of preservation for libraries, for library schools not to offer (if not a complete course) at least some exposure to the student of the problem, is not to really prepare students. The whole question of trying to create an awareness, again throughout the entire profession, means starting at this level. We're not talking about rare book librarians, we're talking about people who must have their own awareness heightened so that they recognize that there is a problem. Since we can't wait for the conservator to appear (he or she isn't going to appear for an awfully long time), they, as librarians, are going to have to develop the preservation programs.

Davis: I think we in library schools don't necessarily have to have courses labeled "preservation" to teach concepts—e.g., courses in library administration and technical services often cover these areas. Because schools don't have courses labeled preservation does not mean they don't have offerings.

Unidentified Speaker: Doesn't the library staff have an obligation to educate their staff and users about preservation? There is a lot that we can do to educate people about not harming books.

Patterson: I think that you have already answered your question. Clearly, one of the responsibilities of a preservation officer or preservation committee is to look at programs to train and educate the library staff about what is proper handling and what is not. There are a wide number of very, very fine slide and tape shows, publications, all kinds of things, designed for the training of the library staff, whether they are students handling books in the stacks or whether they are persons working in processing or binding. There are a large number of programs that are now available or are being developed in a large number of institutions, which, I am sure, you will hear about as we go on in this conference. It is clear that education is one of the primary roles of the preservation officer.

PAMELA W. DARLING

Preservation Specialist
Office of Management Studies
Association of Research Libraries

Expanding Preservation Resources
The Corps of Practitioners and the Core of Knowledge

Recently a small sampling of libraries was asked to comment on a proposal for a preservation information service, which would aggressively disseminate publications and new information about procedures and techniques. One library's response was brief and blunt: "What we need is a corps of practitioners, not more articles!" Another suggested that the availability of information about preservation was no longer the issue, arguing that in fact "sometimes I think we have so much information that we are paralyzed from effective action."

Since a significant proportion of my professional energies has been devoted to the dissemination of "more articles" on the topic of preservation, these cold assertions took me rather by surprise. Defensively, I mentally rehearsed all the arguments supporting the need for accurate, current information to support decision-making and shape procedures in day-to-day preservation program operation; reviewed the ample evidence that staff in numerous libraries know nothing—have never read a single article—about preservation; and reaffirmed my conviction that progress depends on making preservation information as widespread within the profession as information about cataloging or reference.

But as I thought more about it, I came to the conclusion that the critics offered a valuable insight: true though it is that preservation information is still scarce, scattered, primitive, and often inaccurate, the creation of a comprehensive data base on the topic cannot by itself solve the preservation problems of the nation's libraries and archives. Information is valuable only when put to use. Information is a tool, but people do the work. Though the distinction may appear academic, to focus on developing informed people, instead of focusing on information, is an important step in improving our collective ability to respond to urgent preservation needs.

With that distinction in mind, I will describe several current projects and programs which aim to develop informed people, and speculate about some future possibilities.

ARL/OMS Preservation Project

To begin with the one I know best, the Preservation Planning Project of the Association of Research Libraries' Office of Management Studies (ARL/OMS), with which I have been involved since July 1980, is a one-time project aimed at putting "self-help" tools into the hands of people responsible for developing preservation programs. This project is a direct outgrowth of the Collection Analysis Project—CAP—which the Office of Management Studies developed several years ago. CAP studies enable a library to examine a wide range of factors affecting the nature, growth and use of its collections. One of those factors is preservation, and a number of libraries were able to take their first serious look at preservation needs and possibilities in the course of conducting a collection analysis self-study. While the importance of viewing preservation in the context of overall collection development and management cannot be overemphasized, it was apparent that the topic is broad and complex enough to merit the more extensive attention possible through a self-study focused exclusively on preservation. Thus the current project was generously supported by the National Endowment for the Humanities, to design, test and make widely available a preservation self-study process.

The project has both short- and long-term products. Early in the grant period, the OMS conducted a SPEC survey on preservation. (SPEC is the Systems & Procedures Exchange Clearinghouse, a service of OMS whereby ARL member libraries share in-house documents and report on local activities. SPEC surveys are a speedy way to pool information on specific topics of current interest.) While the ultimate purpose of this particular survey was to gather data for use in designing the preservation self-study, there were three immediate byproducts, the SPEC Kit/Flyer packages on *Planning for Preservation, Preparing for Emergencies and Disasters,* and *Basic Preservation Procedures.*[1] Distributed to ARL members, several hundred regular subscribers, and dozens of institutions here and abroad who have ordered individual copies, the SPEC kits offered a glimpse of preservation administration as it is actually being practiced in major libraries today, with policy statements and descriptions of procedures which can serve as models for adapting to many other library situations.

The kits were an early bonus, a way to give people something to work with right away while we were developing more extensive and systematic

tools. That work is now in its final phase, and will result in two complementary products. The first is an assisted self-study manual, the *Preservation Planning Program*,[2] which sounds a bit intimidating but is simply a
set of instructions for conducting a systematic examination of a library's
preservation needs and developing a plan for responding to them. The
second is a compilation of technical information, drawn from a wide
variety of sources, which serves both to educate those staff members conducting the self-study and to guide subsequent implementation of the
plan.

How the Self-Study Works

The self-study process, which has been tested in three different library
settings during the past year, involves a team of four to seven library staff
members in a careful investigation of the library's preservation situation.
The study team is assisted by a consultant, who provides orientation to the
subject of preservation and to the techniques of the study itself, makes
periodic visits to work with the team and its task forces, is available
throughout the study for advice about problems which may arise, and
provides an outsider's perspective on the findings and plans.

The process begins with a review of the library itself—the history and
nature of its collections and users as these affect the condition of its
materials and its responsibility for maintaining them. During this first
phase the study team also informs itself about basic preservation issues,
through reading and exploring in a preliminary way the history of preservation activities within the local library and in the profession. Major
external factors likely to affect plans for future development—building
plans, cooperative relationships, and steadily mounting financial
pressures—are also identified. With this preparation, the study team prepares a background paper, setting forth the scope and priorities for the
second phase of the self-study.

Task forces are then appointed, chaired by members of the study team
but bringing into the study process as many as twenty-five additional staff
members for an intensive information-gathering effort. Five major areas
are examined. The first is the physical environment affecting materials in
the collections, which is studied by assembling data on the nature of
facilities and spaces throughout the library and by monitoring temperature, humidity and light levels in representative spaces. This task force
prepares a report on present conditions with recommendations for ongoing monitoring to identify seasonal problems and patterns, and for various
short-term and long-range measures for upgrading the environment.

The second task force studies the physical condition of the collections
themselves. This is a major topic addressed through development of an

inventory of the physical types of materials held throughout the system, and by sampling the condition of representative items from the major categories identified in the inventory. This process lays the foundation for the body of statistical and evaluative data which must be accumulated over a more extended period in order to shape preservation program priorities and justify the reallocation of funds that will be essential to support expanded preservation programs.

The third area is that of the library's preparedness for accidents and disasters affecting the collections. This task force looks at facilities, geography, climate, and the history of previous disasters in order to assess the library's current vulnerability; identifies areas in which preventative measures ought to be taken; and prepares a preliminary "disaster plan" for coping with emergencies which might threaten the collections.

The fourth area of study, sometimes handled by a task force and sometimes by the study team itself, is that of the organizational factors and current procedures which affect the physical condition of materials. This involves identifying preservation activities, often disguised under other names, which are already going on throughout the library—processing, binding, handling, repair, replacement; codifying whatever policies may exist which influence those activities; beginning the arduous task of identifying the current level of preservation-related expenditures. Analysis of this data leads to recommendations for developing comprehensive policies, improving procedures, realigning operations in order to coordinate decision-making, and making preservation a conscious, integral function within the library's ongoing operations.

The fifth area I like to think of as identifying opportunities rather than needs, and serves as a good antidote to the often depressing findings of the other task forces. It is an analysis of the resources which might be employed in an expanded preservation program, resources which are available in-house, on the campus, in the community, in the region, and "out there." The task force develops an inventory of people, products, services, and literature which might be useful in staff training and patron education programs, decision-making about policies, treatment procedures, and supply budget allocations. It assembles the beginnings of a resource file, and develops recommendations for maintaining, updating and making use of these resources in a library-wide preservation program.

In the final phase, the study team takes the work of the task forces and puts it all together, beginning with a description of the current situation which identifies major problem areas, causes, and potential solutions. It then develops a phased plan for responding to preservation needs, a step-by-step process whereby the library can move toward the creation of a comprehensive presevation program within a three- to five-year period. Although the self-study encourages some dreaming about an ideal program, in order to establish long-term goals and bring home the magnitude of the preservation responsibility, the emphasis is on realism: what can be done this year, with existing resources, to improve what we are now doing to materials in our care, and what can be done to increase the resources available in the next few years in order to bring our ability to care for our materials into appropriate balance with needs? The plan, with all its supporting documentation, is then presented to the library administration as the final report of the self-study.

Is It Worth It?

What are the results of such a process? Is it worth all the effort? The effort is very substantial. In the three pilot test libraries, which were asked to keep careful records throughout the study, total hours averaged more than a year of cumulative staff time during the four- to seven-month process. Even with the streamlining that has resulted from the pilot test experience, the commitment of staff time will be a major one for any library undertaking the complete study. Is it worth it? Is it necessary? Wouldn't it be easier to assign one person to the planning job? Couldn't he or she develop a plan for preservation if given a whole year to do it, without disrupting the working lives of two dozen people and the functions of the two dozen units which must do without them while they're off on "that damned preservation study?"

Only libraries which have gone through the process can give you a final answer—their final answer—to such questions. My own response harks back to the question of information *v.* informed people. The preservation study is based on a fundamental assumption that a library can change its way of operating—in this case to improve its care for materials in its collections—only when the people who carry out those operations change their attitudes, broaden their understanding, and expand their knowledge and skills. A formal self-study helps this happen. Involving a broad cross section of the staff in the study not only feeds into it a wealth of experience and knowledge of local library operations that no single individual could possess, but also serves to create within the library a pool of staff members who have been exposed to preservation issues, who have become aware of local preservation needs and resources, who can immediately take back into their daily work a new preservation awareness.

Preservation is not solely the domain of a few specialists, but a job for all of us. A "preserving attitude" on the part of every staff member is essential if the institution as a whole is to come to terms with the awful pressure of deterioration threatening the collections we have spent so much time and money to acquire, organize, and service. In the absence of this attitude, damaging practices will continue. But send a dozen or twenty or thirty people back to the front lines after an intensive period of learning about the threats to their collections and I guarantee you the library will never be quite the same again. Even if the institution can't afford to implement all the recommendations, even if the administration loses its nerve and puts the study report on a back shelf to deteriorate along with the rest of the collections, even if the plan itself was so poorly put together that it deserves to disappear without a trace—even then, the materials in the collections will have a better chance for survival. An informed staff is worth infinitely more than all the information compiled in a report, or neatly filed in a cabinet marked "preservation." The Preservation Planning Program can be an effective step in developing that informed staff.

Society of American Archivists' (SAA) Basic Archival Conservation Program

Another approach is currently underway in the archival field. Also funded by the National Endowment for the Humanities, the Basic Archival Conservation Program of the Society of American Archivists is conducting a series of workshops on conservation theory and practice which will reach, over a two-year period, some 350 staff members in archival institutions throughout the country. Workshop materials will eventually be combined into a manual of practice and procedure for use in further staff training and improvement of conservation-related activities.

Coupled with this grassroots educational effort is a consultant program which provides on-site evaluation of conditions and offers recommendations for basic improvements. This subsidized service will be available to fifty or sixty archives during the grant period, and is particularly useful for small institutions lacking the staff to undertake an extensive self-study.

Regional Programs

Regional programs such as the Northeast Document Conservation Center, the Western Conservation Congress, and the Illinois Cooperative Conservation Project—about which Carolyn Morrow will be speaking— also perform important educational functions, not only providing information in response to specific problems but also advising on the interpretation and application of that information, offering workshops or serving as a meeting ground on which staff from many institutions can gather to share and learn from each other. Through these contacts, and through participation in professional associations such as the American Library Association, the Society of American Archivists, and the American Institute for Conservation, librarians and archivists with preservation responsibilities are building personal networks, creating the invisible college through which we all continue our professional development after we leave school. It's a ragged, patchwork affair yet, with some groups and areas of the country doing rather well while others must go long distances for information and support. But the outlines have been sketched and the patterns—good, effective patterns of communication and accumulating knowledge—are becoming discernible.

Academic Avenues

We are playing a catch-up game, most of us, for our formal professional education took place before the preservation threat was fully recognized, before the development of practical mechanisms for applying the emerging body of theory about causes and cures. Our teachers could not teach us much about preservation because there wasn't much to teach. The new generation is more fortunate. Most library schools now include preservation in the master's curriculum, if not as a separate course, at least in connection with the study of collection management or processing. Students emerging from the good schools are now familiar with the issues, the problems, the terminoloy, and will thus bring that all-important preservation awareness into their new positions. The growth of such basic educational opportunities is clearly reflected in the *Preservation Education Directory*[3] produced by ALA's Preservation of Library Materials Section, which has grown in five years from a one-page flyer to a 33-page booklet.

But for those wishing to devote careers to the preservation of library materials, the preparatory path has been a rather rocky one, since there have been no academic programs or formal credentials. Some conservators—those skilled craftsmen/scientists who treat deteriorated materials in the workshop or laboratory—learned their craft through long apprenticeships, the quality of their preparation therefore depending heavily on the knowledge and skills of their masters, some excellent but some, inevitably, not so good. Others came into library conservation through a side door, via graduate-level museum conservation training programs. The first of these, at New York University's Institute of Fine Arts, was established in 1960. It has since been joined by three others in North America: at the State University College at Oneonta, in conjunction with the New York State Historical Society, known as the Cooperstown Program (begun in 1970); at the University of Delaware in conjunction with the Winterthur Museum (begun in 1974); and at Queens University in Kingston, Ontario (also begun in 1974). Although they all focus on art and museum objects, several graduates who have concentrated on paper or photographic conservation have migrated to the library world.

Library preservation administrators—librarians responsible for the full range of activities including processing, binding, replacement, and brittle books programs for whole collections in addition to the laboratory treatment performed by conservators—have had an even more haphazard preparation. Thus far they have been largely self-taught, learning on the job and through whatever reading and workshop experience they could find, picking each other's brains at meetings and through informal professional contacts. Successful as such measures have been in bringing us to the present stage of development, they are by no means adequate to produce the "corps of practitioners" needed to direct programs in libraries throughout the country.

The Columbia Program

And so it is good news indeed that two graduate programs, one for library conservators and one for preservation administrators, have now begun. With generous start-up funding, chiefly from the National Endowment for the Humanities and the Andrew W. Mellon Foundation, and with assistance from the Carnegie Corporation, the Morgan Guaranty Trust Company, and the H.W. Wilson Foundation, the programs are offered by the School of Library Service at Columbia University in cooperation with the New York University (NYU) museum conservation training program. The conservator program, which began with four full-time students in September 1981 and will expand to a maximum of six, is a three-year course, including two years of course work and intensive laboratory practice followed by a year of supervised internship in a recognized conservation laboratory—a melding of the book-learning and apprenticeship approaches developed successfully by the museum training programs. On successful completion of the course of study, students will receive a master's degree from the library school, and a certificate in library conservation issued jointly by Columbia and the NYU Conservation Center, and will be prepared for beginning positions as professional conservators.

The preservation administration program may be done in two ways, as a one-year advanced certificate by practicing librarians, or as a two-year combined program leading to the library degree and an advanced certificate. The curriculum is packed with the theory and practice of preservation, in addition to study of general librarianship, the history of books and printing, the nature and care of materials, and library administration, and it includes a laboratory component which provides in-depth exposure to the materials and techniques of physical treatment. The administrator students will not become mini-conservators; they will not receive the heavy doses of conservation science, paper chemistry, and lengthy supervised bench practice necessary for those who provide extensive sophisticated treatment for a wide range of materials. But they will learn to establish and train staff for routine binding and mending operations, to analyze and improve procedures for handling and storage, to coordinate decision-making and large-scale systems for the care, repair or replacement of all materials in a library's collections. The first four administrator students completed the certificate program in May 1982.

A Core for the Corps

The foregoing suggests that we have some cause for confidence: the "corps of practitioners" will expand to meet the expanding personnel requirements in the field of preservation. But just what is it that these people are going to practice? Have we a body of theory and practice adequate to meet the complex demands of salvaging massive quantities of rotting materials? To put it bluntly, the core of preservation knowledge is still very small and primitive, and our research and development needs are correspondingly large and sophisticated. Given the distinction between information and informed people, and the mechanisms by which the former is put to use by the latter, let me now identify those areas which seem to me most sorely in need of development, and the approaches to each that appear most promising at this time.

As a framework for these projections, I'd like to share with you a study model developed for the Preservation Planning Program. Its graphic representation appears in figure 1.[4] Though its aesthetic proportions may leave something to be desired, the grouping of causal factors, potential control strategies, and the interrelationships among them all does prove useful in analyzing the present situation and trying to figure out what to do about it. For a review of the basic facts, see figure 1.

Causal Factors

There are three interdependent sets of causal factors contributing to the preservation problem. The first of these arise from characteristics of the materials themselves, the physical and chemical natures of which are, as a general rule, inherently unstable. The rate of natural deterioration varies widely, and each type of material has its own life cycle, its own pattern of responding to and reacting with its environment over time, which is established by the basic molecular character of its components and by the mechanics of its physical structure.

Directly related to the internal characteristics affecting the life of materials are the external factors which constitute the basic physical environment. The temperature, humidity, light, and chemical components of the atmosphere surrounding any object, and the structures which contain

PRESERVATION STUDY MODEL

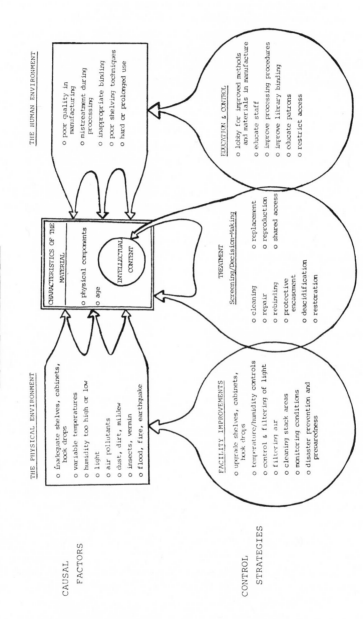

from PRESERVATION PLANNING PROGRAM: AN ASSISTED SELF-STUDY MANUAL, by Pamela W. Darling and Duane E. Webster. Washington, D.C. Association of Research Libraries, Office of Management Studies. Unpublished pilot project draft, Spring 1981, p.18. Final version to be published Spring 1982.

or support it, all influence both the rate and type of deterioration of that object. Changes in temperature and light—two different forms of energy—control the speed at which chemical reactions take place; the chemical nature of the materials themselves and the substances surrounding them define the type of reaction.

The third set of causal factors, also external to the object, is found in the nature of handling and use—binding or packaging techniques, shelving procedures, processing and circulation practices, and the way staff and patrons handle materials. Some effects are chemical, but most effects are physical, that is, they affect the external structure of an object rather than its chemical nature. The susceptibility of materials to this kind of damage depends upon both the internal and environmental factors. For example, paper embrittled through chemical reaction will shatter at a touch; a tight adhesive binding can split when opened under hot, dry conditions; film softened and stretched through prolonged exposure to a projection lamp may be wound too tightly, splitting as it cools and contracts.

The interrelationships among all three sets of factors are complex, and the knowledge that nothing is immortal can lead to an attitude of hopeless helplessness. However, an understanding of the chemical and physical causes of deterioration and of the influence which the material and human environments have on the natural aging processes can point to methods of care which significantly extend the life of library materials.

Control Strategies

Like the causes, the strategies for controlling the preservation problem fall into three related groups. In response to the physical and chemical characterisics of the materials, there are a variety of treatment possibilities which will halt or at least retard further deterioration and may undo some damage. These include cleaning, minor repair, binding and rebinding, deacidification, protective wrapping, and major restoration. In some cases of severe deterioration, physical treatment may be inpractical or economically unjustifiable although the intellecual content of the material warrants continued access. For such items, several possibilities exist for preserving content, through replacement, reproduction in a variety of formats and media, or through securing access to duplicates held elsewhere. Decison-making and provision of treatment are individual, item-by-item functions. Though guidelines and treatment routines for categories of materials may lend efficiency to the operation, the unit costs, in both time and materials, are high. The development of mass deacidification procedures, though vital for the stabilization of paper-based records, will by no means control all the factors affecting the survival of library materials.

Unlike physical treatment, the other two sets of preservation strategies can have a beneficial effect on large numbers of materials at once. Changes in the physical environment can prolong the life of all materials stored and used within that space. Such changes might include enhanced temperature and humidity control, filtering of air and light sources, cleaning, improvement of shelf and cabinet arrangements, redesigning book return structures, and upgrading materials used for storage folders and boxes. Though the total cost for major environmental improvements appears high, the unit cost for prolonging the life of each affected item is quite low. Given the accelerated rate of deterioration in an uncontrolled environment together with the high unit cost of physical treatment, these strategies offer cost-effective insurance that many materials will not be totally lost before individual attention can be given to them.

There are, in addition, several methods for limiting the human potential for damaging materials, through lobbying for better methods and materials in the manufacture of books and other media (especially supporting use of the paper specifications recently developed by the Committee on Production Guidelines for Book Longevity[5]), through staff education and training, improvement of binding and processing procedures, patron awareness programs, and restricing access to some materials.

Development Needs

If this analysis is reasonably accurate, it follows that we've got at least two dozen complementary activities to develop and promote. I'll say no more about most of them, but three taken together, may help us cope with the most perplexing aspect of the preservation problem: the sheer magnitude of the numbers of deteriorated materials.

Environmental control is perhaps the most urgent. Technically, we are well on the way to understanding what the environment ought to be, and how to keep it that way, in order to insure maximum survival for various types of materials. National standards exist for the proper storage of many photographic and magnetic media, and the American National Standards Institute has just established a Z-39 subcommittee to develop such a standard for paper-based records. Climate control systems— knowingly referred to by some as "HVAC" for "heating, ventilating, and air conditioning"—are becoming increasingly sophisticated. The technology already exists to create a life-sustaining mini-environment under the most adverse conditions, at the bottom of the sea or in outer space, so it must be technically feasible to control the many mini-environments in which library materials are housed. The technology is there, but two more ingredients are needed if it is to be used: (1) effective operational models and systems for applying the technology to the variable conditions that exist in a thousand storage spaces, and (2) money. Two examples will illustrate the research and development activities that I believe may bring the ingredients together.

First, adequate control of complex library environments must be based on data derived from regular monitoring of several factors in many locations. During the pilot testing of the Preservation Planning Program at the University of Washington in 1981, the environmental task force took some preliminary steps toward accumulating and manipulating such information by processing its findings through a simple data base management system on a microcomputer. As microcomputers become ever smaller, smarter, and cheaper, it ought to be possible to expand this approach, creating library-oriented environmental control software that would swiftly identify problem spaces and patterns of conditions, and pinpoint the most significant variables in particular areas. Microprocessor links between monitoring devices and climate control equipment could extend the familiar thermostat principle to regulate a variety of environment conditions automatically, on a continuous basis.

Second, consider the relationship between enviornmental conditions and the rates of deterioration for different sorts of materials. We have a handy rule of thumb which says that the rate doubles with every 10°C increase in temperature. But how might we apply this rule to create accurate projections of the cost in lost materials over x period of time at one temperature level or another? Careful sampling procedures might provide a profile of the deterioration rates for various categories of materials in a particular collection. Further testing could enable us to quantify the effects on those rates of altering this or that environmental factor. Price indexes for replacements and treatment cost figures could be combined on the financial side of the equation. With such information it ought to be possible to develop a formula for comparing the cost of controlling the environment with the price of failing to control it. There are many variables; I'd hate to have to do it on an abacus, or even this year's pocket calculator. But the new high technology office toys seem made for such a game, and the rewards of winning could be very great indeed.

From Universal Bibliographic Control (UBC) to Universal Preservation

Another area in which I see exciting development possibilities also relates to the alluring new information technologies. The capture, compact storage, and retrieval of massive quantities of sound, graphic images, and textual data appears to be moving swiftly out of the realm of science fiction. The Cataloging Distribution Service of the Library of Congress, working in cooperation with the research arm of Xerox, has equipment now in place for transferring the entire stock of 5.5 million pre-MARC printed catalog cards onto two dozen LP-size optical discs. The capture device "reads" the image by scanning at very high speed, converting what it "sees" into electronic impulses related to precise coordinates on a sliced-up grid containing 480 lines-per-inch. (Standards for high-quality micro-filming call for a resolution of 120 lines-per-inch. Television operates on a similar grid of about 120 lines-per-inch, so this new process can record four times the detail of the clearest television picture you've seen.) As the image is "digitized," the term for this electronic encoding, it is first recorded on a conventional magnetic disc, the "slices" lined up end-to-end. Access points or indexing tags—the LC card number, for example—are added to the string of slices for each image, and this composite data is then "writ-ten," or etched, by laser onto a thin film of metal sandwiched between two layers of glass.

Copies of this master optical disc can then be "read" by converting the codes back into an image viewed on a screen or printed as a high-quality facsimile reproduction. This process can even record and reproduce color, in a manner analogous to the three-color separation technique used in conventional photography. There are implications for interlibrary loan, for remote access in multiple locations, and for publishing. There are also remarkable preservation possibilities. The technology is there for a com-pletely new approach to salvaging the intellectual content of deteriorated material, until now accomplished chiefly through microfilming. But tech-nology is not enough; again, it must be employed within a well-designed system, and supported by apparently enormous sums of money. How to bring these pieces together?

To answer this question we must first look at the third topic that I believe to be crucial for the development of effective large-scale preserva-tion programs—the bibliographic structure. If you've ever dealt with preservation filming or brittle books replacement programs you know how important bibliographic control is, and how painfully inadequate our present systems are for such work. Intelligent decision-making about preservation treatment or replacement alternatives depends upon speedy, comprehensive access to current data about the existence and condition of other copies or related editions. Today's data base is far from comprehen-sive; it is not current; and access to its scattered components, manual and automated, is slow and cumbersome. Although computer-based catalogs lend plausibility to the librarian's dream of Universal Bibliographic Con-trol, and optical disc storage technology stimulates an even shinier vision of Universal Textual Preservation, years of hard, painstaking work are necessary if we are to reach such goals. It does no good to store tons of information in a machine unless you can get it out again when you need it. Intricate layers of file structures, indexes, registers, and links must be carefully put together if the terminal screen is to do its magic when I push the buttons. These systems are already being created. If they are to support collection management and preservation activities in addition to acquisitions, cataloging, and reference services, the designers need to know what kinds of special information each record might need to contain, and how it will be manipulated in carrying out those activities.

Recently, the Research Libraries Group (RLG) Preservation Committee tried to spell out exactly these design requirements in recommending enhancements to the RLIN (Research Libraries Information Network) data base. The final document deals exclusively with bibliographic support for preservation microfilming activities, and will certainly be of tremendous value as RLG, LC, OCLC, and the rest work more and more closely in building a national information network. But the committee had to abandon its original plan which was to have encompassed condition statements and preservation treatment reports as well as microform information. The reason for this, I believe, is that we have not yet figured out how to systematize the processes of evaluating condition and deciding on appropriate treatment. We must do that if we are to develop affordable programs for either mass treatment or electronic storage.

We must develop uniform condition descriptors, a common terminology for categories of treatment, and shared sets of criteria for screening materials and sending them down this or that path to restoration, format conversion or oblivion. To avoid wasteful duplication of effort on some things while others vanish for lack of attention, we must divide up the universe and assign primary responsibility for preserving chunks of it to many different libraries. RLG is struggling toward this; the Association of Research Libraries is beginning to consider it; some informal agreements exist within regional systems and arise from *de facto* recognition that *x* collection is simply the best that there is on the topic. But it's all pretty primitive, and we run the risk of being lulled into complacency by scattered reports that this group or that is working on the problem. Much fundamental thinking remains to be done, followed by much cooperative design, testing and redesign, in order to develop a practical system for employing both automated bibliographic control and compact text storage technologies in the service of preservation.

And so the final challenge is that of coordinating our efforts, sharing developments fully and swiftly so that we may build on each other's work, keeping always in mind the ultimate goal even as our attention is devoted to perfecting one small component. To that end we must nourish and invigorate our communications networks, so that time spent in one place to assemble the information needed for a particular preservation activity need not be duplicated in another. The widening gap between institutions with established preservation programs and those with none must be closed, for all must participate in making the fundamental decisions that will shape the nation's preservation programs.

Having come full circle, let me close by reiterating the importance of collecting and aggressively disseminating information about preservation at all levels of the profession. As individuals we have an obligation to share our own theoretical insights and practical discoveries with our colleagues through speaking, writing, and the informal contact that takes place during professional meetings, workshops, and conferences such as this. Our institutions must be active in reporting local preservation efforts, and quick to take advantage of information developed by others. Our systems and networks and consortia must work together to keep us well-informed, so that the corps of practitioners and the core of knowledge may grow together.

NOTES

1. Association of Research Libraries. Office of Management Studies. *Planning for Preservation* (SPEC Kit #66). Washington, D.C.: ARL, July/Aug. 1980; _____ . *Preparing for Emergencies & Disasters* (SPEC Kit #69). Washington, D.C.: ARL, Nov./Dec. 1980; and _____ . *Basic Preservation Procedures* (SPEC Kit #70). Washington, D.C.: ARL, Jan. 1981.

2. Darling, Pamela W., and Webster, Duane E. *Preservation Planning Program: An Assisted Self-Study Manual for Libraries.* Washington, D.C.: ARL, 1982; and Darling, Pamela W. comp. *Preservation Planning Program: Resource Notebook.* Washington, D.C.: Association of Research Libraries, 1982.

3. American Library Association. Resources and Technical Services Division. *Preservation Education Directory: Educational Opportunities in the Preservation of Library Materials, 1981,* edited by Susan G. Swartzburg and Susan B. White. Chicago: ALA, 1981.

4. Darling, and Webster, *Preservation Planning Program,* pp. 16-20.

5. Council on Library Resources. The Committee on Production Guidelines for Book Longevity. "Interim Report on Book Paper." Washington, D.C.: CLR, 1981. *See also* "Making Books Last." *Publishers Weekly* 219(29 May 1981):19-22.

DISCUSSION

Unidentified Speaker: What kind of statistics are available about how many items are being preserved?

Pamela Darling: There is nothing systematic available yet. There are a number of reasons for that, one of them being that we do not yet have that shared set of descriptions of treatments or shared understandings of what constitutes preservation. There is a lot of preservation going on in a lot of libraries that don't know they have a preservation program. The single thing that you can get statistics on for practically everyone is commercial binding, because we've been set up for years to count that, but most other things are not reported separately. In fact, in most places, there is not a separate count even kept for replacement when it is done for preservation purposes. It is simply buried in the acquisitions statistics somewhere.

David Farrell (Indiana University, Bloomington): What is being done about the special problems connected with the preservation of East Asian materials?

Darling: I probably can't say very much because I don't know a great deal about it. I think that there are problems with format and there are problems, obviously, with bibliographic control since most of the materials are not included in the regular bibliographic systems at present.

I am not aware of any *unique* problems about East Asian materials but that doesn't mean there aren't some. If you're talking the Orient, that is one thing; if you're talking about Southeast Asian, that's another. There are certain areas of the world where we all know that the quality of the paper is just really "the pits." There is very little that can be done to keep those things going more than ten to fifteen years, so that there are probably large categories of publications from certain areas, or at least certain types of publications from those areas, which, like newspapers, we will have to convert to some other form before we even add them to the collection because they won't last.

Roberta L. Hudson (R.B. Hayes Preservation Center, Fremont, Ohio): Is there a way to adapt the preservation and planning program self-study process to a small staff?

Darling: It is clearly designed for the larger institutions. I believe it would be possible, however, to take the principles that are involved, and the general procedures, and to cut the thing back in some of its detail. I would have to think about it to tell you exactly how it would be done, but I do think that the basic process, the elements of things that are to be examined and the process for analyzing the information you have and working toward a phased plan, are quite applicable to any kind of institution.

Gerald Gibson (Library of Congress, Washington, D.C.): I don't believe that there is presently a screen capable of showing the resolutions required for reading of the optical disc material.

Darling: The screen will only show, I think, a quarter of the resolution that is actually stored in the machine. There simply are not available now the cathode ray tubes, or whatever they are, that have that kind of refinement. The significance about the resolution capability from our point of view is not really so much what we see on the screen but the fact that the information is stored to that level of detail and it's stored in electronic and digitized form so that, even though it begins to degrade, it can be restored perfectly, because all the machine knows is "on" or "off" in this particular little tiny, teeny spot on this page. Is or is there not a mark? And so it's just on-off; it's a blip or it isn't, and that blip can degrade considerably before it disappears altogether so that you can go back and reconstruct the record in a way that is completely different from the possibilities that we've had, for example, when a microform begins to fade or lose its image.

Gibson: You have to produce a hard copy to read it. At present, it doesn't have the resolution that people will accept.

Darling: I think again a lot of it depends on the type of material that you're talking about. There's a lot of basic textual data that is perfectly acceptable at the lower levels, but on the other hand there are certain kinds of things where you absolutely must have that additional thing, and so we will have to be clever and smart about deciding which are the areas to concentrate on first. I don't know what the likelihood is of the screening capability coming up to the ability of the disc storage in ten years or so. I suppose they can develop that, but, in the meantime, we can begin with something like LC cards which are an obvious and excellent application for the current abilities of the machine. There are a lot of exciting possibilities, but we need to be careful in not getting so carried away by some dazzling dream of preserving everything that we lose sight of the immediate requirements of our work.

CAROLYN CLARK MORROW

Conservation Librarian
Southern Illinois University at Carbondale

National Preservation Planning and Regional Cooperative Conservation Efforts

This morning, I would like to present a chronology of national preservation planning, describe some notable developments in the area of regional cooperative conservation efforts, and suggest the types of activities that are feasible on a cooperative basis.

In 1964, Gordon Williams conducted a study for the Association of Research Libraries (ARL) to plan for a national program for the preservation of research library materials. The Williams report, endorsed in principle by ARL in 1965, recommended that libraries establish a central agency to "insure the physical preservation of at least one example of every deteriorating book and make photocopies of the preserved originals readily available to all libraries."[1] The proposal went over like a lead balloon. It was still the boom years of the sixties, money was easy, and libraries were intent on building collections. So what if a few dusty volumes lay crumbling? Furthermore, the logistics of establishing a central agency were overwhelming. The 1964 report was definitely ahead of its time.

In 1972, the Association of Research Libraries came out with a second report, written by Warren Haas, and entitled *Preparation of Detailed Specifications for a National System for Preservation of Library Materials.* It had been eight years since the 1964 ARL report. Those intervening years had seen the culmination of research efforts at the Barrow Research Laboratory in Richmond, Virginia, with the publication of a series of studies investigating the permanence and durability of the book.[2] This concrete evidence, printed in black and white, had helped to heighten an awareness of the problem of paper deterioration. After all, statements such as "97 per cent of the book papers produced during the first half of the twentieth century have a life expectancy of fifty years or less" could not help but turn

37

a few heads. Also between the two ARL reports, in 1969, the Graduate Library School of the University of Chicago held their thirty-fourth annual conference on the topic of "deterioration and preservation of library materials."[3] It was clear from the nature of the papers presented, that the profession of librarianship was determined to be optimistic. It was not until much later that librarianship faced the frightening realization that they had perhaps waited too long to act.

The catastrophic floods in Florence, Italy, in November 1966 also occurred between the two ARL reports. The ensuing destruction and damage focused international attention on the preservation of cultural materials. Conservators from all over the world rushed to Florence to aid in recovery and reclamation efforts and the experience of working together to solve conservation problems gave the field its first taste of the powers of collective action.

So by 1972, it seemed the time was ripe for more planning by ARL. In its second report, ARL dropped the idea of a "central agency" and prepared instead "Suggestions for Action" including the topics of Research, Education and Training, Preservation and Conservation Efforts in Individual Libraries, and Collective Action. The gist of the report was that preservation should be viewed as part of the broader goal of access to information. Presumably, libraries made a conscious decision to preserve by collecting the material in the first place. By allowing materials to deteriorate beyond the point of usability, libraries were limiting access to information. Under the topic of Collective Action, the ARL report called for a group of ten to fifteen libraries to join together to carry out certain specific preservation projects as a model for an eventual national plan. Paramount would be the development of a coordinated system of individual preservation collections based on well-defined subject areas. The report maintained that "by not aspiring to preserve everything, and concentrating instead on discrete subject areas, some real progress becomes possible."[4]

ARL had good reason to assume that the timing was right for such collective action. The oldest and largest research libraries had begun, in the late sixties (with much wringing of hands), to tackle the problem. In 1967, the Library of Congress unified preservation and binding activities into a single Preservation Office, promising greater emphasis on the application of scientific principles and sound administrative methods.[5] In 1970, the Newberry Library established a Conservation Laboratory under the direction of Paul Banks. Exemplary leadership and an unerring sense for pinpointing the important issues made the Newberry program an early moving force in the field, though a separate Conservation Department did not emerge until 1975.[6] Also in 1970, the New York Public Library published its *Memorandum on the Conservation of the Collections* and launched a Conservation Division.[7] The *Memorandum* was the first attempt to formally to assess conservation needs and determine priorities. Yale followed suit in 1971 with a Preservation Office.[8] Columbia was laying the groundwork for preservation reorganization as a result of a study completed in 1970 by the management consulting firm of Booz, Allen, and Hamilton. Its Preservation Department formally made the organization chart in 1974.[9]

The second ARL report received serious attention because libraries were beginning to act. They were beginning to act because they were no longer able to ignore the awesome prospect of millions of simultaneously deteriorating documents. However, the ARL report also wisely pointed out that success would ultimately hinge on "finding a permanent way for research libraries to take effective collective action," and that in the "final analysis, the research libraries of the country lack a capacity for collective action that is suitable to the dimension of the job to be done."[10]

In 1973, a significant vehicle for national preservation planning was established. With broad representation from the conservation field, the National Conservatory Advisory Council (NCAC) emerged to provide a "forum for cooperation and planning among institutions and programs concerned with the conservation of cultural property in museums, historic properties, libraries, archives, and related collections." An original mandate of NCAC was to consider the advisability of creating a national institute for conservation. In its role as an advisory body, NCAC has sought to identify national needs in areas such as training, research, and standards. By issuing and distributing reports, NCAC has expanded an awareness and understanding of conservation problems.

Early in 1974, the New York Public Library and the libraries of Yale, Columbia, and Harvard joined forces to form Research Libraries Group, Inc. (RLG)—a separate corporation owned and operated by its members. RLG is dedicated to solving the "double problem of rising costs and dwindling funds for the operation of research libraries by coordinating activities and pooling resources." The significance of RLG is that it represents an integration of preservation with dissemination and access— in part fulfilling the recommendations of ARL's second report.

By 1976, the National Conservation Advisory Council had issued their first major report, *Conservation of Cultural Property in the United States.* The report outlined national needs in conservation and made recommendations for national conservation planning. Those recommendations included a call for a nationwide cooperative effort to preserve our national artistic and historic heritage; establishment of a permanent national advisory council, a national institute for conservation, and a network of regional conservation centers; increased training for conservators and education for curators and administrators; increased scientific support; and the development of standards. The report projected that a national institute could fulfill much of the national need by providing information, training, education, and coordinating research and the development of standards.

Optimism about the possibility of cooperation in the specific arena of library and archives conservation reached a peak in December 1976 with the National Preservation Planning Conference held at the Library of Congress. For two days, forty-one invited participants and nineteen LC staff members struggled with the "what," "who," and "how" of preservation. Frazer Poole, chairman of the conference, summed up their major objective when he said, "After years of worry and talk, we must establish a plan of action."[11]

Much of what went on before 1976 in the area of national preservation planning stressed that since libraries do not have the resources to preserve everything, they must first decide what needs to be preserved. This was where collection development was supposed to meet preservation and decide what would have the chance to survive for the users of the future. By 1976, a decade of experience in national planning for preservation had shown that libraries were bogged down pondering the "what." Warren Haas, author of the 1972 report (where he urged libraries to determine discrete subject areas worthy of preservation) found himself saying in 1976 at LC, "don't worry about selection and priorities,..." they will "take care of themselves once we have developed a national capacity that provides a set of preservation options." He called for a small steering committee to steer us "towards action, not planning."[12] Following the Planning Conference, in July 1977 the Library of Congress formally named a National Preservation Program Officer and began to plan for those services that LC could provide in the way of national direction to aid a nationwide preservation effort.

No small amount of change and reorganization at the Library of Congress (not to mention moving) has stymied the National Preservation Program these last several years. However, the new chief of the Preservation Office and National Preservation Officer, Peter Sparks, plans to spend the next six months exploring the future direction and emphasis of the program. Assistant Chief Lawrence Robinson will administer the day-to-day mechanisms of the Preservation Office.

According to Dr. Sparks, a revived National Preservation Program will definitely expand its publications program and continue its intern and education program. It will also continue the encouragement of cooperative microfilming projects. New components to the program will probably include a formal technical consulting service and information center.

LC's preservation program has always been in a sense, national; exploring theoretical and managerial solutions to the Library of Congress's own preservation problems and developing applied technology has worked for the benefit of all libraries. The National Preservation Program will enhance LC's national role and provide national direction to preservation by actively communicating the methods and technology explored at LC and putting out models that other libraries can work from.

Following the landmark planning conference in 1976 at LC, 1977 and 1978 were busy years of workshops, seminars, and more workshops. Although not formal cooperation, these sharing and expanding experiences strengthened the informal people network that kept conservation awareness and efforts growing. The publication *Conservation Administration News*, for example, grew out of a 1978 Columbia University institute and has become a significant information sharing tool.

In 1977, the American Library Association, Resources and Technical Services Division (RTSD) formed a Discussion Group on the Preservation of Library Materials to "informally discuss common problems concerning the preservation of library materials."[13] By the annual meeting in June 1980, Preservation of Library Materials Section (PLMS) was launched as a new section of RTSD. With PLMS, preservation has an official voice in the national organization of librarians.

In 1978, the National Conservation Advisory Council published two significant documents having implications for national preservation planning. *The Report of the Study Committee on Libraries and Archives: National Needs in Libraries and Archives Conservation* sought to "identify and describe the problems existing in the field as a necessary first step to seeking solutions to these problems."[14] The committee concluded with seven recommendations for national action in the area of preservation and called for the "proposed national conservation institute, the national preservation program of the Library of Congress, and other bodies" to address them without delay. The recommendations included: (1) formulation of guidelines for environmental and condition surveys, (2) increased education and training efforts, (3) increased research, (4) a flow of sound and balanced conservation information, (5) establishment of regional or cooperative centers, (6) a vigorous program to preserve the intellectual content of deteriorated materials through reproduction, and (7) the development of standards. Today, it is gratifying indeed, to note that there is progress on every front.[15]

A fifty-five page *Discussion Paper on a National Institute for Conservation of Cultural Property* was also issued by NCAC in 1978. Its purpose was to further delineate the possible functions of a national institute and stimulate interest and input from the conservation profession. Members of the American Institute for Conservation (AIC) (the professional organization of conservators) discussed the proposal at annual meetings in 1979, 1980, and 1981. Concerns expressed by the profession were that a national institute would drain already depleted funding sources, that it would require major support from the federal government and yet be unduly restricted by government controls, and that it would perhaps unfairly limit the access of private conservators to services in favor of institutions. The unseemly, but practical question of how funding would be obtained in an era of shrinking federal support for the arts was also raised. Conservators further expressed concern that the proposed institute would not advance the high standards adhered to by the conservation profession and promulgated in AIC's *Code of Ethics.*

After nearly eight years of discussion and revision, NCAC published in April 1982 a detailed *Proposal for a National Institute for Conservation (NIC) of Cultural Property* and has begun to seek funding. NIC is conceived as a private organization with some government support, but receiving at least one-half of its funding from the private sector. It will serve the three major functions of information, education, and scientific support. Information Services will include a reference and research library, consulting, dissemination, and publication. Education Services will encompass training of new conservators, seminars to educate the users of conservation services, continuing education opportunities for conservators, and communication of conservation concerns to the public. Scientific Support Services will concentrate on developing standards for testing materials, devising analytical tests, and conducting basic and applied research according to the priorities established by the field. It is not envisioned that the NIC will duplicate or supplant already existing facilities or capabilities, but rather will have a strong coordinating and contracting element. NIC will, however, absorb NCAC at its inception. The proposal for NIC includes details of staffing, equipment and space needs, and budget and calls for a phased implementation of services over a three-year period.

At the beginning of 1979, the Research Libraries Group amended its charter and began to expand its membership. Today, with twenty-five full members thoughout the United States, RLG's potential for effective cooperative action in the area of preservation is greatly enhanced. Most recently, RLG's Preservation Committee is developing specifications for inputting master negative information into RLIN (Research Libraries Information Network). Enhancements to RLIN allow members to enter item-specific information about the existence of master microforms and service copies and the intent to film specific items. RLG's Preservation Committee recommends that enhancements to RLIN be compatible with other automated systems and that the system be capable of furnishing an RLG list of microfilm masters. The implementation of RLG's plan to share preservation microfilming information is truly reflective of a national preservation program.[16] They have received a grant from NEH (Oct. 1982) to begin inputting. The basis of the project, of course, is the New York Public Library's present project to input its master negative file. RLG also plans to institute a cooperative filming program and is currently studying possible categories of materials to be filmed and operational details such as bibliographic control and standards for filming, processing, and storing master negatives. Future activities of the committee may include a resource manual of standards and designation of preservation responsibility in conjunction with primary collecting responsibility. Simply by addressing preservation and conservation concerns, however, RLG engages in a very basic form of cooperation, peer group pressure, and is undoubtedly responsible for increased and upgraded preservation efforts in some of the largest research libraries in the country.

A discussion of the chronology of national preservation planning begins to sound rather repetitive. Words such as *information, coordination, training, support,* and *standards* occur again and again in the planning documents of the last decade. Many of us with a sense of urgency may wonder: When will there be some action?

It may be that ten years, or even twenty, is not very long to address such a mammoth and complicated task as preservation of the nation's intellectual resources. We have made real progress in developing conservation awareness and sophistication among those in a position to act and we are moving toward responsible collective action-albeit slowly. It might be useful, even uplifting to ask: What do we have today, in 1981, in national preservation action that we did not have even five years ago?

We have at Columbia University the first academic program to train library conservators and preservation administrators. We have a detailed proposal for a National Institute for Conservation that includes the concerns of libraries and archives. We have a National Preservation Program at the Library of Congress that promises to be responsive to the needs of the nation's libraries. We have in the Research Libraries Group a vehicle for cooperative action that will provide a model and a beginning for national cooperative activities. We have important work going forward in the area of standards (for example, permanent/durable paper, binding, and environmental storage). We have real breakthroughs in the application of conservation science to preservation problems (for example, mass deacidification, cold storage of photographic materials, and vacuum-drying of water-damaged library materials). We have exciting possibilities in new technology that can be used to record and preserve information. We have an official section of the American Library Association dedicated to addressing preservation concerns. And finally, we have a steady increase in preservation activities and commitment in the nation's libraries. We *have* a lot of action on the national preservation scene.

If we accept, as we must, that we will never have enough time, money, or staff to preserve everything that has deteriorated or is deteriorating now, then we must have coordination of preservation activities on the national level. However, as we all realize, planning, or even action, on the national level (however encouraging, or even grandiose as in the case of the proposed National Institute for Conservation) does not solve today's nitty-gritty, down-home problem with deteriorating collections. These are problems that for years librarians have affectionately been calling book confetti, yellow snow, or (as a librarian in my library is fond of saying) peanut brittle. Pamela Darling put it best in introduction to *Library Journal*'s 1979 series on preservation when she said, "A 'national' preservation program decreed and directed from some central source of power/knowledge/funds is neither practical or desireable at the present time."[17] Instead, she suggested a nationwide effort emphasizing communication and cooperation. She went on to say, "Only after learning how to create viable preservation programs on a small scale are we going to build an effective large-scale program."[18] As we heard this morning from Pam [Darling], both the Association of Research Libraries and the Society of American Archivists have put this philosophy into action. Likewise, in the last decade, significant regional and local activity has moved us much closer to the level of knowledge and sophistication needed to grapple effectively (and efficiently) with today's and tomorrow's preservation problems.

The most notable development in the area of cooperative or regional conservation has been the experience of the Northeast Document Conservation Center (NEDCC). NEDCC was formed (as the New England Document Conservation Center) in 1973, but was conceived as early as 1965 by Walter Muir Whitehill and George Cunha at the Boston Anthenaem. The center was established under the New England Interstate Library Compact with start-up funds from the Council on Library Resources. It is administered by the New England Library Board, which consists of six state library agency heads or their designated representatives.

Today, NEDCC has evolved into a successful cooperative venture.[19] In new larger quarters in Andover, Massachusetts, they serve several hundred clients and provide professional treatment for a wide variety of materials. They also offer field services such as mobile fumigation, disaster assistance, on-site consulting, surveys and collection evaluations, and workshops.

From its inception, it was hoped that NEDCC would serve as a prototype for other regional centers to spring up around the country. Eight years later, they are still the only treatment center devoted to library and archival materials. Why? Mainly because the development of a treatment center is a complicated and expensive undertaking and because experts have vigorously warned against the too rapid rise of multiple centers before there are enough people to staff them. Additionally, NEDCC is essentially devoted to highly specialized item-by-item treatment of materials.

Although conservation has traditionally been associated with the treatment of rare books and unique materials, raising the conservation consciousness of librarians and administrators has resulted in a shift in focus to the long-term maintenance of whole collections and preservation of the intellectual content of deteriorated materials. Can an administrator in good conscience support a regional treatment center when the library can only afford to send a few special items for treatment each year and when the bulk of the collection is in desperate need of preservation attention? NEDCC itself has responded to this shift in focus by expanding its consulting and training activities and by working closely with clients to help them select materials for treatment within the framework of a rational overall plan. Fledgling cooperative and regional efforts around the country are emphasizing those activities that can help libraries develop viable local programs to cope with the preservation problem.

Demonstrating what can be accomplished in cooperative conservation in a very discrete region is the Book Preservation Center serving the New York metropolitan area.[20] Hosted by the New York Botanical Gardens Library and using the facilities of its workshop, the center has, since 1979, built a very successful cooperative program. The center's purpose is to "help librarians plan and implement in-house preservation programs within the very real limitations of space, money, and staff."[21]

After visiting the participating libraries, the center developed its package of services based on common needs. A series of workshops was held to demonstrate very basic procedures followed by a second series to teach more complex techniques. Participants were furnished with information sheets and illustrated instruction sheets. These handouts formed the basis for a manual to be published in 1983. The center has also compiled an extensive information file and even provides assistance to libraries in setting up in-house work areas. A three-year grant from the National Endowment for the Humanities (NEH) is enabling the center to continue its workshops in New York, as well as hold workshops in other locations around the country. To date, the center is entirely supported by grant funds and provides service free of charge to participating libraries. From modest, but highly effective beginnings, the Book Preservation Center hopes to expand to include cooperative purchasing of supplies and restoration work on individual items for other libraries.

A notable example of regional cooperative planning was the Western States Materials Conservation Project.[22] The project began as a year-long saga to determine conservation needs in the states west of the Mississippi River and to develop a coordinated plan for conservation in the West. At twenty state meetings, 454 people participated to identify existing conservation programs, define needs, and suggest action. Three areas of concern were identified: conservation information and education; conservation services; and research, standards, and legislation. These three concerns formed the themes for discussion at the two-and-a-half-day Feasibility Colloquium at Snowbird, Utah. Two representatives from each state meeting attended the colloquium where the group voted to form the Western Conservation Congress and adopt a three-phase plan for regional cooperation.

As conceived at Snowbird, the Western Conservation Congress would, in its first phase, provide information to its members through a clearinghouse. Components of the clearinghouse program would include directory information (such as people and services), notices of training and education offerings, development of conservation administration tools and information packets, and a consulting service. The second phase calls for creating a more sophisticated package of services, and the third phase for creating a network of conservation laboratories in the West.

To date, the Western Conservation Congress, under the guidance of a steering committee, is exploring avenues for funding and using volunteers to maintain contact with its two hundred members. A catalog of conservation reference materials in the West that can be loaned has been compiled. If the Western Conservation Congress can either obtain outside funding or muster a significant monetary commitment from its members, it will have a chance to survive and fulfill its potential.

Similar in design to the Western States Materials Conservation Project, but on a smaller scale, the Midwest Regional Study for Materials Conservation was conducted to identify persons interested in conservation in a six-state region of Indiana, Kentucky, Michigan, Ohio, Pennsylvania, and West Virginia. Planning meetings were held at three locations and the study's final report outlines possible avenues for cooperation.

With direction and encouragement from the state libraries, statewide cooperative planning and activities are going forward in Colorado, Illinois, and Kentucky.

In Colorado, a statewide plan, *Towards a Cooperative Approach to the Preservation of Documentary Resources in Colorado* was completed in 1981 by Howard Lowell under contract with NEDCC and with funding from the Library Services and Construction Act (LSCA). The published plan is the culmination of a planning and survey process that started with recommendations made during the Colorado meeting of the Western States Materials Conservation Project and included development of a self-assessment manual for libraries, conservation education and training experiences conducted in Colorado, and surveys of a representative sample of libraries to determine common problems and needs. The plan calls for a separate preservation position in the state library to be responsible for the coordination of preservation activities in the state. In the interim, the staff position charged with collection development has had the preservation responsibility added to it.

In Illinois, as the result of a formal Needs Assessment Survey conducted in fall 1980, Southern Illinois University at Carbondale developed a proposal for an Illinois Cooperative Conservation Program (ICCP) and was successful in the fall of 1981 in securing LSCA funds on the recommendation of the Illinois State Library Advisory Committee. The program takes advantage of the cooperative mechanism that exists in ILLINET (the Illinois Library and Information Network) to enhance long-range library development by the addition of a conservation component.

ICCP has built upon the outreach activities of Morris Library's conservation program and, with input from a Program Advisory Committee, is bringing conservation services to all types of libraries in Illinois. The program offers an information service, publishes posters and information sheets and held eight workshops around the state. Other components of the program include an emphasis on disaster preparedness, the development and dissemination of training materials, and coordination of conservation and preservation activities throughout the state.

In Kentucky, George Cunha is at it again as chairman of a Conservation Advisory Committee appointed by the state librarian. The committee is surveying libraries and archival repositories in the state to gather information on existing conservation resources as the first step toward a long-range program for Kentucky. The committee has recommended and had approved both an expanded disaster assistance service and the establishment of a Conservation Clearinghouse as part of the Public Records Division of the Department of Library and Archives.

All libraries face the need to preserve the mass of deteriorating materials as well as arrange for the physical treatment of special items. Based on our experience in cooperation to date, it may be that the most viable arrangement for providing conservation services is a regional treatment center that can also dispense information, engage in training and consulting activities, and coordinate regional cooperative projects.

An important concept in cooperative conservation is that, whatever services are available cooperatively, they must be in addition to activities taking place at individual libraries. With organizations such as ALA's Preservation of Library Materials Section, innovative programs such as ARL's Preservation Planning Project and SAA's Basic Archival Conservation Program, and cooperative ventures such as the Book Preservation Center and the Illinois Cooperative Conservation Program, we are assured of having the tools needed to direct conservation activities and a forum for discussing common concerns. What is also vital to the preservation effort is informed library administrators who are willing to reorganize and upgrade the preservation and conservation function within their own libraries and commit funds. Cooperation is not a substitute for local action but an enhancement. Cooperation enables libraries to avoid needless duplication of effort, share scarce expertise, and afford services that may be unfeasible or prohibitively expensive on their own. For example, a group of libraries might cooperate to provide centralized cold storage for important but little-used research materials, but each individual library should also have proper environmental conditions for the rest of its collection. Training materials developed by a cooperative conservation center would greatly facilitate the implementaion of sound conservation procedures at individual libraries.

Another important concept behind successful cooperation is that librarians and curators must be well informed about conservation in order to arrive at intelligent decisions about the best use of cooperative services. For example, a book that is extremely fragile and brittle should not be sent to a conservation treatment center for restoration unless the paper format is essential to understanding the work, or the physical book is important as an artifact. Even more basic, a certain level of sophistication about conservation is necessary for libraries even to recognize the potential benefits of cooperative conservation.

Based on the experience of cooperative ventures to date, it seems that a key to success is the existence of an already established vehicle for cooperation. A formally organized and politically and financially secure basis for cooperation will lend itself to fewer problems of funding and long-term commitment. The sanction of an official body such as a state library, or regional system or network, can insure a broad base of support for cooperative action and can help keep momentum going in lean times. For example, the Northeast Document Conservation Center is authorized by the New England Interstate Library Compact, a regional political subdivision whose purpose is to plan and implement cooperative projects between libraries in a six-state region. NEDCC receives 10 percent of its annual budget from the Compact. The Research Libraries Group is an independent corporation formed by its members and dedicated to sharing resources; it concerns itself with preservation as a part of the total goal of dissemination and access.

On the other hand, a regional or cooperative center can be organized solely for the purpose of providing conservation services to its membership. Its success then depends on the members' continuing commitment to the venture, its businesslike operation, and the quality of the work generated by the conservation staff. For example, the Conservation Center for Art and Historic Artifacts in Philadelphia is an independent, nonprofit treatment laboratory that specializes in the treatment of art and historic artifacts on paper. Its nonprofit status also allows it to receive grant funds.

The benefit of a supportive host institution is often crucial to the initial development and continued success of a cooperative conservation venture—providing that the host does not impose undue restrictions or interfere with policy or operations. Part of the success of the Book Preservation Center can undoubtedly be attributed to its having a "home" at the New York Botanical Gardens Library. Likewise, the Illinois Cooperative Conservation Program would in all probability not have made a beginning without the support of Morris Library and Southern Illinois University.

Regardless of formal organizational structure, the services offered by a cooperative venture must reflect the members' needs, their willingness to pay for services, and the peculiarities of the region. If members are concerned with the maintenance of audiovisual materials, then a center must address their concerns. Members' willingness to pay a reasonable fee for services is a reflection of their commitment to the concept of conservation; a center that relies entirely on grant funds for support fosters unreal expectations and may have a difficult time getting even modest support if grant funds disappear. The cooperative mechanism successfully employed by a Book Preservation Center located in the Bronx and serving libraries in a 625-square-mile area would probably not work for a Western Conservation Congress that plans to serve libraries in a 1.8 million-square-mile region.

What kinds of services are feasible on a cooperative basis? Basically, they can be divided into five different types: information, consultation and surveying, cost-sharing, coordination, and treatment.

Information

Every planning document and needs assessment survey that has explored cooperative conservation has emphasized the need for basic and specific information. People want to know: What are the optimum storage conditions? How can environmental conditions be improved? How do I monitor the environment? What standards exist for library materials? What is the state of the art of mass deacidification? Who has conservation expertise in my region? Where can I locate vacuum-drying facilities? What is needed in a disaster preparedness plan? What are the best supplies and who sells them? Where can I get more training?

Information can be offered in a variety of ways and, as the most basic service, costs for providing information are most logically absorbed in membership fees. A newsletter can keep libraries up to date on techniques, opportunities, and research. An on-line directory can match needs with people and services. Training materials such as slide/tape shows and manuals can be compiled and distributed. A lending library can make a reference and research collection available to all. And perhaps the most satisfying and expedient..."Hello, this is *x* library, can you tell me...?" Likewise, regional conservation centers would have a need for reliable technical information that would be developed and dispersed by the National Preservation Program or the proposed National Institute for Conservation.

Consultation and Surveying

Shared expertise in the form of a consultant service can help members of a cooperative venture identify problems and determine directions. Collection surveys define and quantify individual situations and the accompanying report can suggest improvements and serve as a basis for rationalizing increased funding for the local preservation effort. An inspection of the building might reveal the most economical plan for improving air exchange, upgrading systems for filtration of airborne pollutants, or adapting existing air-conditioning systems for humidity control. A consultant could survey present treatment practices and make recommendations for upgrading and expanding routine repair operations. A specific, valuable collection might warrant piece-by-piece examination by a conservator with recommendations for treatment, discussion of options, and cost estimates.

Consultation services can be a routine task of staff employed by a cooperative center. Costs can be prorated depending on the complexity of the consulting task, or consulting and surveying services included as a privilege of membership. Or more simply, a cooperative center could serve a liaison function and arrange for fees and services from outside consultants, or merely put libraries in touch with appropriate experts.

Cost-Sharing

The dictionary definition of *cooperation* stresses economic cooperation and mutual profit. Conservation services that are financially unfeasible for the individual library or infrequently needed can be made available through cost-sharing or a pooling of resources. Cooperative purchasing of supplies or equipment can reduce costs. For example, there is no reason for every library to own a $8,000 fumigator that may be used only a handful of times in a year. Likewise, polyester encapsulation could be performed more efficiently at a cooperative center that owned the $12,000 machine that neatly and quickly seals the edges of the envelope. Specific research contracted for by a cooperative center would be for the benefit of all libraries. Cost-sharing activities can be as simple as sharing the cost of an information service, or as elaborate as a cooperative preservation microfilming project or regional cold storage facility.

Coordination

Coordination of regional preservation activities is a logical role for a cooperative center to assume. Preservation microfilming projects can be coordinated so that duplication of filming is eliminated. A cooperative center can also coordinate training and education opportunities. For example, staff from member libraries can attend intensive, short-term training sessions at a center. General workshops can be periodically offered at convenient locations. The technology of conservation is often at a level that overpowers local expertise and new developments are continually being offered as the panacea for all our problems. A cooperative center could screen new technology and coordinate specialized services such as vacuum-drying, conservation rebinding, and mass deacidification.

Treatment

The literature of cooperative conservation is replete with warnings about the establishment of regional treatment centers. This cautionary stance is advanced for a number of very valid reasons. First, fully-trained conservators are scarce; there are simply not enough qualified professionals available to direct the workshops of very many regional centers. Second, technical support staff must be trained in-house—a time-consuming and costly undertaking. Third, the cost of equipping a full-scale treatment facility is great. And fourth, "at-cost" treatment sounds great, but at-cost can still cost a lot. For example, some economies of scale are possible for some types of treatments; however, many operations take a given number of hours to complete satisfactorily regardless of whether it is on a profit or not-for-profit basis.

Not to be all discouragement—some simple operations can be performed at a cooperative treatment center as a prelude for more complicated treatments after the center is fully staffed and functioning. For instance, protective enclosures such as rare book boxes, portfolios, simple wrappers, and polyester film envelopes can be an appropriate and inexpensive option for libraries. Or, like NEDCC, a center might offer a microfilming service to provide archival-quality film for difficult-to-film materials. This type of basic conservation work can be done by conservation technicians trained and supervised by a conservator. More complicated restoration treatments for very valuable books, manuscripts, maps, and photographs could be gradually added to the repertoire of a center. Actually, it has been convincingly argued that the scarcity of trained professionals is all the more reason for the existence of regional centers. Otherwise only the few and lucky elite will have access to these specialized services.[23]

Except for NEDCC, existing cooperative treatment centers are primarily for the treatment of museum materials. Most centers, including NEDCC, have been established with the assistance of a large start-up grant to defray the cost of equipment and give the center a grace period of several years. Ann Russell, Director of NEDCC, has suggested that realistically, a treatment center should receive some form of partial subsidy on a continuing basis.

A center normally charges for services on an hourly basis. Overhead is included in the billing rate. Most centers charge higher fees for work done for nonmembers. For example, the Rocky Mountain Regional Conservation Center charges a 25 percent higher rate for nonmembers. There are many possible arrangements for billing treatment services. The Conservation Center for Art and Historic Artifacts offers contracts with members for single item treatments, intermittent treatments, or annual or multiyear arrangements.

At NEDCC there are no "fixed" costs for treatment because of the wide range of damage that can accrue to materials due to variations in the physical properties of paper, leather, etc., the environment in which the item was stored, and the use or abuse to which the item was subjected. A member first submits a document for pre-examination and the center prepares an estimate which is in turn submitted for the member's approval. The success of a center may depend on the ability of its conservators to estimate the cost of each individual job accurately.

What is standing in the way of the development of multiple cooperative regional centers that offer a variety of information, education, coordination and treatment services?

The number one impediment is cost. Since libraries are impoverished these days, they exercise extreme caution when advised that they will have to pay for a new (even if it is vital) service. The bottom line is, of course, priorities. But who can blame the library administrator faced with the rapid rise in the cost of serial subscriptions and the rapid fall in the morale of staff who receive inadequate salary increases? With standstill budgets, an administrator is wanting to commit even modest funds to preservation would be forced to take funds away from something else.

On the other hand, libraries have found money to improve bibliographic access to resources. And some would say that to plan and implement an elaborate and expensive automated system for bibliographic access without also providing for preservation is shortsighted. It may be that once we have perfected systems to identify and locate bibliographic items exactly, we will go to the shelves (or in a cooperative system send someone in some distant library to the shelves) only to find the physical item disintegrated. Then we have to go back and update the file, right?

Cooperative preservation and conservation can and should exist on a number of levels. Preservation planning and coordination on the national level is imperative, as is the measured development of a network of regional centers that are responsive to regional needs and that reflect national priorities. There is no simple or cheap answer to the preservation problem, but if we accept the preservation challenge, then perhaps cooperation can be an important enhancement to our efforts.

NOTES

1. Williams, Gordon R. "The Preservation of Deteriorating Books: Part I: Examination of the Problem." *Library Journal* 91(1 Jan. 1966):51-56.

2. W.J. Barrow Laboratory. *Permanence/Durability of the Book,* 7 vols. Richmond, Va.: W.J. Barrow Research Laboratory, 1963-74.

3. Winger, Howard W., and Smith, Richard D., eds. *Deterioration and Preservation of Library Materials* (Proceedings of the Thirty-Fourth Annual Conference of the Graduate Library School,f 4-6 Aug. 1969). Chicago: University of Chicago Press, 1970. Published originally in *Library Quarterly* vol. 40, Jan. 1970.

4. Haas, Warren J. *Preparation of Detailed Specifications for a National System for the Preservation of Library Materials.* Washington, D.C.: Association of Research Libraries, 1972. (Reprinted in *Information–Part 2: Reports, Bibliographies,* vol. 2, nos. 1-2(1973):17-37.)

5. "Preservation Office at LC." *Library of Congress Information Bulletin* 26(2 Nov. 1967):721-22.

6. Schur, Susan. "Library/Conservation Profile: The Newberry Library." *Technology and Conservation* 6(Summer 1981):22-31.

7. *See* Baker, John P. "Preservation Programs of the New York Public Library. Part I. The Early Years." *Microform Review* 10(Winter 1981):25-28.

8. Walker, Gay. "Preservation at Yale." *Conservation Administration News,* no. 1(June 1979):1, 6, 8.

9. Byrne, Sherry. "Columbia University: Pioneer in Preservation." *Conservation Administration News,* no. 7(June 1981):1, 4, 5.

10. Haas, *Preparation of Detailed Specifications.*

11. Library of Congress. "The Preservation Program of the Library of Congress." In *A National Preservation Program: Proceedings of a Planning Conference* (held 16, 17 Dec. 1976). Washington, D.C.: LC, 1980, pp. 16-26.

12. Ibid.

13. American Library Association. Resources and Technical Services Division. *Manual of Procedures.* Chicago: ALA, 1977.

14. National Conservation Advisory Council. *The Report of the Study Committee on Libraries and Archives.* Washington, D.C.: NCAC, 1978.

15. Ibid.

16. Research Libraries Group. Preservation Committee. "Research Libraries Information Network. Design Requirements for Preservation Support Enhancements: Microforms." Mimeographed. Stanford, Calif.: RLG, 1981.

17. Darling, Pamela W. "Towards a National Nationwide Preservation Program." *Library Journal* 104(1 May 1979):1012.

18. Ibid.

19. Russell, Ann. "Regional Conservation: A New England Example." In *Preservation of Paper and Textiles of Historic and Artistic Value II,* edited by John C. Williams, pp. 25-32. Washington, D.C.: American Chemical Society, 1981.

20. Reed, Judith. "A Nucleus of Guidance, A Center for Preservation." *Library Scene* 9(Sept. 1982):12-13.

21. Ibid.

22. Day, Karen. "A Conservation Plan for the West." *Conservation Administration News,* no. 6(Feb. 1981):1, 6-8.

23. Bruer, J. Michael. "Regional Cooperation for Disaster Preparedness." In *Disasters: Prevention and Coping,* edited by James Meyers and Denise Bedford. Stanford, Calif.: Stanford University Libraries, 1981.

DISCUSSION

Gerald Lundeen (Graduate School of Library Science, University of Hawaii, Honolulu): I think I heard you say that the NEDCC was the only regional treatment center. The Pacific Regional Conservation Center does offer treatment and services to libraries and museums in the state of Hawaii and the Pacific region.

Carolyn Clark Morrow: Yes. So does the Conservation Center for Art and Historic Artifacts. What I said was "devoted to"; that was *begun* on that basis.

Lundeen: Right. That I believe is its primary mission.

Morrow: In Hawaii?

Lundeen: Yes.

Morrow: I'm mistaken then, if you say its primary mission is library materials.

Lundeen: Library *and* museum.

Morrow: Museums tend to have what they consider more precious materials, so even NEDCC, especially because its conservator comes from a museum background, has attracted a lot of museum work.

Tom Kilton (Library, University of Illinois at Urbana-Champaign): You were mentioning the RLG (Research Libraries Group) plan to have a list of microform masters that would go into RLIN. First, is there any cooperation planned between this effort and the present *National Register of Microforms* records at LC; and secondly, if it does go on-line into RLIN, will libraries who are not members of RLIN have access to the information, to maybe offprints or some other means?

Morrow: Yes, the plan I saw talked about at least the potential for a published list. They also emphasized that the system will be compatible with other automated systems so that they would be able to be used by other RLG members. I know there are RLG people here and maybe they would like to speak to that.

Nancy Gwinn (Research Libraries Group): What Carolyn has said is correct. The design requirements for enhancing the RLIN data base with regard to microforms called for the ability to retrieve records for master negatives and produce, from that, a union list in some form of hard copy, either COM or paper—it's uncertain. The requirements are just that—requirements. Our systems people are now looking at that document and beginning to work on the specifications that would allow for that to happen. It's still unknown what the cost will be. It's still unknown what the demand is. So there are a number of questions to be answered but the

Preservation Committee is well aware of the need to disseminate this information outside the partnership. RLG doesn't think it can solve the preservation problem alone any more than can any other institution or group of institutions, so they are looking at this as a national responsibility and hoping that, in fact, it can be meshed with other efforts. If we can make our programs and plans known, then other people can use that in deciding what they want to do, and perhaps we can carve the problem down to manageable size. As far as the *National Register* is concerned, it would be very nice if we could take the whole file that exists there in the Register office (and I've been to look at it and have seen it—it's a nice alphabetized, integrated file), and just convert it through a retrospective conversion process to machine-readable form. It would be a mammoth project to do that and it would require a lot of editing of the file before it could be easily converted. It's not something that can be scanned like the card stock in the Card Division which is all nice and clean with a nice access number. The RLG Board has now stated that, as a priority for RLG, members will look to converting their own files of master negatives and contributing the cataloging to RLIN. We would like to draw the Library of Congress into this, if not for the whole register file, then at least for the files that exist in LC's own preservation microfilming office, of the things that it has itself filmed, which, of course, is a substantial amount of material. And we do have, as a member of our Preservation Committee, Peter Sparks, who is the new Preservation Officer at LC, and we are exploring with him the possibilities of doing this. I do not know what the prospects are because it involves LC's agreeing either to produce tapes or to input directly into RLIN through terminals and they do not now have the capacity to do that. But we are talking about it. That's for the retrospective part. As far as the future of the *National Register* itself, I'm sure that you've all seen announcements of the possible automating of the *National Union Catalog* which would incorporate the *National Register* in some form. There is a lot of work going on now among the utilities talking about contributing records to the *National Union Catalog* in tape form. Those records, of course, would include any cataloging of microforms or master negatives that is done, so through that circuitous route, those records would eventually reach the *National Union Catalog*, and one might say that that would become the union catalog for master negatives as well as everything else. But how quickly that might, in fact, transpire is still a question and it's unclear. Also, whether there would be a product like the *National Register* produced from the *National Union Catalog* or if everything would be in one grand list of some sort is still not determined. So there are still lots of questions. But RLG is really looking at the retrospective problem of capturing the records that exist. We at least do have the published volumes of the *Register* that have been produced so far. It will be up to the Library of Congress, to a certain extent, to determine the future and whether or not this can be worked into the *National Union Catalog.*

CAROLYN HARRIS

Head, Preservation Department
Columbia University Libraries

Preservation of Paper Based Materials: Mass Deacidification Methods and Projects

Introduction

When I was first asked to update my 1979 *Library Journal* paper on mass deacidification processes, I thought it would be simple. I could just write "nothing's happened," and go on my way, or just say "there's not yet a good process" and leave it at that. But I found that there is still a lot of controversy regarding deacidification within the preservation profession. In the first month of research into new developments in mass deacidification, I heard or read "morpholine is the only viable process," "I looked at the Canadian Archives project, it looks great," "diethyl zinc is the only way to go," "VPD is the best method of deacidification." I began quickly to realize that the issue has not been settled—and probably won't be for some time.

My other thought, that nothing has happened since 1979, I found was also not true. There have been several developments; two of the three processes are being tested right now, and information will soon be available on their efficacy and licensing for commercial use. I know that this has been said for years, and it may be several more years before one is commercially available, but no longer because there is not a viable working process. We are still in a transitional stage, nothing is yet in an actual operational phase.

First, let's review what a mass deacidification process is, what it does, and how it will benefit libraries that have millions of brittle books. Well, it won't. Mass deacidification does not return a book to its original condition. Deacidifying a brittle books leaves you with a brittle book. "Many researchers dream of finding a fountain of youth"[1] for books, said Richard

Smith, in 1979. But a mass deacidification process cannot guarantee eternal life for books, it can only prolong the life of books that are in a nondeteriorated condition. The book will last longer because the paper is more permanent, but that does not make it more durable so that it can stand longer use.

The term deacidification is actually a misnomer. Acid in the paper is neutralized (the paper is not actually deacidified) and is buffered—i.e., an alkaline reserve is introduced—so that new acid formed in the paper through further degradation or introduced from polluted air will also be neutralized in the future. Acid in paper, introduced in several ways, whether from alum rosin size, bleach used in manufacturing, or in lignin as part of the ground wood pulp, is the catalyst which causes the chemical breakdown of paper. As a catalyst, it is not used up in the chemical reactions and, therefore, is always present to cause further deterioration.

Mass deacidification is the process by which a bound volume or stack of loose sheets can be neutralized and buffered as a whole. The neutralization agent is introduced into the volume as a gas or a liquid which penetrates the entire volume. The gas or liquid is pulled into the paper under a vacuum, the paper deacidified, and the waste products pulled out and destroyed.

There are a few points I would like to make about deacidification processes in general. First, they are highly technical in nature, as you will see in a moment, and require skilled engineers and technicians to set them up and operate them. These professional people are expensive. But these processes' technical apparatus require skills not taught in library school. For this reason, and other safety and health considerations, an off site technical facility will be necessary except in the largest libraries. Besides personnel costs, there are equipment, chemical and handling costs that will necessarily require either cooperative ventures among libraries or a commercial basis of operation.

Second, as I have said, a brittle book would benefit very little from mass deacidification. The ideal time to deacidify a book is when it is new, in good condition, and not yet deteriorated. I think it will be difficult to persuade librarians that a new book needs this kind of attention. It will require a conscious decision that this book has long range value, meets long-term research needs, and is necessary to the collection for permanent retention. An interest is developing in providing mass deacidification services among commercial binders. The paper could be deacidified when the book or serial is bound or rebound, at the time the book is disbound. The book has already been sent outside the building, and the procedures for handling these materials are well-defined. One could perhaps safely assume that if a monograph needs rebinding, it has been used, and therefore is necessary to the collection. However, at the costs estimated, $5 per book added to an estimated cost of at least $6 for binding, could we justify deacidifying volumes sent for binding, or would there have to be another set of selection criteria? Also, because of the still largely undetermined effect on book structures, bindings, inks, and adhesives, one must still be cautious about sending very valuable books or unique manuscript materials for deacidification. Beside the possible effect of the deacidification process, one must take into account the need for security outside the library. So for the forseeable future, we are faced with several unanswerable questions.

Back to the topic at hand. George Kelly of the Library of Congress and Jonathan Arney, recently of Carnegie-Mellon and now in the paper industry, have identified criteria necessary for a good mass deacidification process. I have borrowed from their lists with slight adjustments and combined information from various sources to compile the following list of criteria for a mass deacidification process:

1. Is the book completely penetrated in a reasonable time?
2. Is the book paper uniformly neutralized?
3. Is the book paper at an adequate pH level?
4. Is an alkaline reserve left in the paper?
5. Does the agent react chemically with the paper and not volatilize out?
6. Is an odor left in the book?
7. Is the treatment process toxic to humans or the environment?
8. Is the treated paper toxic to humans?
9. Are new problems introduced or paper characteristics changed?
10. Is the treatment economically feasible?
11. Can the process be done in-house?
12. Are there exceptions, i.e., books that should not be treated?

The four processes I will be discussing are the vapor phase deacidification, Barrow morpholine, the Wei T'o liquified gas, and the diethyl zinc process.

Vapor Phase Deacidification (VPD)

Although I was not specifically asked to talk about the Langwell VPD method, I am disturbed that it is still being produced and sold, and would like to discuss it briefly.

VPD, or vapor phase deacidification, is sold either as pellets encased in cheesecloth pouches to be placed in archival storage boxes, or in thin porous envelopes which can be used to interleave a book. The solid pellets vaporize to permeate the paper with an alkaline gas which neutralizes the acid in the paper. The pH is raised only to 5.6—not high enough to be really effective. No buffering agent is left in the paper, so there are no long-term effects. The VPD process is being marketed by Interleaf, Inc., in Minneapolis, and advertisements for it have appeared in recent issues of *Library Scene* and other library publications.

The primary problem with VPD is that the main agent is cyclohexylamine carbonate (CHC), which hydrolyzes (reacts with water in the air) to cyclohexylamine, one of the cyclamates and a well-known carcinogen. This is a health hazard to both library staff and library patrons, because the gas doesn't react chemically with the paper but volatilizes out. Most suppliers have discontinued the sale of VPD. Nancy Gwinn in her article about the Council on Library Resources and preservation reported that Process Materials Corporation has discontinued carrying it,[2] and I would like to reiterate that it should not be used. Langwell's development of the VPD process and its subsequently identified health risks led the Barrow Laboratory scientists to investigate other chemical substances.[3]

Librarians should recognize that they could be liable in a lawsuit if persons were to develop health problems, and this consideration should discourage the use of hazardous substances such as VPD in libraries and archives. Pro VPD articles have been appearing in the literature lately, and there is controversy about the health risks; but until further research is done, and definite documented information is available, I recommend that it not be used.

Morpholine

The Barrow morpholine process has also been very much a topic in the news lately. The recent articles on preservation by Pamela Darling and Sherelyn Ogden[4] in *Library Resources & Technical Services* and by Nancy Gwinn,[5] "CLR and Preservation" in *College & Research Libraries* review the significant contributions W. J. Barrow made to the field of preservation, as does the article by David Roberson[6] in the second volume, *Preservation of Paper and Textiles* published by the American Chemical Society. Barrow was one of the first to recognize and quantify the rate of deterioration of paper and the role of acid and environment in its chemical deterioration. He was also one of the pioneers in the treatment of paper. In many ways, because he was the first and because the field has moved in more technical directions some of his methods have since been discredited. An example of this is cellulose acetate lamination of paper, which if not done to specifications can cause further deterioration and is nonreversible for all practical purposes. He is, however, credited with the two step aqueous deacidification method widely used today. But one of the discredited projects of the Barrow laboratories is the morpholine mass deacidification process.

It has been difficult to lay to rest the topic of morpholine. The Council on Library Resources (CLR) which has put more than $1.67 million into the Barrow laboratory,[7] has patented the process, and vested the patent in the Research Corporation, a non-profit firm which handles many academic patents. CLR has not yet responded to the latest research which would lead them to discontinue promoting the process, but there has recently been a noticeable change. They had been willing to give the equipment, still in the Virginia State Library, to libraries which might find the funds to test the process, and have encouraged libraries to do so. The Research Libraries Group Preservation Committee talked about testing to be done at Stanford or Johns Hopkins, but after consideration, the topic was dropped. In the Winter 1980 issue of *American Archivist,* a Technical Note was published which indicated that the Pacific Northwest Conservation Laboratory of Port Orchard, Washington, would be setting up a deacidification unit using morpholine.[8] However, according to Robert Goldsmith of Research Corporation: "the only work that has been done utilizing our process was done at the Virginia State Library."[9] That project did not come to fruition, as far as I can tell.

With the publication of Nancy Gwinn's article and the Roberson article, the controversy has again surfaced. But more information is now available from current research which shows the limited usefulness and the health hazards of morpholine.

The Library of Congress Preservation Division Research and Testing Laboratories tested paper treated with morpholine in the early 1970s. The test results show that morpholine volatilized out of the paper within two weeks, and more quickly under humid artificial aging conditions. There is also the problem that morpholine leaves no alkaline reserve or buffering agent in the paper and therefore does not prevent future degradation from new acid produced by or introduced into the paper. The process would probably add ten years to the life of a book, but it would have to be repeated at intervals in order to preserve a book over a longer period of time.

The statement by Roberson that a "recent test of twenty treated books at the Library of Congress show that their pH has not declined in two years,"[10] was brought into question by George Kelly of the Library of Congress. He said they had not done any recent testing. Peter Sparks, Chief of the Library of Congress Preservation Division, has also indicated that the implications of the statement that the "Library of Congress Research and Testing Office tested the process extensively and generally corroborated the findings of the lengthy and thorough testing previously carried out by the Barrow lab,"[11] are not true. Having seen the test results from the Library of Congress in the 1977 Barrow final grant report, some of which are discussed in my earlier article, I can also verify that. Because of this implied recommendation of morpholine by the Library of Congress, Peter

Sparks is currently researching morpholine as a chemical substance and intends to publish the results of his research in the near future. In a recent article on an experiment using morpholine to deacidify textiles, it was indicated that it caused discoloring and accelerated loss of strength. (Kerr, N. et al. "Reinforcing Degraded Textiles: Effect of Deacidification on Fabric Deterioration." In *Durability of Macromolecular Materials*, (ACS Symposium Series, no. 95), edited by R.K. Eby, pp. 357-69. Washington, D.C.: American Chemical Society, 1979.)

The most important issue with respect to morpholine is the risk to the health of both staff and patrons which might accrue, especially in cases where libraries might contain many treated books. Because the morpholine volatilizes out of the paper into the atmosphere, it is important that the chemical be harmless and innocuous. As both Nancy Gwinn and the *American Archivist* Technical Report indicate there is no evidence that morpholine is mutagenic or carcinogenic by itself, or that it combines with nitrites in polluted air to create nitrosomorpholine, a carcinogenic substance. However, there is significant evidence that it will convert in the presence of nitrites under aqueous acid conditions (such as in the human stomach) to the carcinogenic state. Nitrites are widely used as food preservatives and are probably present in all stomachs, and breathing morpholine assimilates it into the body thus possibly setting the stage for the critical conversion. This may be overstating the case, but in a test of seven animals, rats showed 100 percent cancer tumor formation when morpholine and nitrites were introduced into their stomachs.[12] We are all aware of the shortcomings of this type of research and the small test sample, but there does seem to be a significant correlation. The Library of Congress staff reported that they developed headaches and nausea when testing morpholine. My feeling is that, overstated or not, we do not want to create any possible risks to our staffs or users. Minimum government standards for the volume of morpholine in the air (20ppm) are met under morpholine process conditions, but it is rumored that the government will be reevaluating that standard, and that the feeling is that any level of morpholine in the air is unsafe, especially in nonventilated areas with stagnant air.

It is ironic that the Barrow scientists began looking at morpholine as an alternative when the VPD process was recognized as a hazardous substance, and that morpholine has now been also recognized as hazardous. Of course, no guilt can be assigned. At the time the Barrow lab was working with morpholine, it was used industrially in many common household products, and was approved as a food additive.

Beside the fact the the morpholine process doesn't really work, and that it is a health hazard, in a humid atmosphere it smells like dead fish. I also hope that it will soon become a dead issue. If you want to know more about the morpholine process, how it was developed or how it works, I refer you to the references in my 1979 article, and Nancy Gwinn's article gives an excellent account of the history and development of the process in the Barrow laboratories.

Wei T'o Liquified Gas

Mass deacidification has long been one of Richard Smith's research and development interests. His 1970 dissertation for the University of Chicago Graduate Library School addressed the topic of nonaqueous deacidification. In 1972 he patented a nonaqueous process in the United States and Canada. His company, Wei T'o Associates, markets this product as a solution or a spray. Wei T'o is the "ancient Chinese God who protects books against destruction from fire, worms and insects, and robbers, big or small," according to the company letterhead. The deacidification agent in Wei T'o is methyl magnesium carbonate. This same agent is used in the mass deacidification process.

In 1974, Richard Smith was asked by Jan Pidek, head of the Records Conservation Division of the Public Archives and the National Library of Canada, to direct the installation and testing of this mass deacidification process using Wei T'o as the deacidification agent. In 1977, an article on the design of the system was published in the American Chemical Society's work, *Preservation of Paper and Textiles*[13] edited by John Williams. When I recently interviewed Jan Pidek for this paper, he said that the tests had taken longer than anticipated, but that they were very pleased with the results. They were looking for perfection, and had nearly gotten there. I asked about the publication of the test results. He said they were still testing, and wanted to be sure not to jump the gun—as he felt others had done in this field. He anticipates that they will soon go into systematic operational use and within the next six months should have information available for publication. This information will include costs, personnel necessary, testing results, and other types of data that require operational experience. The Canadian project has involved local engineers and technical personnel working with Richard Smith, using his product.

This process is basically different from the morpholine or the Library of Congress diethyl zinc process because it requires that the deacidification agent be introduced as a liquid that impregnates dried books under pressure instead of as a gaseous agent. The solvent in this mass process is methanol and dichlorodifluoro-methane—a nonflammable, nonexplosive, and low hazard chemical. It will clean and rapidly wet closed books; can dissolve and transport the deacidification agent; can be readily removed from books; and it is easily recovered. The paper is buffered with a magnesium carbonate reserve.

This process is actually the least controversial of the three. Problems exist because the books must be moistened by the solvent. As Richard Smith says: "Actually the books are flooded; they are absolutely soaking wet all the way through,"[14] but the deacidification medium is widely used by paper conservators, somewhat modified at the Library of Congress, and the chemistry is recognized to be sound. Because this process does seem to be viable, and the Canadian test successful, a discussion of how it works is useful.

First the books are selected for treatment. Because of the need to wet the books and the solvent used, some books are inappropriate for treatment. These include books containing ball point ink and laminated plastic or artificial leather bindings which might be effected by moisture or heat. Any alcohol-soluble ink causes problems too, as do 'some colored inks. The print may offset or feather while wet. The selected books are loaded into several wire baskets which hold ten to fifteen books. They are dried for twenty-four hours in a warm air dryer, then loaded into a vacuum dryer to be dried overnight. It is necessary that the books be completely dry because if the deacidification agent reacts with moisture, it precipitates out to a solid state. About twenty-five dried books are loaded into the process chamber at one time. The air in the chamber is evacuated, the pressure equalized between the process and storage tanks, and the deacidification solution pumped out. The books are thoroughly wetted by increasing the pressure. The excess solution is drained out and flash drying commences by evacuating, recovering and condensing the solvent vapors. Richard Smith mentions that this is analogous to the working of a refrigerator. A vacuum pump removes the residual solvent. The books are warmed by warm air, the pressure raised so the doors can be opened, and the books removed. The books are then packed into cardboard cartons and allowed to regain moisture and return to room temperature overnight.

Because of the nature of the solvent, the paper does not swell, and thus does not stress the bindings.

Richard Smith has published this process in several places, and articles are available which go into much greater detail about the mechanics of the system. I am not sure what the next step for implementing this process is. Jan Pidek indicated that the National Library of Canada and the Public Archives of Canada will probably license the process and make it available to other libraries. We are still some time away from test results from the National Library of Canada. Conservation professionals who have seen the setup in Canada think it could be a useful process. It was indicated that there are not any other libraries thinking about using the process at this time. The mechanics of increasing the scale will have to be addressed and could create unforeseen problems. The process will also have to be shown to be cost effective. Estimated costs right now are $4 per book.

The conservation profession feels that objective information is not available. George Kelly remarked in the *Cambridge Conference Preprints* that, "We will look forward to the opportunity to evaluate the results for the pilot trials when they are published." Very little has been written on the Wei T'o liquified gas process except by Richard Smith. To date, an unbiased description of the process or its results has not been published. This has caused a tendency for skepticism in the field, and the publication of results from Canada by less-biased researchers, scientists, and engineers are eagerly awaited. We are in a "wait and see" holding pattern at this time.

Richard Smith says that it is possible that this process can be expanded to include paper strengthening agents for brittle paper, fungicides and other rodent and insect repellants. Richard Smith is doing further research into these possibilities, and tells me he is currently looking for funding.

Diethyl Zinc

Peter Sparks, Chief of the Preservation Division at the Library of Congress, is strongly committed to putting the diethyl zinc process into operation. After many obstacles have recently been overcome, it seems that it will be an effective, viable, mass deacidification process. Further large-scale trials will be held at the NASA Goddard Space Flight Center chamber in Green Belt, Maryland, in April (originally they were planned for October or November, but have been bumped by the space shuttle).

George Kelly, Robert McComb and John Williams, research scientists in the LC Preservation Division Research and Testing Office, began working on developing a mass deacidification process in 1971. They had experimental results that the amines (e.g., morpholine) were ineffective in the long run because they volatilize out of the paper. They turned to an organo-metallic compound, diethyl zinc. By 1972 they were publishing early test results . The first large-scale trials were held in 1978 in the General Electric Space Center in Valley Forge, Pennsylvania. General Electric had been using this chamber to dry flood wet books, were familiar with libraries, and at that time were interested in further services to libraries. There were three trials in 1978, with interesting results.

The processes seemed to work well, but two major problems surfaced. One was the deposit of irridescent ring formation on book covers packed in contact with each other, and the other was the tendency of the diethyl zinc deacidified paper to age more quickly than usual under exposure to ultraviolet light in humid aging tests. The problem with the covers was solved by mechanical means in succeeding trials; spacers of hardware mesh between the books kept the rings from forming. The light sensitivity problem was solved chemically by modifying the process to leave zinc carbonate rather than zinc oxide as the alkaline reserve. This was accomplished by adding carbon dioxide in a damp state into the chamber after the excess diethyl zinc was destroyed.

The essential points of the process are as follows: 5000 books are loaded on loosely packed shelves spine down for easier gas penetration; spacers of hardware mesh are placed between the books. The books are warmed and dried in a vacuum chamber for three days in order to remove all traces of water. This is very important because diethyl zinc is explosive in the presence of water. After the chamber is at full vacuum, with no leaks (diethyl zinc ignites on reaction with air), the chemical reagent is added. Diethyl zinc is a sensitive leak detector, even an extremely tiny leak will show up as white smoke in the chamber. The smoke settles on the books in the form of a white powder which is a nuisance to clean off. After three days exposure to the vapor, under pressure, the books are completely penetrated, deacidified and buffered. The excess diethyl zinc is then removed from the chamber by adding alcohol. There are to be some variations of this part of the process which will be worked out for the next trial run. The vapor is tested to insure that all the diethyl zinc is gone, and the organic vapors are then pumped from the chamber and moist carbon dioxide is pumped in. After twenty-four hours, the moist carbon dioxide has hydrolyzed the diethyl zinc cellulosate to reform the cellulose and leave zinc carbonate as the alkaline reserve. The chamber is again pumped out and the books removed.

The treatment cycle lasts eight days. As you can see, it is very important that the chamber be monitored for any type of leak. This is not a process that can be done in a library basement. It is, however, a process that can be done in any vacuum chamber, and there are vacuum chambers large enough to hold a Polaris missile.

Test results show that the pH of the book paper is raised to 7.8 and an adequate two percent alkaline reserve is left. This is a relatively mild process which makes it more applicable to items with colored inks. Because the agent is introduced in a vapor state, it does not involve wetting the books and there is little danger of offsetting printed images or of the feathering of ink.

Some anomalies have shown up in the latest test results. Groundwood papers showed increased degradation under dry aging conditions, but performed well under humid conditions. The next series of tests should give further information. Peter Sparks has indicated that the Library of Congress is considering asking several libraries to contribute books for testing so some independent testing on penetration, pH and aesthetic considerations can be done.

The only testing to date has been at the Library of Congress. Test results have been widely published in the library preservation media together with full discussions of both the problems encountered and the solutions to those problems.

Because the diethyl zinc reacts chemically with the paper and remains in the paper as zinc carbonate, health risks should not be a problem with the treated books. Peter Sparks is researching this further now.

Since 1979, several administrative problems have surfaced. General Electric (GE) no longer has any plans to use the space chamber for books— whether drying flood wet books or for mass deacidification. The GE chemist, Dick Schoulberg, who worked on his project, was very apologetic, but felt that due to the new management nothing could be done at this time. Rumor has it that the chamber is for sale, if anyone is interested. They feel that there isn't any profit in it, and they have been unwilling to take the risk of an incident with the chemical diethyl zinc. The newest approaches to the shipping, handling and costs of diethyl zinc might change their minds. The Library of Congress has turned to government owned NASA chambers. Peter Sparks assures me that there are several that should be available. A commercial library binder indicated interest in offering this service, but felt that the fact that the Library of Congress has gone to internal chambers has effectively kept the private commercial sector out. It remains to be seen what will happen. There are probably chambers available, but where and how available is yet to be determined. The Library of Congress is exploring this process with large industrial firms who may want to set up centralized service centers.

The primary administrative problem has been the transport and handling of diethyl zinc. As I have mentioned, it is a very volatile substance, igniting on contact with air, and explosive on contact with water. The manufacturer, Texas Alkyls, a division of Stauffer Chemical, had been for some time unable to find a satisfactory means of shipping the chemical. They were not willing to take the liability risks of having their truck blow up on the highway; and diethyl zinc tended to corrode standard containers. The problem has recently been solved as indicated in the "Annual Report of the Librarian of Congress, 1980" as published in the *Library of Congress Information Bulletin:* "Continued work by Stauffer Chemical Company, however, has indicated a possible solution to the supply of diethyl zinc in a 50/50 mixture with mineral oil. Hazard tests on this mixture are under way and a laboratory sample is scheduled for testing in May."[17] According to Peter Sparks, this testing was done, and the mixture with mineral oil was successful. The oil nullifies the properties of the diethyl zinc, and as they have very different boiling points, the diethyl zinc can be removed as a gas simply by hooking up a line and pulling a vacuum. Some questions have come up as to the supply of diethyl zinc; Texas Alkyls considered discontinuing its manufacture, but have been persuaded to continue and have come up with cheaper methods of production.

The Library of Congress is moving very quickly to complete another large scale test in the Spring. Funding has been obtained and all is ready to proceed. The intent is to license the process for the private sector. Peter Sparks indicated that there are several interested parties, and that it should move very quickly from here. A report at ALA in Philadelphia (summer 1982) should be available with results of these trials. One question that remains to be seen is whether librarians will be willing to pay the $4 to $5 per book plus handling and shipping. It may be cheaper if larger numbers of books are done at one time in larger chambers. The ideal candidates will be the nonrare books that are still new and relatively undeteriorated, both because of the offsite requirements and the nature of the process. The next few years of experience at the Library of Congress will show us the way. LC has budgeted $50,000 for books from their collections to be deacidified in 1983 and more for 1984.

Conclusions

In my research, I tried to get realistic analyses of the situation from various scientists, conservators and other people in the field. I don't know whether I got any views that were realistic. And I'm not sure what the future prospects are. I think one would need a crystal ball to call this one. My best analysis of the situation is:

1. VPD use should be discontinued; no longer sold, or used.
2. The morpholine process should be dropped because it doesn't work and there are health risks pending further research.
3. We will have to wait to see about the Wei T'o process. It has still not been tested or used on a large scale, and test results are not yet available.
4. Diethyl zinc process will be further tested in the Spring. The problems of available chambers, liability, safety and environmental risks related to its use will have to be solved. It looks like they will be, and this process probably has the most possibilities on a truly mass scale.

In their January/March 1981 *Library Resources & Technical Services* article, Pam Darling and Sherelyn Ogden said, "A degree of skepticism, and even despair, was creeping into the literature by the late seventies as major breakthroughs in the mass treatment area continued not to take place."[18] Imagine my consternation when reference 44 in that article was my 1979 *Library Journal* article. Well, they were right, and I still tend to be skeptical about mass deacidification. But, in many ways, I am more optimistic today than I was two or three years ago because there has been considerable progress in at least a few related areas. More librarians have come to understand that mass deacidification can only be one small part of any preservation program, and won't solve all, or even most, of our problems, although it may help prevent future ones.

Mass deacidification is not the fountain of youth we're seeking and can't ever be. Our future depends on the developing awareness of publishers, the economics of paper making, the development of information storage techniques such as optical disks, environment controls and complete preservation programs, which may, and probably will one day include mass deacidification.

ACKNOWLEDGMENTS

This paper has been written with information obtained in interviews with Peter Sparks, George Kelly, Dick Schoulberg, Jonathan Arney, Frazer Poole, Richard D. Smith, and Jan Pidek, who were very generous in cheerfully giving up-to-date analyses of the situation with each mass deacidification process.

NOTES

1. Smith, Richard D. "Progress of Mass Deacidification at the Public Archives." *Canadian Library Journal* 36(Dec. 1979):329.

2. Gwinn, Nancy. "CLR and Preservation." *College & Research Libraries* 42(March 1981):108.

3. Ibid.

4. Darling, Pamela W., and Ogden, Sherelyn. "From Problems Perceived to Programs in Practice." *Library Resources & Technical Services* 25(Jan./March 1981)9-29.

5. Gwinn, "CLR and Preservation."

6. Roberson, D.D. "Permanence/Durability and Preservation Research at the Barrow Laboratory." In *Preservation of Paper and Textiles of Historic and Artistic Value II* (Advances in Chemistry Series, no 193), edited by John C. Williams, pp. 45-55. Washington, D.C.: American Chemical Society, 1981.

7. Gwinn, "CLR and Preservation."

8. "Book and Document Preservation Process." *American Archivist* 43(Winter 1980):98-99.

9. Robert Goldsmith to Harris, personal communication, 22 April 1981.

10. Roberson, "Permanence/Durability," p. 54.

11. Gwinn, "CLR and Preservation," p. 109.

12. Lijinsky, William. "N-Nitrosamines as Environmental Carcinogens." In *N-Nitrosamines* (American Chemical Society Symposium Series, no. 101), edited by Jean-Pierre Anselme, p. 107. Washington, D.C.: American Chemical Society, 1979.

13. Smith, Richard D. "Design of a Liquified Gas Mass Deacidification System for Paper and Books." In *Preservation of Paper and Textiles of Historic and Artistic Value* (Advances in Chemistry Series, no. 164), edited by John C. Williams, pp. 149-58. Washington, D.C.: American Chemical Society, 1977.

14. Smith, "Progress in Mass Deacidification," p. 330.

15. Kelly, George. "Nonaqueous Deacidification: Treatment En Masse and for the Small Workshop." In *The Conservation of Library and Archive Materials and the Graphic Arts Abstracts and Preprints* (1980 International Conference on the Conservation of Library

and Archive Materials and the Graphic Arts). Cambridge, England: Society of Archivists and the Institute of Paper Conservation.

16. Waters, Peter. "Archival Methods of Treatment for Library Documents." In *Preservation of Paper and Textiles II,* pp. 45-55.

17. Boorstin, Daniel. "Annual Report of the Librarian of Congress, 1980." *Library of Congress Information Bulletin* 40(5 June 1981):200.

18. Darling, and Ogden, "From Problems Perceived," p. 18.

BIBLIOGRAPHY

(Mass Deacidification, 1979-81)

General

Darling, Pamela W., and Ogden, Sherelyn. "From Problems Perceived to Programs in Practice: The Preservation of Library Resources in the U.S.A., 1956-1980." *Library Resources & Technical Services* 25(Jan./March 1981):9-29. (A general article on the history and status of preservation; contains brief information on the history and development of each of the three mass deacidification processes.)

Vapor Phase Deacidification

Campbell, Gregor R. "Take Action—Protect Your Books from Acid Deterioration." *Library Scene* 8(March 1979):27. (Pro VPD article; tries to imply guilt in not using easily available deacidification agent.)

Kavin, Mel. "The President Ponders: Deacidification Methods." *Library Scene* 10(Sept. 1981):20. (Written in response to Werner Rebsamen's "Must All Library Materials be Acid Free?" *Library Scene* 10(March 1981); and letter to the editor, *Library Scene* 10(June 1981). Pro Vapor Phase Deacidification, feels health risks overstated.)

Morpholine

Anselme, Jeane-Pierre. *N-Nitrosamines* (Symposium Series, no. 101). Washington, D.C.: American Chemical Society, 1979. (Technical information on the health hazards of amines, including morpholine in reaction with nitrite compounds.)

"Book and Document Preservation Process." *American Archivist* 43(Winter 1980):98-99. (Announces use of morpholine process by Pacific Northwest Conservation Laboratory; discusses and dismisses health hazards.)

Gwinn, Nancy. "CLR and Preservation." *College & Research Libraries* 12(March 1980): 104-26. (Account of CLR's involvement with the Barrow laboratories; detailed information on the development of the morpholine process; does not include most up-to-date health information.)

Roberson, D.D. "Permanence/Durability Research at the Barrow Laboratory." In *Preservation of Paper and Textiles of Historic and Artistic Value II* (Advances in Chemistry Series, no. 193), edited by John C. Williams, pp. 45-55. Washington, D.C.: American Chemical Society, 1981. (On the Barrow Laboratories; one paragraph on the morpholine process which misrepresents the Library of Congress' position.)

Wei T'o

Rebsamen, Werner. "A Genuine Break-through in Mass Deacidification." *LBI Technology Newsletter* vol. 1, March 1981. (Rehash of Smith articles; description of the process.)

Smith, Richard D. "Mass Deacidification at the Public Archives of Canada." In *The Conservation of Library and Archive Materials and the Graphic Arts Abstracts and Preprints,* p. 131. Cambridge, England: International Conference on the Conservation of Library and Archive Materials and the Graphic Arts, 1980. (Brief description of the mechanics of the process.)

_____ . "Progress in Mass Deacidification at the Public Archives of Canada." *Canadian Library Journal* 36(Dec. 1979):325-32. (Statement on why books should be deacidified; description of mechanics of the process and its development.)

_____ . "Preservation: Library Need and Industry Opportunity, Part II." *Library Scene* 9(March 1980):10-14. (A not so long version of the *Canadian Library Journal* article.)

_____ . "Preserving Our Books; A Chemical Problem." *ChemTech* 11(July 1981):414-17. (With a chemical slant.)

Diethyl Zinc

Kelly, George B. "Mass Deacidification with Diethyl Zinc." *Library Scene* 9(Sept. 1980):6-7. (Development and description of the process; includes recent improvements; thoughts on future developments.)

_____ . "Non-Aqueous Deacidification: Treatment En Masse and for the Small Workshop." In *The Conservation of Library and Archive Materials*, pp. 126-30. (Includes description of each process, but concentrates on diethyl zinc; includes criteria for mass deacidification systems.)

Kelly, George B., and Williams, John C. "Inhibition of Light Sensitivity of Papers Treated with Diethyl Zinc." In *Preservation of Paper and Textiles*, pp. 109-17. (The problem of faster aging of treated paper under ultraviolet light in humid conditions; design of experiment, data and solutions.)

DISCUSSION

James Orr (Hertzberg-New Method, Inc., Jacksonville, Illinois): Some time ago when General Electric (GE) had the deacidification program at their Germantown plant, there was a good deal of interest by a number of our customers in the East Coast area to get into a deacidification program. At that time we had some discussion with GE as to whether we could use their chamber. They were evaluating the program. At the same time, we were evaluating it knowing that probably we would handle a great deal of valuable and rare material. So before we progressed, we figured that it would be wise to protect ourselves from possible liability. So, we asked the various libraries that were interested in this if they would be willing to sign a release in the event (maybe not in my lifetime, but in time to come) that something would happen to that material as a result of the deacidification. And at that time there wasn't too much enthusiasm. This turned everybody off. Just about that time the people who manufactured the gas said it was too dangerous to transport so they discontinued the whole thing. We have been trying to follow this very closely as well as developments at the Library of Congress.

There still seems to be quite a bit of interest in deacidification. This takes me back to my old question: I wonder how many people here, to embark on this program, would be willing to sign a release that even if something happened to the material in due time that they would be willing to go along on an experimental basis? That is my question.

Carolyn Harris: I'm not sure that I would. Do you want a show of hands? (*Editor's note:* There was no response.) That may be your answer. That may be one of the problems with setting up a mass deacidification program.

GERALD W. LUNDEEN

Associate Professor
Graduate School of Library Science
University of Hawaii

Preservation of Paper Based Materials: Present and Future Research and Developments in the Paper Industry

Introduction

The essential nature of paper[1] has changed very little since its invention in China in A.D. 105. It consists of cellulose fibers suspended in water and formed into a matted sheet on screens.

While handmade paper methods have changed little over the centuries, the modern machinemade paper is a very complex, and highly capital-intensive mix of craft, science and engineering.

Cellulose is a naturally occurring polymer, that is a long chain-like molelcule made up of a large number of smaller (monomer) units. In the case of cellulose, the monomer units are anhydro-glucose molecules. The number of units in a cellulose molecule (known as the degree of polymerization or DP) varies with the source and treatment of the material. Cotton and flax cellulose have approximately 7,000 to 12,000 units while cellulose derived from refined wood pulp which has been chemically separated from the lignin binder in wood and bleached have about 2000 to 3000 monomer units per cellulose molecule.

Cellulose occurs in fibrous form. The fibers are made up of both regular, ordered crystalline regions and irregular, less dense amorphous regions. The flexibility and ability to absorb moisture derive from the amorphous regions.

The beating of cellulose fibers in water develops microfibril fuzz on their surface which causes the fibers to stick together when the formed sheet of paper is dried.

Paper made with only cellulose fiber acts like a blotter. It absorbs water readily, swelling in the process. Ink tends to feather on such paper. To overcome this, papermakers add a size to the paper in order to make it more resistant to fluids. The amount of size needed depends on the printing process. Offset printing, which is now the most widely used process for books, requires more than other printing methods.

Filler materials or loadings are added to paper pulp to increase opacity and ink receptivity. Fillers such as clay, calcium carbonate, titanium dioxide, or other white pigments, while they keep the printing from showing through the other side, do nothing for the strength of the paper but in fact detract from it by interfering with fiber-to-fiber bonding. Printing and book papers are often coated with a composition containing a white pigment and an adhesive such as starch or casein in order to improve brightness, surface smoothness, and printing quality. Colors and a wide range of other additives are often added for special purposes.

A Brief Historical Overview

From the beginning, sources of good quality cellulose were inadequate to the demand. The search for cheaper and more plentiful sources is one of the continuing themes in the history of papermaking.[2] In early days, clean white cotton and linen rags were the principal source of cellulose.

The machines such as the hollander, developed to speed the pulping process, replaced beating with grinding action with a resulting shortening of the fibers produced.

The discovery of chlorine by Scheele in 1774 and the recognition of its bleaching properties allowed colored and dirty rags to be used in addition to clean white ones. Unfortunately, the bleaching process degrades the fiber.

Early papermakers sized their paper by dipping the paper in dilute solution of gelatin. The introduction of alum-rosin size and its rapid adoption by almost all papermakers was the next major setback to paper quality. In 1807 Moritz Friedrick Illig found that rosin soap could be added to the beaten fiber suspension and precipitated by adding alum. The paper made from this mixture became sized in the same step as the sheet formation and only required drying, thus eliminating an extra dipping and drying step. From the point of view of the paper manufacturer this was a marvelous advance and alum has been considered the papermaker's cure-all up to the present. From the librarian/archivist's and conservator's perspective this was the greatest in a series of calamities to befall on the process of papermaking.

The quest for other sources of cellulose led to the discovery that wood cellulose could be used to produce acceptable paper. Wood cellulose fiber is bonded together by lignin. When wood is ground mechanically to produce paper, the lignin and other wood byproducts such as hemicelluloses are left in the finished product. The result is a low-grade, relatively weak and chemically unstable paper such as that used in newsprint.

Processes were developed during the nineteenth and twentieth centuries to treat wood pulp chemically to remove lignin and other impurities. These treatments are harsh and degrade the cellulose fiber in the process; however, bleached chemical pulps are stronger and more stable than paper made from groundwood (mechanical) pulp or from semichemical pulps, though not as strong as rag fibers.

Paper permanence began to decline sharply at about the time wood pulp was displacing rags as the main source of fiber. This has caused many people to think that high-quality, permanent paper can only be made from rags and that paper made from rags is necessarily better than that made from wood pulp. This has been shown not to be the case. In fact, it has been determined that the major cause for the decline in permanence was the introduction of alum, which just happened more or less to coincide with the transition to wood fibers.

While the chemical pulping and bleaching of wood fibers is certainly responsible for a decrease in the polymer chain length and a lower strength in the paper, the decrease with time of whatever strength the paper had when new is less attributed to these treatments and can be explained primarily by two synergistic chemical processes which attack the paper over time—acid catalyzed hydrolysis of the cellulose polymer linking bond, and oxidation. There are, in addition to these, a host of other degradation processes to which paper is susceptible.

Causes of Paper Degradation and Current Research

William K. Wilson and E.J. Parks in a detailed examination of aging of paper list the following reactions which might occur during the natural aging of paper:

(a) hydrolysis;
(b) oxidation;
(c) crosslinking;
(d) changes in order, or crystallinity, due to changes in moisture content;
(e) photolysis;
(f) photosensitization;
(g) photo-oxidation.[3]

The study of the chemical reactions in paper is difficult. One can measure changes in physical properties, but attributing these effects to specific reactions is not something that can always be done with a high degree of certainty. More than one reaction is likely to be occurring and these often interact.

Accelerated Aging Methods

The processes which degrade paper are relatively slow at room temperature. Even poor-quality paper will last for twenty-five years. Raising the temperature increases the rate of these processes so they can be conveniently studied in the laboratory in a reasonable time period. Special aging ovens with very good temperature and humidity controls are employed. The practical range of temperatures which can be used to give measurable rates of degradation is from about 70° to 100°C. After aging, loss of strength is commonly determined by use of standard tests. The most commonly used is the TAPPI MIT Folding Endurance Test. A 1.5 cm.-wide strip of paper under 1 kilogram (or, in some laboratories, 0.5 kilogram) of tension is folded repeatedly through an angle of 270° until it breaks. The required number of folds is taken as a measure of the paper's strength. By measuring the degradation of samples of a paper over the 70-100° range it is possible to extrapolate to room temperature to predict the useful life of the paper under normal storage conditions. These tests show that seventy-two hours at 100°C is equivalent to about twenty-five years at room temperature. Other tests that are frequently used measure tensile strength and extensibility, tearing strength, and light reflectance.

The accelerated aging approach has been used for several years and much of the research on longevity of paper is based on such experiments. Comparisons with long-term aging experiments has shown it to be a viable method of studying paper aging.[4]

Hydrolysis

Cellulose is fairly stable in neutral and alkaline media but is readily hydrolyzed in acid, the rate increasing with hydrogen ion activity (decreasing pH). This acid catalyzed hydrolysis results in cleavage of the monomer to monomer bond, thus fragmenting the polymer chain and weakening the paper. The presence of oxidized groups in the cellulose causes it to be more readily hydrolyzed. Acid hydrolysis takes place in the amorphous regions of the cellulose fiber. The cellulose chains, once broken, tend to crystallize making them more brittle. The fibers are weakened but the fiber-to-fiber bond is affected less seriously. New paper tears by pulling apart the fiber-to-fiber bonds giving a fuzzy tear; aged, degraded paper tears by fracture of the fibers giving a clean tear.

The principal source of acid in book paper is alum. Up until very recently almost all book papers contained alum rosin size and much of this paper has a pH of 4.5 or less. Such paper has a useful life of twenty-five to fifty years. Another important source of acid is pollutants in the air, particularly sulfur dioxide and oxides of nitrogen. The presence of trace metals (iron, copper, manganese) in the paper play a role in this by catalyzing the oxidation of sulfur dioxide to sulfur trioxide which, with water, produces sulfuric acid.

Chlorinated compounds such as residues from chlorine bleaches can generate hydrochloric acid.

Some of the products of paper oxidation are acidic.

Deacidification is becoming a well-established practice though research continues. Researchers at the National Archives are studying liquid phase deacidification with methyl magnesium carbonate looking at ways to improve this process. Research at the Library of Congress on gas phase deacidification with diethyl zinc is progressing to final pilot testing in a 5000 book per charge chamber. There is reason to expect this method will move soon from research to practical implementation.

Oxidation

Cellulose and especially other organic constituents of paper are susceptible to slow reaction with atmospheric oxygen. The reaction produces peroxides which decompose and promote further oxidation. The oxidation is catalyzed by metal ions such as copper, cobalt, manganese and iron, and ozone in polluted air acts as a strong oxidizing agent. Copper sulfate is sometimes used as a slimicide. It should not be used in the manufacture of permanent paper. Hypochlorite and chlorine bleaches leave the cellulose more susceptible to oxidation.

The relative importance of hydrolysis and oxidation to the degradation of paper varies with the kind of paper and environmental conditions, but both are important. For alkaline papers oxidation is the major mode of degradation.

One of the criticisms of some of the accelerated aging tests is that it is a gross measure which doesn't provide information about how the paper is degrading. Some recent work at Carnegie-Mellon Institute Research[5] has addressed the question of the relative importance of oxygen-dependent and oxygen-independent deterioration. The relative importance of these two processes was found to depend on the moisture content, the type of paper, the temperature, and the physical property monitored. They found that oxygen-dependent deterioration is more important for newsprint than for rag paper. Yellowing was caused primarily by oxidation; tensile strength loss was caused primarily by oxygen-independent reactions. In all cases, both processes contribute significantly to the deterioration.

The atmospheric oxidation process was found to be inhibited by a decrease in acidity. This means that alkaline paper will not only prevent hydrolysis, but will offer some protection against oxidation as well.

Chemiluminescence Studies

Some recent research conducted at Battelle Columbus Laboratories[6] used the very weak chemiluminescence (light produced as a result of a chemical reaction at environmental temperatures) accompanying the degradation of paper. The author introduced this technique to Battelle when he worked there as a research chemist in the late 1960s. The light emission which accompanies the degradation of a wide range of organic materials is, where the detailed mechanism has been determined, associated with the oxidation of the materials. It seems reasonable to assume that the chemiluminescence observed from paper is due to oxidative degradation but this has not been determined.

Though there have been some long-term studies which support the validity of accelerated aging methods, there have been some concerns about extrapolating results at elevated temperatures to room temperature. The chemiluminescence method, because of its extreme sensitivity, permitted measurements down to room temperature. Temperature dependence results for the chemiluminescence experiments were in agreement with accelerated aging experiments in the 70-100°C range done with the same papers at the Library of Congress. These results thus give support to conclusions drawn from accelerated aging experiments.

In addition to looking at effects of temperature, samples of paper were cycled between moist and dry atmospheres. This produced a striking increase in light emission when the humidity was changed. This suggests, as has long been supposed, that fluctuating humidity is detrimental to paper.

Effects of Reducing Agents

Partial oxidation of paper makes it more readily hydrolyzed. Researchers at the Library of Congress[7] have studied the use of sodium borohydride to reduce the oxidized functional groups. It was found that such treatment improved brightness of paper as well as brightness retention, in addition to increasing folding endurance. Sodium borohydride has been found to be an effective addition to alkaline pulping liquors but is too expensive to be used in the quantities required to make it effective.[8]

Changes in Crystallinity

As mentioned earlier, cellulose consists of crystalline regions characterized by regular order and disordered amorphous regions, the latter being responsible for the ability to absorb moisture and for flexibility of the fibers. Some recent research at the Institute for Paper Chemistry[9] suggests that crystallization processes may be an important factor in aging of cellulose fibers.

Heating sample pulp to 170° for two hours, a treatment similar to what pulp experiences in a typical pulping process, showed a deterioration in all papermaking properties. The degree of crystallinity was measured using X-ray diffraction methods. The treated pulp showed a significant increase in crystallinity. Tensile strength decreased by 20 percent, burst by 30 percent and tear strength by 45 percent. Water retention characteristics declined to 60 percent of original values. All of the changes reflect an increase in crystallinity. The small degree of chemical degradation resulting from the treatment was not sufficient to account for the observed change.

Elevated temperatures enhance molecular mobility and accelerate the ordering process. The presence of water was also found to promote the crystallization process.

The degree of polymerization of the cellulose was also found to be important. Ordering increased with decrease in molecular weight or degree of polymerization. Samples with a degree of polymerization (DP) greater than 1000 were unaffected by exposure to water at room temperature while samples with a DP less than 100 crystallized on exposure to the moisture content in the laboratory atmosphere.

These findings have several implications for conservation. Chain scission due to acid hydrolysis causes a reduction in the degree of polymerization giving not only an inherent reduction in the tensile strength of the fibers but also enhanced opportunities for crystallization with resulting embrittlement.

The effect of the ordering process must be considered in the interpretation of accelerated aging results. The temperature dependence of ordering and of the chemical degradation processes may well be quite different. The amount of moisture in these tests will very likely influence the rate of each of the processes differently.

Photochemical Deterioration

Light, particularly light in the ultraviolet region of the spectrum, is damaging to paper. Pure cellulose is very resistant to photochemical attack, but many of the impurities in paper, especially lignin, are sensitive to light. Lignin in groundwood paper, such as newsprint, yellows very rapidly on exposure to sunlight primarily due to photochemical oxidation. Rosin size, the presence of metal ions, and chemical bleaching all contribute to increased photochemical attack on paper. A variety of reactions are caused by the absorption of light, including oxidation. Depending on the paper and other conditions, paper may yellow and darken or bleach when irradiated. Some of the products of photochemical attack (primarily peroxides) are themselves thermally and photochemically unstable, causing further degradation.

It has been found that the introduction of small amounts of iodide in the form of hydrogen iodide gas may afford protection against oxidation.[10] This has prompted researchers at the Library of Congress to consider the possibility of introducing antioxidants into paper by gas phase techniques.

Crosslinking

Hydrolysis, oxidation and reactions of the products of these processes, plus reactions of a variety of functional groups in cellulose and other ingredients in paper cause crosslinking (the bonding of separate cellulose molecules at various points on the chains). A degree of crosslinking improves paper strength, but too much results in embrittlement.

Current Developments in the Paper Industry

The major development today in the paper industry is a trend to alkaline paper. The Library of Congress has been monitoring the pH of books coming into its collection and finds that about 25 percent of the American books and about 50 percent of the European books are made of alkaline paper. Five years ago less than 1 percent of the books tested were made with alkaline paper.[11]

Alkaline paper is paper made in a neutral or slightly alkaline system and contains calcium carbonate as a filler. The calcium carbonate acts as a buffer, neutralizing any acid which may develop in the paper over time. Alum-rosin size is not compatible with alkaline papermaking. Since the 1950s with the introduction by Hercules Corporation of a synthetic alkaline sizing material, Aquapel, it has been possible to size alkaline papers in the machine. There are now several alkaline sizes available.

The Europeans have been leading in the move to alkaline paper, because calcium carbonate is less expensive in Europe and because energy and fiber costs are significantly higher. The alkaline process provides cost savings in these areas. Several American companies are currently producing alkaline paper and the number is growing as the industry learns to operate with the new processes and as its many advantages are recognized.

The reasons for this trend are economic. Paper consumption is conservatively expected to double in the next twenty-five years. During this period fiber and energy are expected to double in real cost and the cost of water is expected to triple.[12]

Alkaline papermaking offers a potential savings in all of these areas plus a number of other advantages.[13]

—A stronger paper is produced permitting savings through weight reduction, increased filler content, the use of weaker, less-expensive fibers or the elimination of dry strength resins.

—Waste water and byproducts can be recycled, reducing pollution control cost and conserving resources.

—Calcium carbonate is already widely used as a pigment in paper coating. The alkaline process allows easy recycling of such papers.

—The machinery lasts longer. The acid process is corrosive, and recycling waste water in this process increases the corrosion problem and causes scaling problems. An alkaline papermaking environment is noncorrosive, extending machine life and reducing maintenance costs. With a single paper machine costing upward of $50 million, this can be significant.

—A higher brightness is achieved. Calcium carbonate, in addition to its acting as a buffer, is a pigment with high brightness.

—Calcium carbonate is cheaper than the titanium dioxide it replaces.

—The waste water is at about pH7 so neutralization of effluent discharge is not required.

—Energy may be conserved in three areas—drying, refining, and in some cases process waste water temperature control. Alkaline paper has been found to drain faster, thereby reducing drying costs. The improved strength of the paper can permit a reduction in refining with a subsequent energy savings.

Some mills maintain high stock temperatures. One mill, on changing from acid to alkaline papermaking was able to reduce its effluent discharge from 14,000 gal./ton to 5,000 gal./ton. The energy savings in not having to heat 9,000 gal./ton to 150°C amounted to more than $10/ton.[14]

—Alkaline paper recycles better, giving a stronger recycled product.[15]

—No capital expenditure is required to convert. The same machinery is used in both acid and neutral or alkaline papermaking.

—Productivity is increased as a result of reduced down time of machinery due to maintenance problems or periodic cleaning. The alkaline process is cleaner.

—The product resists aging.

Not all of the above advantages are likely to be realized in any individual mill. The particular benefits gained will vary, depending on local conditions, the grades of paper being produced, and other factors. An example cited in the literature[16] showed a savings of $42/ton in primary raw materials and a savings in reduced water consumption of $15/ton, giving a $57/ton savings (10 percent of the cost of the finished product).

The lasting quality of the paper carries little or no weight with the producers. They are in general convinced that permanence will not sell paper.

Barrow, working with chemical and paper companies, showed many years ago that permanent/durable paper could be produced commercially from wood pulp. Alkaline sizes have been available for more than twenty years. Librarians, archivists, and publishers must take some of the blame for not forcing the industry to provide permanent/durable alkaline paper and for not using it when it was available. To put things in perspective, however, it should be remembered that only about 15 percent of the total paper production is for printing purposes,[17] and only a little more than 1 percent is book publishing paper.[18] Fortunately, the economics of the process are sufficient to prompt many of the producers to switch to alkaline paper production and the problem of rapid decay of paper may be solved by default in the course of the next twenty-five years or so.

There are some problems to be overcome in making the transition to alkaline paper. The conversion itself is expensive, requiring retraining of workers, cleaning of equipment, and a completely new set of additives (dyestuffs, starches, defoamers, retention aids) need to be introduced. Paper which contains lignin (groundwood paper) has problems—the pulp is sticky and brownish in color and the resulting paper is reduced in brightness. By making the proper adjustments however, groundwood paper can be made with neutral or alkaline size and calcium carbonate filler. This is being done increasingly in Europe. The sticking problem (press sticking) is present, though to a lesser extent, even using pulp free of lignin. Release agents are added to counteract this. The feel of the paper may be different.

Though alkaline paper seems to be well established, there is still research to be done to improve the process, and since most companies are fairly new to the process there is promise for measurable improvement as they learn more about it. Overall the advantages outweigh the problems and those producers who have switched say they would not change back.

Converting to alkaline paper is sufficiently costly and disruptive that it requires a total commitment at all levels from the top management down to assure success. It is a complex and expensive transition, but one that pays dividends in the long run.

One economic pressure working against high-quality alkaline paper is the cost of wood and the desire to get maximum yield from the wood used. Groundwood gives about a 90-95 percent yield, compared to a 40-50 percent yield for good-quality paper. Thus there are economic pressures to use groundwood paper. A newer method, Thermo-Mechanical Pulping, is growing rapidly.[19] It requires more power, but its yield is as high as regular stone groundwood and the paper is strong enough to be used alone. (Groundwood pulp is generally blended with higher quality chemical pulp for added strength.) Thermo-Mechanical Pulp, like groundwood, contains the lignin and other materials from the wood which contribute to its poor lasting qualities. For certain types of publications the situation will probably get worse even though alkaline paper is becoming more available. This is seen in Europe where many magazines, brochures, and ephemera are being printed on groundwood paper. Groundwood paper is being used increasingly in textbooks and some reference books. These papers are almost always coated, which significantly increases their longevity although they cannot be called archival. A groundwood paper which uncoated might last twenty-five years will, if coated, still be handleable after fifty and perhaps up to seventy-five or one hundred years.[20]

Another trend in papermaking is the increasing use of hardwoods.[21] Hardwoods are more plentiful and are cheaper than softwood. Paper from hardwoods generally gives better printing quality, but is weaker.

Oxidation

The problem of paper oxidation has received less attention, and less effort is being expended in the industry to deal with it. As with acidity, the concern in the industry is not with paper longevity but with other factors such as brightness and reduced yellowing. Some efforts are being made to reduce metal ion levels in paper. As noted above, these catalyze paper oxidation and the oxidation of sulfur dioxide to sulfur trioxide.

Bleaching

Bleaching of pulp is another area of change and exploration.[22] The effluents from bleaching plants are a major problem. Environmental pollution controls together with other changes in paper technology are causing paper companies to look for better methods of bleaching. Historically, chlorine, calcium hypochlorite, and chlorine dioxide have been popular bleaching agents. Oxygen bleaching was introduced on a commercial scale in 1970. Oxygen bleaching allows for simpler pollution control methods, but the bleaching is not as effective.

Some experimentation with ozone as a bleaching agent has been done. New bleaches and new methods will very likely be introduced in the future. The implication for permanence and durability are not clear at this point. Whatever changes are made will no doubt be made for reasons other than the effects on paper longevity.

Standards for Permanent/Durable Paper

Though librarians and archivists can claim little credit for the move to alkaline papermaking they should be able to exert influence in the use of this paper for the books and other paper materials that they collect.

Requirements for permanence and durability should be included in specifications for items being purchased. There are established standards which can be referenced in purchase orders, and to which paper manufacturers can look to for guidance. To be informed customers, purchasers should be familiar with the appropriate standards.

American Society for Testing and Materials (ASTM) standards of interest are:[23]

D3290 Bond and Ledger Papers for Permanent Records

D3458-75 Copies from Office Copying Machines for Permanent Records

D3301-74 File Folders for Storage of Permanent Records

D3208-76 Manifold Papers for Permanent Records

The National Historical Publications and Records Commission provides standards for paper, printing and binding.[24] Barrow Research Laboratory published specifications for permanent/durable paper.[25]

Current activities in this area include the work of the Committee on Production Guidelines for Book Longevity which operates as part of the Council on Library Resources. This group, made up of representatives from publishing, paper manufacturing, and library preservation programs, has recently issued an "Interim Report on Book Paper."[26] The report offers guidelines on paper which are adapted and simplified from the standards set by the National Historical Publications and Records Commission, the Library of Congress, and the ASTM/ANSI Standard Specification for Bond and Ledger Papers for Permanent Records. The report also addresses the question of what types of publications should be printed on such paper and what categories might be considered lower priority with respect to permanence. Some commercial sources of acid-free paper are listed.

Other collective efforts toward creating a conservation-conscious and informed consumer include the activities of the Association of Research Libraries, Preservation Committee and Office of Management Studies; the Preservation of Library Materials Section of the American Library Association's Resources and Technical Services Division; the Study Committee on Libraries and Archives of the National Conservation Advisory Council; the Society of American Archivists; and the American Association for State and Local History.

Conclusion

While we still have much to learn, and there is room for further progress, it is not only possible, but it is in the papermaker's own economic interests to produce permanent/durable paper. Such paper can reasonably be expected to last several hundred years instead of the twenty-five to fifty years for modern acidic book paper. There is thus no excuse for producing books and other publications of lasting importance on anything other than paper meeting existing standards for permanence and durability. There is reason to hope that this will finally happen. It is up to every librarian, publisher and paper consumer to insist that it does and to use whatever influence we have to speed this process.

NOTES

1. Browning, B.L. "The Nature of Paper." In *Deterioration and Preservation of Library Materials,* edited by Howard W. Winger and Richard D. Smith, pp. 18-38. Chicago: The University of Chicago Press. Also published in *Library Quarterly* 40(Jan. 1970):18-38; Sutermeister, Edwin. *The Story of Papermaking.* Boston: S.D. Warren Co., 1954; Bolam, Francis, ed. *Paper Making.* London: Technical Section of the British Paper and Board Makers' Association (Inc.), 1965; and Casey, James P., ed. *Pulp and Paper: Chemistry and Chemical Technology,* 3d ed. New York: John Wiley & Sons, 1981.

2. For a historical review *see* Williams, John C. "A Review of Paper Quality and Paper Chemistry." *Library Trends* 30(Fall 1981):203-24; *see especially* pp. 205-06.

3. Wilson, William K., and Parks, E.J. "An Analysis of the Aging of Paper: Possible Reactions and Their Effects on Measurable Properties." *Restaurator* 3(1979):37-61.

4. _____ . "Comparison of Accelerated Aging of Book Papers in 1937 with 36 Years Natural Aging." *Restaurator* 4(1980):1-55.

5. Arney, J.S., and Jacobs, A.J. "Accelerated Aging of Paper, the Relative Importance of Atmospheric Oxidation." *TAPPI* 62(July 1979):89-91; and _____ . "Newsprint Deterioration—The Influence of Temperature on the Relative Contribution of Oxygen-Independent and Oxygen-Dependent Processes in the Total Rate." *TAPPI* 63(Jan. 1980):75-77.

6. Kelly, G.B., et al. "The Use of Chemiluminescence in the Study of Paper Permanence." In *Durability of Macromolecular Materials* (American Chemical Society Symposium Series, no. 95). Washington, D.C.: ACS, 1979, pp. 117-25.

7. Tang, Lucia C., and Troyer, Margaret A. "Adding Stability to Alkaline Papers." *Proceedings of the Technical Association of the Pulp and Paper Industry* (1981 Papermakers Conference). Atlanta: TAPPI, 1981, pp. 77-84.

8. Casey, *Pulp and Paper,* p. 485.

9. Atalla, Rajai H. "The Crystallinity of Cellulosic Fibers." In *Preservation of Paper and Textiles of Historic and Artistic Value II* (Advances in Chemistry Series, no. 193), edited by John C. Williams, pp. 169-76. Washington, D.C.: American Chemical Society, 1981.

10. Kelly, G.B., Jr., and Williams, John C. "Inhibition of Light Sensitivity of Papers Treated with Diethyl Zinc." In *Preservation of Paper,* pp. 241-49.

11. Kelly to Lundeen, personal interview, Washington, D.C., 28 Oct. 1981.

12. Hagemeyer, R.W. "The Impact of Increasing paper Consumption and Resource Limitations on Alkaline Papermaking." In *Preservation of Paper,* pp. 241-49.

13. Thomas, Joseph. "Alkaline Printing Papers: Promise and Performance." In *Deterioration and Preservation,* pp. 99-107; Dumas, David H. "Recent Progress in Alkaline Sizing." *Proceedings of the Technical Association of the Pulp and Paper Industry* (1981 Papermakers Conference), pp. 41-47; and Williams, "A Review of Paper Quality."

14. Thomas, "Alkaline Printing Papers."

15. Williams, John C. "Retaining the Strength of Secondary Fibers with Alkaline Calcium Carbonate Fillers." *Paper Trade Journal,* 30(Nov. 1980):33-34; and McComb, Robert E., and Williams, John C. "The Value of Alkaline Papers for Recycling." In *Proceedings of the Technical Association of the Pulp and Paper Industry* (1981 Papermakers Conference), pp. 65-70.

16. Hagemeyer, "The Impact of Increasing Paper."

17. Evanoff, Philip C. to Lundeen, personal communication, 14 Nov. 1981.

18. The Committee on Production Guidelines for Book Longevity. "Interim Report on Book Paper," April 1981.

19. Evanoff to Lundeen, personal communication.

20. Evanoff, Philip C. "Trends in Paper Making Affecting Permanence." Chillicothe, Ohio: Mead Papers, n.p.

21. Ibid.

22. Casey, *Pulp and Paper*, p. 633.

23. American Society for Testing and Materials. *1979 Annual Book of ASTM Standards, Part 20, Paper: Packaging: Business Copy Products.* Philadelphia: ASTM, 1979.

24. *U.S. National Historical Publications and Records Commission.* Washington, D.C.: National Archives.

25. Barrow Laboratory. Technical Notes. "Barrow Laboratory Research." *American Archivist* 38(July 1975):406-16.

26. Casey, *Pulp and Paper*.

DISCUSSION

Philip A. Metzger (School of Medicine, Southern Illinois University at Carbondale): I was interested in your figure of 25 to 50 percent of the new books being on alkaline paper. With the introduction of mass deacidification does that mean that essentially 25 to 50 percent of the books that might be mass-deacidified might not really need it?

Gerald Lundeen: The books that are being considered for mass deacidification are books that have been in the collection for some time. The only ones that are found to be on alkaline paper are the ones that have been coming into the collection within the last five years, but mostly within the last one or two years.

Metzger: But aren't those really the prime candidates for mass deacidification before they degrade?

Lundeen: It has been suggested that books that are printed on alkaline paper ought to be so identified. The publisher ought to make a statement in the book saying, "This book is made from paper meeting such and such standards." That way we won't unnecessarily treat these books, as you point out. Along with that question, identifying books for deacidification or treatment that are not so identified by a statement from the publisher requires testing the paper with pH detectors. The problem of identifying books that may require treatment because of acidity (if the books are not identified by the publisher as being printed on permanent durable paper) forces us to use a chemical test of some sort to see whether it's acidic or basic. You can have acidic paper that is coated with calcium carbonate, and, if you use the wrong sorts of tests, it will test basic even though the core of the paper is acidic. And so that's something you've got to be careful about. That's one of the reasons for recommending that publishers provide this information in books that they have printed on permanent paper.

D.W. Krummel (Graduate School of Library and Information Science, University of Illinois at Urbana-Champaign): I think one of your statements does need qualification. The library profession—Verner Clapp in particular—has been calling for an improvement of that situation. Library publications directed toward permanent library collections (e.g., the imprints of G.K. Hall and Scarecrow, in particular) conspicuously mention the quality of the paper. We've had less success in working with the publishers who are not directed primarily toward library markets. But since the late 1950s I think we have had a significant impact. I think that should be made a part of the record, but I'm not sure what impact, if any, we've had on the new machinery which has been developed that dramatically changed the character of paper.

Lundeen: That's a good point. I didn't mean to slight that, and when I said we couldn't claim much credit for the transition to alkaline paper, it's not from lack of trying. As Don [Krummel] suggested, we've been calling for a transition for a long time but economics are what, for the most part, carry the weight with the papermakers. There are some exceptions in terms of papermakers, too. S.D. Warren has been making alkaline paper for many years (since the late 1950s). Recognizing that permanence is important, few other paper companies have been doing this as well but the majority of the papermakers are convinced only by dollars.

Charles Davis (Graduate School of Library and Information Science, University of Illinois at Urbana-Champaign): I was wondering about the effects of low temperature. Has anybody extrapolated with enough confidence to assert that we should move our archives to Greenland?

Lundeen: I'm not sure if I'm remembering my numbers right but I think the suggestion has been made that if we reduce the temperature by 25 degrees Celsius below room temperature, paper that normally would last on the order of 50 years or so is extended to 4000 years. And by going another 25 degrees lower, you get another 40,000 years or thereabouts. Some measurements were done on paper from the expedition of Scott, who froze to death at the South Pole. His materials were left there. Notebooks from that expedition were retrieved sometime in the late 1950s and this paper has been examined and compared to essentially the same kind of paper to see what the effect was of this prolonged storage in Antarctica. The effects are not nearly as dramatic as was expected based on those projections. There was a stabilizing effect due to the low temperatures but it wasn't nearly as much as we would have expected based on the extrapolations that people have been making.

Larry Hall (Alma College, Alma, Michigan): You made a few references to variations of humidity and their effect on paper longevity. Could you speak to that further?

Lundeen: This is a question which is still up in the air. The accelerated aging tests have been done in essentially two different modes, one with dry air with essentially zero humidity. People have criticized that as being unrealistic because you don't store books in dry air. The other series of tests have been done in 50 percent humidity and these, likewise, have been criticized because that's perhaps a bit high although maybe not that far off, depending on where you live. In Hawaii that's a little bit low. Measurements comparing the accelerated aging tests with long-term tests seem to indicate that really some place in between is probably the best condition, but where in between hasn't been decided yet—maybe 10 to 20 percent humidity for the accelerated aging tests. There are some fairly well accepted guidelines for storage under normal temperatures and relative humidities, and there, around 50 percent or so is accepted. A more crucial problem may be fluctuations in humidity which cause paper to be stressed by absorption and desorption of moisture.

GERALD D. GIBSON

Head Curatorial Section
Motion Picture, Broadcasting and Recorded Sound Division
Library of Congress

Preservation of Nonpaper Materials

Present and Future Research and Development in the Preservation of Film, Sound Recordings, Tapes, Computer Records, and Other Nonpaper Materials

When asked earlier this year by Erik Barnouw, the man who was originally to have given this paper, if I would allow my name to be suggested as a possible alternate since he would be unable to be here, I said yes. After spending some six months of work and thought on the subject, I fear that if I were asked the same question today that my answer would be a polite, but firm, no. The reason for my change of attitude is not that I feel the topic is unworthy. To the contrary, I feel it is of major importance to all libraries and archives of which I am aware. Nor is my present feeling on the subject due to an unwillingness to be involved in the work, since it is a substantial part of my present position, and is one of the aspects of the job which I find both particularly enjoyable and rewarding. Rather, my reservations on the topic are due to the especially broad scope of my topic and the time limitations which have had to be imposed on delivery of this paper. To give a reasonably thorough report on the present research and development of the preservation of any single format with which we as librarians must work would barely be possible in this one session. To broaden the scope to anticipate future research and development severely compounds the assignment. To do so for all nonpaper materials is truly impossible.

To compound my reservation I looked at the schedule and agenda of the institute. Of the twelve papers to be given, only this one specifically deals with nonpaper materials. Before allowing myself to become even more paranoid, I stopped and reviewed the position that nonpaper materials actually hold in libraries and to realize just how long they have been there. Until the last decade of the nineteenth century the only nonpaper in virtually all libraries was that associated with books or as furnishing for a library: the wood, leather, and metal of bindings; animal skins used before or as a substitute for paper; the wax used in seals and in color pigments; marble in statuary; etc. In fact, it was not until 1945 or later that most commonly accepted nonpaper formats were considered anything other than throwaways allowed into the library world in the United States. Also, I had to remind myself that I, too, am a paper based, book trained musicologist and librarian and that I held to that training and bias until taking a position in 1966 as sound recordings' librarian at the Sibley Musical Library of the Eastman School of Music.

Nonpaper materials are still considered by many—some might say most—of my traditionally trained colleagues as "nonlibrary" materials. Until very recent years the Oral History Project of Columbia University, the prototype for many such programs in this country, used sound recordings only as a means to simplify the collection of data. These recordings were then transcribed and collected into typescripts, whereupon the sound recordings were either erased to be used for another project or were destroyed.

Until 1877, civilization did not have the ability to record and playback sound. The camera was not invented until 1840. Though sound recordings were present in libraries as early as the turn of this century, it was not until 1958 that a generally accessible archival collection of sound recordings was established in a U.S. library. (Note: There were classroom collections in colleges and universities, as well as a fairly extensive collection of commercial classical music recordings and field recordings of ethnic materials available at the Library of Congress, but access to them generally required either special affiliation or advance notification of interest and special arrangements for playback.) Even though moving pictures were accepted as copyrightable items as early as 1897, they could come in only as "paper prints" (or photographs) and not as film. The Museum of Modern Art (MOMA), New York, established its film library in 1935, proclaiming motion pictures as worthy of research and scholarship, though primarily for their content as "art." As an archival medium, the motion picture was not generally accepted and collected until after World War II. Prints and photographs fared little better, even though there was an established collection at the Library of Congress as early as 1897. With the exception of a few areas, like census records, public opinion surveys, and bibliographic data, the collecting and storing of computer records as primary research data is still in its infancy.

As late as 1950, nonpaper materials—pictures, audio, machine data—represented less that 10 percent of the 28,691,350 items in the total collections of the Library of Congress. By 1980 this had grown to more than 20 percent of a collection of 76,945,360 items. Thus, during an acknowledged period of information explosion—a phrase generally used by librarians to mean an increase of paper based materials—the nonpaper collections of the national library dramatically increased by a factor of 5.4 while paper collections were increasing by a factor of 2.4; put another way, nonpaper materials increased by twice as much as paper materials during this vital period for libraries. Preliminary information from a broad range of libraries indicated that they, too, have experienced similar collection growth during this period.

The assigned title for this paper specified the media to be covered as film, sound recordings, tapes, computer records, and, in the event that something has been left out, other nonpaper materials. My approach will be slightly different, grouping the media as pictures (moving and still, regardless of their form or base material), audio, machine data, and a broad, miscellaneous "other." This "other" category will include materials that I assume generally would be included in the consideration of the preservation of unusual paper objects—maps, for example—or types of materials that would more properly belong in a museum preservation course: musical instruments, furniture, carpets, paintings. As much as I feel it desirable to include them in this paper, time does not allow me to discuss the preservation of these materials, nonpaper though they may be. However, any library which accepts these types of materials, whether to furnish a rare book room, to sponsor a series of musical concerts on their own instruments, or simply to keep a patron happy, has an obligation to see to their proper preservation.

My coverage of nonpaper media, with one exception, will be directly proportionate to my understanding of the likelihood of finding that format in a library collection. The exception will be for that substance whose deterioration might have a catastrophic effect upon virtually all other materials, paper and nonpaper alike, which are held in libraries: cellulose nitrate based film.

I will attempt to give some realistic idea of the component parts of the general media listed above, review the principal preservation problems which they currently face, and cite the storage conditions and preservation procedures recommended today. If there is a particular publication which has been tried and proved generally reliable, I will cite it. Because the container and/or label is of such significance for many nonpaper objects, and because it frequently is an inseparable part of the item, I will occasionally consider its preservation properties as well. Finally, I will review the more promising current research and development related to the preservation of nonpaper materials and share some speculations about the future prospects for storage and preservation both of original materials and the data they contain.

Picture materials can be grouped into motion pictures, microforms, stills, and video recordings. Motion pictures can, in turn, be subgrouped into film widths, such as the standard 8, 16, 35, and 70mm widths; positives and negatives; fine grain masters; separate picture and sound track and composite picture and track; black and white and/or color; carried in strips, open reels, cassettes, and cartridges. Motion pictures are most frequently encountered which have a base of either cellulose acetate (hereafter called acetate), polymers of the polyester type, with polyethylene terephthalate (hereafter called Estar) being the more common of the polymer group, or cellulose nitrate (hereafter called nitrate). A gelatin suspended emulsion layer, for black and white film consisting primarily of either diazo or light sensitive silver salts, known commonly as silver halides, or for color film consisting of several emulsion layers, is held on the base by a thin adhesive layer.

Microforms are most commonly found in 16 and 35mm, as microfiche or in reels, cassettes, or cartridges. They are also available in black and white and also color, although color microfilm is comparatively uncommon due to cost and color instability. They are made of materials similar to those of motion pictures and in the same wide variety of generations and formats.

Stills are similar to the two formats just described, but while negatives are on a transparent film or glass base, positives are most likely on paper. The image may be in the form of a print or intended for projection and magnification as with motion pictures and microforms. Also in existence, but not included in this paper, are such older photographic techniques as daguerreotypes, tintypes, ambrotypes, collodion-coated glass plates, and albumenized paper.

The last of the genre "pictures" to be considered is video recordings, the newest of this family and the most varied. The fixation of a television program may have the properties of motion picture film, as in a kinescope; it may be a magnetic image on tape or disc; or it may be a signal stored on a video disc. Digital versus analog signals are the latest competitors in the media contest.

The principal thing we must know about digital and analog is that for every generation it is removed from the original recorded event, an analog signal loses information. By the time a film is copied six generations away from its original source, the human eye can easily see visible deterioration of the quality of the image and of the information being presented. There is no generation loss in reproducing a digital signal, regardless of the number of generations one may get from the source. A one-on-one comparison of the original and a copy 100 generations away should present no change in quality or quantity of digitally transmitted information.

There are presently three types of video disc. As with most other nonpaper formats, picture and nonpicture alike, the player built for one type of system will probably not play the discs from the other two. If we were public consumers we could wait to get the machine that finally, if ever, wins out. Unfortunately, libraries must collect and make available materials wanted and needed for research. As with other nonpaper materials, if the data is important enough, this usually means acquiring the material in the form then available, and acquiring and maintaining the necessary equipment to play it.

The first of the three disc systems on the market was LaserVision, originally made only by Magnavox, but now available as well from U.S. Pioneer, and, in industrial versions, from Sony and MCA DiscoVision. It is the one least like the conventional phonograph, since its 12-inch discs are read by lasers, not stylii, so there is no physical contact to wear out the discs. The recording is under the disc's transparent surface and the laser reads the bottom of the disc from the inside out. This system uses a Constant Angular Velocity (CAV), which is to say that the longer groove at the outside edge of the disc takes no longer to play than does the shorter groove at the inside margin of the disc. This allows for such "extras" as perfect still frame, slow motion, fast motion, and direct access to any individual frame. Unfortunately, it also means that the playing time of the disc is roughly 30 minutes per side as opposed to the approximately 60 minutes per side of the Constant Linear Velocity (CLV) discs. Or, it may hold roughly 54,000 still frames.

The RCA Selectavision, introduced in the spring of 1981 using CLV, is more like the conventional audio phonograph. Its sylus senses variations in electrical capacitance as it rides over microscopic pits in the bottom of the disc's grooves. For protection against dust and scratches, the Selectavision disc is covered by a rigid plastic sleeve that stays on until the disc is in the player. This system has no true still frame, slow motion, or fast motion. Its sound and picture quality are presently a bit lower than that of LaserVision, and the first few players on the market do not have the stereo sound capability of LaserVision. The Selectavision mode disc (also known as Capacitance Electronic Disc, or CED) has been adopted by Zenith, Hitachi, Toshiba, Sears, Sanyo, Ward, and Radio Shack.

I have not yet seen the third system, although it was to have appeared sometime in the fall of 1981. Called VHD, or Video High Density, it reportedly will be manufactured by Panasonic, General Electric, JVC, Quasar, Sharp, and Mitsubishi, and will require a similar protective jacket to the RCA Selectavision. Like LaserVision, it has no physical groove walls. Instead, its track is defined by tiny rows of recorded guide pulses, so it is being listed as offering the same extra features as LaserVision.

There are two main types of videocassette formats, VHS and Beta. The chief differences are tape speed, cassette size, and the path through which the tape is threaded inside the machine. Since VHS tapes are in slightly larger cassettes and run at slightly slower speeds, their maximum playing time is a bit longer (six hours as opposed to Beta's five). Beta's simpler tape path makes such operations as shifting between play and fast forward quicker and more convenient.

In addition to these two video tape recorders utilizing cassettes, there are, also, open reel and cartridge fed recorders. Open reel, cartridge, or cassette differ primarily in the way the tape is held for playing, as well as in the manner the tape is fed through the machine. In addition, there are wide variations within virtually all three video tape formats in the width of the magnetic tape, coming as wide as two-inches, or as narrow as 1/4 inch.

For our preservation information purposes, the primary differences between video tape pictures and video disc pictures are:

1. the ability to record and play, or, as the industry calls it, to "write and read." The video disc systems now generally available only "read" what has already been "written." Magnetic tape, regardless of its packaging, has "write and read" capability; and
2. the LaserVision disc, and presumably the VHD system, offers the potential of not being damaged by the act of "reading," since the stylus does not come into contact with the encoded information. All other systems, whether video disc or tape, as well as all the parts of the other members of the "Picture" family, require direct contact of equipment and the carrier in order to make the data human readable and retrievable. This, obviously, has far reaching repercussions for preservation of all data.

Audio materials are grouped into discs, cylinders, mechanical devices, film, and wire and tape.

The disc group varies in size from approximately one-inch to twenty inches or more in diameter, and from 1/64 of an inch to 1/4 or more of an inch in thickness. They have been made of hundreds of the solid substances presently known, including plastics, shellac, glass, wax, metal, rubber, tinfoil, wood, paper, and even chocolate candy. They also come in a combination of these: a core of metal, wood, glass, plaster of Paris, or paper, or a combination of these, and a playing surface of plastic, acetate, wax, or shellac. Their signal may be analog or digital, recorded either acoustically or electrically, using either a lateral or a vertical cutting and playback stylus. They play at speeds of less than 10 to greater than 100 revolutions per minute (RPM). Their stylii have a tip radius from .0005 to 35 mils, with intended tracking weights of less than 0.25 of a gram to several or more pounds in a groove that varies from microgroove to standard/coarse goove widths, with all variations in between and beyond. The modern commercial "LP" disc is fairly standardized. This has not always been the case. If the manufacturer were using a different recording and playback signal and needed specific tracking, signal configuration and packaging to accomplish the desired end, the manufacturer created a new system—for example hill-and-dale and lateral grooves. Multi-channel sound was realized by using binaural, bilateral, encoded, and enhanced mono; or, to insure that the public used their discs, manufacturers did such things as putting a large square spindle on the record machine so that the buyer of the machine would have to buy records with a similarly shaped hole. Each of these variants, whether of size, speed, stylus size and pressure, type of recording, direction of tracking, et al., requires a specific, working machine for information retrieval. Just as with most other nonpaper formats, an attempt to play a disc on the wrong machine will result in varying degrees of damage to the information-carrying package.

Cylinders are the earliest form of sound recordings. They were the only successful form of recording sound for the first fifteen or so years of the history of the phonograph, and they were an accepted form—in some areas they were the preferred form—until well into this century. Though most people today would recognize almost every other form of sound carrier covered here today, few would make the connection between cylinders and sound.

Cylinders come in a range of sizes almost as varied as those just mentioned for discs. Their recording signal and mode are, however, generally limited to hill-and-dale and mono, although the number of grooves varies.

The mechanical, or music box devices, are far too numerous to mention in any depth here. Their triggering devices were usually a disc, barrel, or strip of wood or paper with either indentions, protrusions, or simple cutouts intended to trigger an action: the plucking of a series of tuned springs, the opening of a pipe, the release of a hammer, the opening of a wind channel, etc. The instruments which were so activated were as varied as the modern player piano, a music box, a mechanically played violin, a church organ, or an entire orchestra of string, wind and percussion instruments.

Film audio materials utilize the same base materials as those found in motion picture film: acetate, nitrate, and polyesters, with all of the inherent problems of each. The recording signal can be either in a cut groove or a strip of magnetic tape applied to the film. In addition, there is optical sound: a photographic line of varying width and frequency in transparent film. When in a cut groove, it carries the same type of hill-and-dale and/or lateral cut signal that one finds in the grooves of discs or cylinders. When in a strip of magnetic tape embedded in the film, the signal has the same possibilities as will be shortly listed for audio magnetic tape. The base material, regardless of its makeup, is generally 35mm wide.

Wire and tape audio recordings are grouped together here not because of their base materials, for they are usually quite different, but because of their similarity of signal. They both depend, as does videotape, upon a magnetic signal held in wire, in the wire itself, and in tape, in magnetic particles which have been dispersed in a resin binder. The packaging of both, as with videotape, may be either an open reel, a cartridge, or a cassette.

The wire varies in diameter from 0.7 to 1.2 mils and may be made of virtually any metal wire capable of holding a magnetic charge. Usually, however, it was made of either stainless steel or carbon steel.

Magnetic tape varies from 1/8 inch to 2 inches or more in width and 0.25 to 1.5 mils or more in thickness and has an acceptable playing speed, depending upon the signal to be placed on the tape and the desired level of response which will be minimally acceptable, from 15/16 ips to 60 ips or higher. Magnetic tapes are made on a base material, now usually of polyester, but originally on metal bands and paper and acetate strips. The paper, acetate, or polyester base material is covered in a gelatin which carries the resin binder loaded with magnetizable particles and, hence, the potential magnetic signal. The coating, or gelatin, is held in place by an adhesive layer, or is bonded to and is a part of the base. Both wire and tape can carry either analog or digital signals.

Other than base material, the principal difference in wire and tape is the number of tracks or bands of sound that each can potentially carry. Wire is limited to a single signal. Tape can carry an infinite number of signals depending upon the width of the tape and the size of the tracks thereon. It is not unusual for a modern magnetic tape to carry up to sixty-four different signals. For commercially available audio tape recordings the number is generally limited to a maximum of either four or eight such bands.

An additional difference is the method in which loose ends of each are connected to like materials. To splice a tape, one can either use splicing tape, a hot splice, or an ultrasonic splice. To "splice" wire one simply ties the two desired ends together in a small, tight knot.

Computer records have been stored in magnetic tapes, discs, punched paper cards, cylinders, crystals, and microforms. At present the most common format is magnetic tape utilizing a digital signal. Punched cards appear to be being phased out and the possibilities of crystal storage are just beginning to be realized. Occasionally one sees or becomes aware of analog signal recordings, usually on magnetic tape and used for backup and preservation purposes.

The worst disaster for most nonpaper materials is fire which is the disaster most likely to destroy virtually all possibilities of salvage, since so many of the base materials of modern nonpaper records are petrochemical products. This, of course, is true for virtually all library materials. Yet the greatest potential catastrophic degradation for any likely library item, and the format with the single most susceptibility to heat, much less to fire itself, is cellulose nitrate based film materials. Temperatures of only slightly over 100°F are sufficient to cause nitrate based film, with no visible signs of deterioration, to self ignite. Once ignited it burns at about 15 times the speed of wood, and once ignited it cannot be smothered, since it carries within its chemical makeup enough oxygen to feed its own combustion.

You may well ask how many of us have, or will ever have, nitrate based films in our collections? And if the number is as small as you are correctly thinking it is, then why waste time with this topic? Following a very unfortunate incident at the National Archives' remote nitrate film vaults outside Washington, D.C., in 1978, the Library of Congress became even more acutely aware of the potential disaster of having nitrate in other than a specifically designed and maintained film vault. The National Library was already aware that it had some 90,000+ cans of nitrate based motion picture film which had been maintained in separate, National Fire Protection Association (NFPA) approved vaults. The Library staff had pulled a large quantity of nitrate based still film and stored it under similar conditions. On closer inspection, staff found additional still film, but were confident that there was no nitrate motion picture film in the general film collections. In September 1981, the staff became aware of nitrate in a collection of materials which a very knowledgeable donor had told them held no nitrate, and which had previously been spot-checked to assure all concerned that such was the case. The collection had been placed in a remote area where large parts of the Library's general collection are held. It had been there for several years as specific preselected parts of it were brought out and integrated into the cataloged collection. Then, during September, the Library of Congress staff became aware that one of the reels being processed was nitrate. The entire collection was then inspected and it was discovered that there were an additional ten reels of nitrate based film in the 1200 or so in the collection. Your comment might logically be: "So what? It was only eleven reels of film out of the approximately 250,000 reels of safety film which LC holds." Eleven reels of 35mm film would weigh an average of fifty pounds. A single pound of burning nitrate based film gives off four to five cubic feet of such gases as nitric oxide, nitrogen dioxide and tetroxide, carbon monoxide, and carbon dioxide. Once burning, it cannot be extinguished by normal fire fighting techniques. The only reasonable hope is to contain the fire while keeping the temperature of other nearby items below their flash point. The usual means of doing this, and virtually the only one which seems to work consistently, is to pour large quantities of water on the fire and its area, thus introducing the second great enemy of paper and nonpaper library materials alike: water and flooding.

The Library of Congress currently has four 5 by 7 by 20 feet nitrate film vaults filled with flat nitrate based picture materials. The Smithsonian, also inspecting its immense collections following the 1978 NARS fire, has located enough nitrate based materials to fill almost three similarly sized vaults.

I urge you, if you have any film based materials possibly dating from the mid-1950s or before to contact Eastman Kodak and get their 1950s booklet on identifying, handling, inspecting, and storing nitrate film. The NFPA Code 40 deals with storage facilities for nitrate film and must be followed in every area of the United States of which I am aware. The odds are that you have none, but be sure. The greatest disaster attributed to a nitrate film fire occurred in May 1929, in a Cleveland, Ohio, hospital. The fire, started by a bare light bulb and faulty steam pipes in the X-ray film storage area, burned only some 4900 pounds of nitrate, or the equivalent of roughly 1000 cans of 35mm film, yet killed 125 persons. Virtually all of the fatalities were from the fumes and gases of the burning film, not from the heat of the fire. Reportedly, some of the deaths were as much as 48 hours later as apparent survivors were walking down the street or resting in their homes.

The picture materials most likely to be held by libraries are microfilm, both roll and fiche, 8 and 16mm projection prints of motion pictures, photographic prints, and a growing number of video cassettes.

The recommended storage of service copies of virtually all safety film calls for an area with filtered air, kept dark except when access is needed, with the temperature at 68° to 70°F, and with a relative humidity of 35 to 45 percent. All materials should be staged—allowed to come to ambient temperature and humidity before being taken from the storage area for use and brought gradually back to low temperature when being returned to storage—for at least twelve hours before being used. They should be on hubs, if appropriate, packaged and sealed into poly/foil bags or envelopes, and, for reels of motion picture film, shelved in nonrust, metal cans placed horizontally no more than three high on a shelf. Microforms and stills are usually filed in drawers rather than placed on shelves. All film products should be inspected regularly and, as appropriate to the format, rolled through no less than every three years.

The single largest problem which most libraries seem to have with all film based materials is surface scratches caused through normal use and handling. Of course, more careful handling, better maintenance of the equipment, and more care in cleaning the film and equipment before every use will make a significant difference in this problem. However, a new product recently offered by 3M holds great promise in this area, especially for rare and irreplaceable materials and for heavily used materials. Called "Photogard," it has a very impressive track record to date. The following data has been furnished by 3M. A polymerized silicone, Photogard can be put onto basically any processed photographic material, including glass. Magnetic tapes and optical video discs are presently being tested. It has potential use in the graphic arts, with X-ray and phosphorous screens, in photo finishing, and in all micrographic and motion picture applications. The 3M company does not recommend it for nitrate based film materials because of the use of heat in the application. Coated materials are:

1. *Highly resistant to abrasion.* In the Gardner Falling Sand Abrasion Test there is a 70 percent haze on uncoated film materials, and an 11 percent haze on like coated materials. On coated glass, the haze level drops to 10 percent. Photogard is approximately eleven times less abrasive than polyester.
2. *Highly antistatic.* The "half life" of an electrical charge at 50 percent relative humidity on Photogarded polyester film is 0.1 of one second. Uncoated, the "half life" of an electrical charge under the same conditions is 2000 seconds.
3. *Highly solvent resistant.* Coated film was virtually unchanged by chemicals that destroyed uncoated film.
4. *Easily cleanable.* Pencil, grease, oil, et al., wipe off. Cleaners may be either virtually any cleaning chemical, ultrasonic cleaners, or combinations of the two, with the major exception that all cleaners and machines should be free of wax.
5. *Virtually antibacterial.* Properly precleaned, coated film will support few if any bacteria.
6. *More resistant to ultraviolet (u/v) light fade.* There is a u/v light screen built into the coating, resulting in a decrease in u/v light fade by a factor of 4.
7. *More resistant to darkroom storage fade.* There is a 50 percent reduction in darkroom fade.

Photogard transmits 97 percent of visible light. The very smooth surface obtained by coating film reduces surface light scatter and greatly improves the legibility of a reel of microfilm which the Library of Congress had assumed to be virtually unusable. Obviously, the coating will make no major improvement on scratches which penetrate the emulsion. One other example of the usefulness of Photogard on heavily used film is that from the New York State Museum in Albany, New York. They showed the film *Logging* 8400 times over twenty-five weeks of an exhibit. Their films normally last a very impressive 2016 plays over the six weeks of a scheduled exhibit. After over four times as many showings, the Photogard coated film was still considered to be in an acceptable condition by museum personnel.

The principal negative result of the 3M tests is that there are some increased problems in cold splicing of coated film, but splicing can readily be accomplished by the use of available products and techniques. There is no particular problem with hot or ultrasonic splices.

In the matter of color fading of motion picture film images, Kodak has published its findings on color stability. Using short term tests at high temperatures to predict the density changes expected, they tell us that materials stored at room temperature (24°C/75°F) or lower, with dark keeping storage conditions at 40 percent relative humidity for all colors, have an acceptable density of 0.8 or better for fifteen to twenty years. By lowering the temperature to 16°C/60°F, we can expect 0.8 density or better for fifty or so years; and by going to -18°C/0°F, we go to upward of 1000 years of 0.8 density or better. By lowering the relative humidity to 15 percent we double the predicted dark storage capability by a factor of two. Specified data on particular motion picture products is available from Kodak, Dept. 620DS, Rochester, New York 14650, as is the data from which I took the above statistics.

There is one major problem with the Kodak data: there is presently available little information on the effect of temperature and relative humidity cycling on film when taking it from darkened, controlled atmosphere storage to a projector or printer and returning it to the cold vault. Kodak, of course, recommends the staging of materials coming and going from the cold vaults, but there appears to be little documented information on long term effects of repeated cyclings.

An additional problem in the preservation of film is the separation of the emulsion from the base material. The recommended, and apparently successful, solution to this problem is to maintain humidity and temperature as constantly as possible. If there must be a change in either or both of these vital elements of preservation they should come as slowly as possible, avoiding the sudden changes which take place when adequate staging is not practiced.

The recommended storage for all magnetic tape, regardless of the signal which it carries, its thickness, its width, or its packaging, is:

1. Where possible, use only reel-to-reel tape, on the largest possible unslotted hubs made of metal whose flanges are immediately replaced if they are deformed or out of plane.
2. Package reels in sealed metal cans or sealed boxes of a material such as polyethylene/cardboard/foil/polyethylene laminate. The boxes should be stacked on edge in the shelves. Tape should not be packaged until it is in equilibrium with the stacks.
3. Stack temperature should be maintained at 65° to 68°F and 40 percent plus or minus 5 percent relative humidity (RH) for often used recordings while storage in 50°F at the same relative humidity is recommended for seldom used and particularly valuable recordings.
4. Playback and packaging rooms should be maintained dust free and at the same 68°F/40 percent RH as the stacks. Tapes exposed to other en-

vironments should be staged in the playback environment before playback.

5. Stray external magnetic fields should not be permitted in the stack, playback, and packaging environments. The maximum flux density should be 10 gauss.

6. Playback equipment should be maintained as recommended by the manufacturer, including cleaning, tape transport adjustment, and component demagnetization.

7. A rewind and inspection deck, separate from playback facilities, should be used for packaging and inspection. Winding tension for 1.5 mil tape should be a constant torque of 3-5 ounces at the hub of a 10-inch reel.

8. The best tape presently available for storage purposes appears to be 1.5 mil Mylar base.

9. Tape should be recorded at a maximum level below 2 percent harmonic distortion (4db below normal recording level is usually satisfactory). The first and last fifteen feet of the tape should not be used for program recording, but should have a burst of 10 mil wavelength (approximately 750 cps at 7.5 ips) signal at maximum recording level preceded and followed by several layers of blank tape for inspection purposes.

10. Tape should be aged in the packaging room for six months prior to recording. Recorded tape which has been exposed to other than the prescribed environment should be conditioned in the packaging room for six weeks prior to packaging.

11. Tape should be inspected once every two years, measured from time of last playback, and rewound so that the curvature of the base is opposite to the direction of the previous curvature. This inspection should consist of measurement of print through caused by the toneburst at the end of the tape and a spot check at the tape end next to the hub for coating adhesion or delamination. It need not include playback.

12. Storage shelves should be made of wood or a nonmagnetizable metal free from vibration and shock.

The principal problems associated with magnetic recordings are undesired erasing of the magnetic signal, separation of the emulsion from the base material, print through, and tape breakage. There is no new breakthrough for these problems of the scope and magnitude of the 3M Photogard for film-based materials; the only prevention for them is care in handling and following of the recommended storage and handling procedures given above. For unique or very valuable materials it is always wise to have backup copies stored separate from the service copies. This, of course, presents the problem of generation loss in analog copies. If a master and a service copy are to be maintained, the master should be the item closest to the original and should be used only to create new service copies.

Computer centers have a very desirable backup procedure which, if possible, is recommended for all other tape collections: data banks are backed-up daily, with the backup copy being kept for a specified, overlapping period of time with other such tape copies. Tapes which are kept on site are periodically transferred to a safe storage area for additional backup capability. Since most computer records are digital, there is no loss of information from generation to generation. Thus, at any given time, virtually all of the data bank is available on site, in a backup copy also on site, and in a safe storage area for added protection.

The most frequently encountered sound recordings are 33 1/3 and 45 rpm vinyl discs, 78 rpm shellac discs, and magnetic tapes. The recommended storage for magnetic tapes and their principal problems have just been covered above. The recommended storage criteria for discs are:

1. Store the cleaned disc recording in a sealed sleeve made of a laminate of polyethylene/paperboard/foil/polyethylene of acid free thirty-four point chipboard or better, soft aluminum foil of 0.0001 inch thickness, and polyethylene. The discs should not be packaged and sealed until they are in equilibrium with the intended storage area.
2. Stack temperature should be maintained at 70°F and 45 percent plus or minus 5 percent relative humidity for often used recordings or for service copies, and 50°F and the same relative humidity for seldom used recordings.
3. Playback and packaging room(s) should be maintained dust free and at the recommended conditions for often used recordings. Discs exposed to other environments should be conditioned in the playback area for twenty-four hours before playback and for an equal period in the storage area atmosphere before being returned to storage.
4. Store in a darkened room, where possible, but always away from sunlight and from artificial lighting of the shorter wavelengths.
5. Store all discs in the vertical position without pressure on the disc surface or the opportunity for off vertical attitude, using only clean, unabrasive surfaced packaging as suggested in number 1 above; do not permit sliding contact of disc surface with other surfaces.
6. Play the disc only with a stylus of proper size and weight for the particular disc.
7. If a disc is to receive heavy playing, particularly if it is unusual or unique, make a service copy and use the original as the archival master as above.

The principal problems of preservation associated with disc recordings are warpage, heavy groove wear, breaking and rim chips (particularly of 78 rpm discs and older 33 and 45 rpm discs), and distortion of the playback grooves by fungi. These are generally readily correctable by proper handling, cleaning, packaging, and storage. Probably the single greatest problem in the preservation of disc recordings is groove wear. This can be greatly reduced by proper maintenance of the playback equipment, regular inspection of the stylus condition and weight, and regular cleaning of the disc. In addition, there are a number of products on the market today which treat the playing surface to either harden it to reduce groove wear, reduce the static electricity on the surface of the disc and thus cut down dust attraction, or remove the built up dirt and dust prior to playing. In general, I am very leery of anything which is going onto the surface of the disc that will alter or coat it and which, in all probability, will have to be removed at some point in the future if the disc is to be preserved. One product, however, LAST, has received high praise from many of my colleagues. The Library of Congress is currently considering whether to use the product for its collections.

A major problem with disc sound recordings which is, fortunately, lacking for the generally collected nonpaper materials is the presence of a label, usually paper, affixed directly to the surface of the disc. The paper label, with its glue or heat-seal and inks, introduces an entirely new problem to the preservation of these materials: How does the preservation of paper materials affect the preservation of nonpaper? Most other non-paper materials have something of this problem, for publishers are forced, for reasons of bibliographic control if nothing else, to put identifying and descriptive information on the item or its container. In most cases, only the disc recording has its label affixed directly to its surface. This, also, raises special problems when the item is being cleaned: will the binder dissolve in water; will the paper dissolve; are the inks and dyes water soluable; is the paper acidic; will it support the growth of fungi? In most cases, the answers to these questions seem to be in favor of preservation: the glues may dissolve, as will the inks, dyes, and paper, but they can be protected with a little care in the cleaning and handling process. The paper seems, generally, to be low in acidity and resistant to fungus growth.

Publications of general use which have been evaluated and are considered by most working in the field to be relatively dependable are comparatively few. They include:

Bertram, H. Neal, and Stafford, Michael K. "The Print-Through Phenomenon." *Journal of the Audio Engineering Society*, vol. 28, no. 10, Oct. 1980.

_____ . *Recording Media Archival Attributes (Magnetic)* (Contract No. F30602-78-C-0181 PR NO. 1-8-4008). Redwood City, Calif.: Ampex Corp. 1979 (2d printing 1980).

Cuddihy, Edward F. "Aging of Magnetic Recording Tape." *IEEE Transactions on Magnetics*, vol. MAG-16, no. 4, July 1980.

Eastman Kodak. *Preservation of Photographs*. Rochester, N.Y.: Eastman Kodak, 1979.

_____ . *Storage and Preservation of Motion Picture Film.* Rochester, N.Y.: Eastman Kodak, 1957 (out of print, but selected portions have been reprinted by Kodak).
_____ . *Storage and Preservation of Microfilm.* Rochester, N.Y.: Eastman Kodak, 1981.
Pickett, A.G., and Lemcoe, M.M. *Preservation and Storage of Sound Recordings.* Washington, D.C.: Library of Congress, 1959 (out of print, but LC has announced its intention to reprint).

At present, there seems to be an active interest in the preservation of nonpaper materials. In recent years this has not been the case. The last in-depth work on the preservation and storage of sound recordings, for example, was published in 1959 and has been out of print for the last ten years or so. Currently, work is being carried out or is being actively considered by Kodak, 3M, various governmental agencies and bodies, including the intelligence community, the National Bureau of Standards, the National Archives, and the Library of Congress, as well as professional organizations and associations, including the American Film Institute, the Association for Recorded Sound Collections, the Audio Engineering Society, the International Association of Sound Archives, the Music Library Association, the Society of Motion Picture Technicians and Engineers, and the University Film Association. Of particular interest is the National Bureau of Standards' recently announced five year study of archival stability of polyester film—chemical properties. On an international level, Unesco adopted recommendations for the safeguarding and preservation of moving images at its general conference in Belgrade, in October 1980. In addition, a number of private individuals are personally working on specialized projects, including Art Schifrin with audio cylinders and early movie sound tracks, Henry Wilhelm on color stability, and Steve Smolian with radio transcription materials.

An important event that is taking place today is the development of systems for the storage of digital signals on optical video discs. This is important not only for the preservation of nonpaper materials and artifacts, but for information in general. The life span of an article in an ideal environment is a property which is built into the article when it is manufactured. Proper care cannot extend this potential life, although it can prevent premature failure. The importance of the optical disc is that it permits the storage and retrieval of data without subjecting it to the physical stresses of most current storage and playback. The advantages of this system are those which were cited earlier in this paper when I addressed the LaserVision disc. The disc is read by lasers, thus there is no physical contact with the stored data to wear it out faster than its own built in properties dictate. It uses a Constant Angular Velocity (CAV), thus allowing for perfect still frame, fast forward, and fast backward searches, along with direct access to any single frame. It has the capability to store aural, visual, and machine data in a digital mode, thus preventing loss of data in the transfer from one generation to another.

There are still a number of problems to resolve. Just what is the potential life of the disc? How susceptible is it to fluctuations in heat and humidity? Will its clear surface scratch easily? Will it discolor with age, or from heat and/or humidity? Will the laminated "sandwich" which makes up the disc separate because of heat or other factors? In addition, the present state of video does not allow for direct retrieval of an image with enough clarity and definition for most motion picture researchers, much less for the specialist working with manuscripts, art or maps, to name but three fields dependent upon clarity and resolution of image. Also, the range and fidelity of colors possible with video have been attacked by those working in areas where color is of importance: maps, art, pictographs, etc. Nonetheless, this device seems to be the solution of most of the preservation problems which are faced by every other known library medium, paper and nonpaper alike. We look with great anticipation to the realization of the solution of these problems and want to believe those who tell us that we can have the requisite resolution and color while assuring us that the problems of storage and preservation are really not unsolvable.

We still have the materials we have inherited, however. The optical disc and its solutions, while promising for many lesser applications, cannot conserve those items we must retain in their original physical form. For those items, we must do everything possible to insure that the life span potential built into all the materials placed in our keeping is realized to its fullest possible extent. Otherwise, if ever a permanent preservation system is developed, we will have far less to preserve and share with the future than we received from the past.

The interrelationships between the general needs for space, shelving, storage, structural weight loads, temperature and relative humidity, packaging, and shielding for the varied materials being considered can best be seen in the accompanying table.

TABLE 1
GENERAL PHYSICAL NEEDS FOR MOST COMMON NONPAPER LIBRARY MATERIALS

Type	Temperature (Fahrenheit)	Relative Humidity	Recommended Packaging	No. of Items/ Linear Ft. of Shelving	Weight of Average Item in Pounds	Weight/Linear Ft. of Shelving
FILM						
MoPict* (safety based)						
16mm (1M)	70° ± 5°	40% ± 5%	film in poly/foil bags; heat sealed; film on hubs; nonrust metal cans; cans horizontal, maximum of 3 cans high	3.00	2.33	6.99
16mm (2M)	70° ± 5°	40% ± 5%		1.75	4.95	8.66
35mm (1M)	70° ± 5°	40% ± 5%		3.00	5.00	15.00
35mm (2M)	70° ± 5°	40% ± 5%		1.75	9.16	16.03
MoPict* (nitrate based)						
	50° ± 5°	40% ± 5%	for special vault construction see NFPA Code 40; film should be hand inspected every 6 months shelved in nonrust metal cans; cans horizontal, maximum 3 cans high	same as for similar formats, nonnitrate base		
Stills*	70° ± 5°	40% ± 5%	poly/foil sleeves; heat sealed; in drawers			
Micro*	70° ± 5°	40% ± 5%	poly/foil sleeves or bags (fiche/roll); heat sealed; rolls on reels; in acid containers			
Video**						
½" Cass	65° ± 5°	40% ± 5%	tape in poly/foil bags; heat sealed; supported center hubs for reel tape; in low acid containers; vertical on shelf; nonmagnetic shelving		1.77	
¾" Cass	65° ± 5°	40% ± 5%			1.71	
1" Reel	65° ± 5°	40% ± 5%			5.00	
2" Reel	65° ± 5°	40% ± 5%			17.50	

AUDIO**

Discs

LPs (10&12)	70° ± 5°	45% ± 5%	poly/foil sleeves; heat sealed; stiff outer sleeve of low acid material; vertical on shelf; full height/width dividers every 5 inches	66	0.51	33.66
45s	70° ± 5°	45% ± 5%		66	0.22	14.52
78s (10&12)	70° ± 5°	45% ± 5%		66	0.60	39.60
16' vinyl	70° ± 5°	45% ± 5%		66	0.60	39.60
16' acetate	70° ± 5°	45% ± 5%		66	0.90	59.40

Tape**

Cass	65° ± 5°	40% ± 5%	in poly/foil bags/lined low acid boxes; heat sealed; supported center hubs for reel tape; heavy, nonslotted hubs; vertical on nonmagnetic shelving; smaller items may be in drawers		0.16	
Cart.	65° ± 5°	40% ± 5%			0.30	
10" Reel	65° ± 5°	40% ± 5%			1.77	
7" Reel	65° ± 5°	40% ± 5%			0.73	

Cylinders	68° ± 5°	45% ± 5%	poly/foil lined low acid center supported stiff boxes; filed in drawers, 1 level deep; vertical position	11 per sq. ft.	0.27	4.32 per sq. ft.

MACHINE DATA

same as for mag materials

*For film based materials image stability (especially color images) Kodak recommends considerably lower temperature (0°F or lower, dependent upon acceptable level of image fade) and relative humidity of 15%.
**For audio and mag based video materials, approximately 50° ± 5°F is recommended for archival storage.

TABLE 1—*Continued*

Type	Filtered Air	Shielding Recommended	Dark Storage	Staging if Stored in Lower than Work Area Temp/ Relative Humidity	Inspection/Rewind where Applicable
FILM					
MoPict (safety based)					
16mm (1M)	Yes	U/V*; mag/RF** for	Yes	Yes	Every 3 years
16mm (2M)	Yes	mag strip sound	Yes	Yes	Every 3 years
35mm (1M)	Yes	mag strip sound	Yes	Yes	Every 3 years
35mm (2M)	Yes	mag strip sound	Yes	Yes	Every 3 years
MoPict (nitrate based)	Yes	U/V; heat	Yes	Yes	Every 6 months
Stills	Yes	U/V	Yes	Yes	Every 3 years
Micro	Yes	U/V	Yes	Yes	Every 3 years
Video	Yes	U/V; mag/RF non mag shelving	Yes	Yes	Every 2 years

AUDIO

Discs

LPs	Yes	U/V	Yes	Yes	No
45s	Yes	U/V	Yes	Yes	No
78s	Yes	U/V	Yes	Yes	No
16″ vinyl	Yes	U/V	Yes	Yes	No
16″ acetate	Yes	U/V	Yes	Yes	Every 12 months for loss of plasticizer
Cylinders	Yes	U/V	Yes	Yes	No
Tape	Yes	U/V; mag/**RF**; non mag shelving free from vibration	Yes	Yes	Every 2 years

MACHINE DATA
same as for mag data

*U/V—ultraviolet
**RF—radio frequency

DISCUSSION

William Aguilar (student, Graduate School of Library and Information Science, University of Illinois at Urbana-Champaign): Recently in a stereo review journal, I was reading about a new product by Sony Corporation. This product was a 35mm camera that was rather unique in that it did not use any film; instead it used some type of magnetic device. The image was played back on a television screen. I'd like to know if you could tell us anymore about this device and its impact on the microfilming industry.

Gerald Gibson: Though I have not seen the item to which you refer, the main impact would seem to be in the home photographic market. As I understand the product, it is not a 35mm image, nor even a photographic image. Rather it is a magnetic recording to be played back via a video system. With it comes all of the problems of resolution, of clarity, and of color which any other magnetic video system presents to its users. If you want a general image, or at least do not need one with greater resolution than your video screen furnishes, then you will probably be OK. If you wish detailed information or storage capability, this type of image gives you the same problems as other magnetic video signals. For example, the film I showed here today was first copied onto video cassette by the Library's video lab. Usually their work is quite good, so I do not think that was where the problem lay. In any event, the video cassette copy was unusable for public presentation. You could not see a useful picture unless you were close enough to touch the screen. It lacked the level of clarity that exists even with a poor 16mm copy. I do not think there is any serious consideration of the device you mention for use in preservation.

WILLIAM T HENDERSON

Binding and Preservation Librarian
University of Illinois at Urbana-Champaign

Preservation and Conservation Decisions in the Local Library

In the course of the second semester last year, I received a note from the University Librarian, Hugh Atkinson, with which was enclosed a note from a faculty member in the Department of Sociology. This faculty person had located in the library's stacks an old and worn volume which he found to be very important and informative. In his note, he asked whether the library was interested in faculty opinion as to what might be worthy of preservation, and he indicated his interest in our doing something to prevent the loss of this valuable volume. Mr. Atkinson asked me to look into the particular matters involved and to report both to him and to the faculty person.

In checking with the staff of the Bookstacks, I learned that, as a result of the interest of the writer of the letter, the book had been routed to storage which meant that it would be filmed or photocopied if and when it was requested again. As a result of this special interest, the volume was pulled from its place enroute to storage and given immediate attention as to its needs for preservation.

The volume turned out to be a pamphlet published in 1913 which had been inserted into a grey photomount pamphlet binder apparently soon after its arrival in the library. The pamphlet itself was brittle, but not broken or badly discolored. It lacked a title page (possibly it never had one). There were no illustrations. The original cover which had been pasted to the front of the pamphlet binder had become brittle and broken along with the binder, but had lost none of its printed information. Our conservation and photographic services units determined that the best procedure in this instance was to photocopy the entire pamphlet, bind the copy in a new pamphlet binder with acid-free end papers and discard the original. This was done, including the making of a copy of the original cover to serve as a substitute title page in the new binder.

When the new copy was ready to be returned to the Bookstacks for shelving, I wrote two notes (one to the faculty member and one to the University Librarian) reporting on the entire process and indicating that there was in operation in the stacks a program by which staff listen to faculty and other users and route materials so as to assure special handling and eventual preservation.

I've recounted this experience because it illustrates the involvement of people at several points in a large library staff engaged in ongoing preservation efforts. Those involved were a library user, a library administrator, those responsible for servicing the volume involved, the conservation staff, and the photographic services staff. Each individual or group played a particular role in working out treatment for the volume. The only thing which marks this incident as special is the direct personal involvement of the library's chief administrator. In my experience, all of these same groups and individuals are essential in preservation activity if preservation and conservation of the collections is to become a reality.

For a period of years, I have been aware that the decisions regarding preservation which I have made, which I have shared in making, or which have been made by others have not all been of the same nature. The level or levels within the library's staff hierarchy of the persons involved make some decisions differ from other decisions; however, these levels of involvement are not the heart of the problem. The thing lacking was a clear way to designate other distinctions which seemed necessary in attempting to analyze such problems and decisions. I found little help in my reading or sharing experiences with others in attempting to work in this area. In reading the proceedings of the 1976 conference on *A National Preservation Program* at the Library of Congress, I was therefore quite interested to discover that Daniel Boorstin in opening the conference suggested a division of the questions comprising the problem of preservation. He characterized two rather distinct types of problems as epistemological and technical.[1] He further described the epistemological questions as being social questions, meaning that they are questions relating to the interests of those who will use, administer, and service the materials comprising the collections. I must admit that the term *epistemological* sent me to the dictionary because it has been some time since I had studied formal philosophical language. At this point, it becomes necessary to understand Boorstin's exact meaning and intention in interjecting this term into the vocabulary of library preservation. Epistemology is defined as "the study of the methods and grounds of knowledge especially with reference to its limits and validity; broadly: the theory of knowledge."[2]

After some reflection on this definition, I have concluded that this is probably a happy choice of terms, given Boorstin's qualification that by the term *epistemological* he means that these questions in their broad sense are social questions as well as questions of knowledge because they pertain to the society for which recorded knowledge is preserved as well as to the knowledge itself.

Under the heading "epistemological questions" we can collect those concerns which have to do with the need to preserve materials in the collections of libraries and archives. These are the questions of what we should attempt to preserve in a general sense as well as the questions which inevitably arise relating to budgeting, staffing and equipping our institutions to do the work of preservation. In general these epistemological questions involve more than the conservator, the preservation librarian, and others on a library staff with responsibility for the care and keeping of the collections. All of these persons are included, but these questions also call for participation by those who use the materials—the sociologist in my introductory remarks and others like him engaged in research, teaching and other activities requiring the use of libraries and archives. Often these persons have very deep and specific knowledge of the materials of a particular specialized subject area. Further, these problems, by their very nature, involve library administrators, budget officers, and those involved in raising funds for the institution among whom may be board members, friends' groups, and possibly even individual donors.

Boorstin's other major heading, "technical questions," which he further defined as physical questions, permits the gathering of those questions and concerns which have to do with the physical nature of library and archival materials and the activities and processes which can be used to enhance their continued usefulness.[3] These are the questions and decisions of preservation-minded librarians and other library staff as well as of conservators and preservation specialists as they consider the physical condition and requirements both of particular materials and of whole collections.

Despite the tone of the above sentences, these concerns are not mutually exclusive. All, or nearly all, of the groups and individuals referred to in the foregoing remarks are concerned with preservation in general, with the determination of preservation policy, with the establishment of budgets, deployment of staff and the other ways and means involved in planning and doing the work of preservation. Epistemological questions, as they are answered, inform those doing the work; and, in the other direction, information about processes and procedures, new developments, new needs, and gaps in the ability of an institution to deal with these problems inform those whose role is primarily administrative in nature. Actually, trying to distinguish between the two with great precision is very difficult because neither the people concerned nor the functions separate with any great neatness. The distinctions made are for purposes of discussion and description and should not be carried over too rigidly into a working situation.

In the paragraphs which follow, several questions or problem areas which fall under one or the other of these two broad headings are discussed. Though the discussion centers first on epistemological questions and then upon technical concerns, their interrelated and overlapping natures are quite apparent; however, the usefulness of these terms in enabling one to distinguish between differing preservation problems is apparent.

Epistemological Questions or Decisions

Perhaps the first and most basic of these is the matter of whether or not to take any particular notice of preservation or to institute any kind of preservation or conservation program within an institution. In its shortest and most concise form this question might be phrased, "Should a library preserve materials?"

There are libraries which at first glance might seem to have little or no need to become involved with preservation because their mission is to provide current materials or current information. Such libraries have no archival function and no intention to be libraries of record. However, even such libraries have the need to preserve their current materials for current use which may stretch over many years; and these institutions will ultimately find it the better part of wisdom to listen to and heed the gospel of preservation, particularly those parts which counsel safe physical handling and storage in clean, air-conditioned, pollution-free, light-controlled quarters. Further, libraries emphasizing current information will have need in many instances for active binding programs to make it possible to keep their materials organized as well as to make them available whole and complete. Almost without exception, they will also have the need to repair and rebind at least occasional items which come to some kind of grief at the hand of even the most careful and well-meaning individuals (both patron and staff). Thus, even though there may be no commitment to keep materials after their current information use is past, there is need for preservation and conservation activity in libraries which might seem unlikely places for it.

The second question, logically, is "What materials will be preserved?" This question is stated in this form because it is still not safe to assume that all libraries will or can conform to the canons of the gospel of preservation relating to provision of air-conditioned, pollution-free, light-controlled quarters. As yet, we have not been able in many libraries to acquire this level of protection for all our collections. The library which has done so is to be counted among the fortunate, and the rest must count themselves among those still striving to meet these basic criteria. It is part of the routine of survivorship among those lacking this level of protection to work for the coming of a better day, however that may be possible. This may include the documentation of present inadequacies, helping set up a departmental library in new quarters with the necessary equipment and controls to provide a safe environment, and working with all who are interested in improving these conditions. Meanwhile, with or without all the collections of a library in ideal environments, all libraries and institutions with archival missions are faced with caring for collections or portions of collections exhibiting physical problems stemming from age and use. Hence, it appears that the question "What materials will be preserved?" is still valid. While it may be that existing quarters are inadequate, there may be parts of collections which can be dealt with in a positive fashion including the institution of improved housekeeping and teaching the staff to handle materials as they work with them in ways which will minimize wear and tear. Materials of great intrinsic value, unique items, and materials of particular research interest all may provide grist for the preservation mill. Working with such limited groups of materials both fills important needs and gives an institution the opportunity to get started with preservation activities.

How, at the present time, a library determines what to preserve beyond these fairly obvious types of things is a question for which there is no one clear answer. Such an answer awaits at least two developments. One is the availability of mass deacidification; the other is the development of priorities both within individual institutions and among groups of libraries, as to what will receive such treatment. Present indications seem to imply that deacidification service may not be too much more delayed, so planning for its use should begin now. There are some relatively obvious groups of materials in almost all institutions which may be good candidates for initial consideration. Included are those select collections often termed "reference collections" and sometimes called "core subject collections" which are frequently kept close at hand for heavy use by those providing reference service and/or working closely with researchers and students in particular subject fields. To be able to treat such collections so as to assure their continued usefulness and availability would be a major achievement. The gradual emergence of networks presenting the profession with working groups of libraries already formed and already quite dependent upon each other could easily expand their sharing into preservation and conservation by beginning to formulate plans for coordinated programs on a regional or other logical basis designed to assure geographic distribution of materials while sharing the work of preservation. Within regions, libraries could have primary preservation missions dependent upon their strengths, thereby relieving the libraries involved from the need to attempt to preserve all their holdings equally. Such an endeavor will require the efforts of library users, librarians with many specialties, and library conservators with knowledge both of collections and of the emerging techniques. Also required will be an evaluation of collections of a type we have not had in the past, but one which can utilize past experience in judging the quality of library resources. Such a program will also require ingenuity in other areas and a great deal of determination to succeed before any materials are actually deacidified and back on the shelves.

At some risk of seeming to have answered before having asked it, I submit that the third question in this group of concerns under the heading epistemological questions is: "How will these materials be preserved?" I make this disclaimer because my remarks about deacidification and preservation planning may seem to have already provided an answer. However, I doubt that it will be so simple and direct if and when we get to the time that libraries generally have access to deacidification on a collection-wide basis. The reason is that deacidification will not be a whole cure, but will be a great help in arresting the progress of embrittlement for those things which are not yet brittle or which are not yet too brittle to be used. However, deacidification will not restore strength to paper already too deteriorated for use. Thus the question of methods of preservation remains.

In considering how materials will be preserved we have our past experiences as well as whatever indications of the future we can discern to guide us. Past experience indicates that brittleness can be dealt with in several ways which are familiar but which possibly may be reiterated without too much fear of belaboring the obvious:

1. Preservation-minded staff all across the library to handle materials in ways appropriate to their condition and to extending their usefulness;
2. Quarters adequate for providing safe physical handling and safe storage environments for materials whatever their format, size or medium;
3. Staff specializing in preservation to provide information and training for nonspecialist staff, to provide service for materials needing repair and restoration, and to provide quality control of all preservation activities;
4. An in-house facility for preservation staff to work effectively and efficiently;
5. A binding program, ordinarily based on commercial library bindery services, to provide basic protection and organization for individual volumes;
6. Services of skilled commercial hand binders/paper conservators to perform necessary work on materials of special worth and to amplify the effectiveness of the in-house conservation staff.

While these six points provide at least a description of what can be done now to permit an institution to deal with its collections and their physical deterioration thoughtfully and appropriately, they are offered neither as a preservation program nor as a cure for brittleness. These are simply techniques that libraries have utilized and are utilizing to deal with materials as they age and become increasingly subject to embrittlement. Taken as a whole, these techniques require a continued sizable allocation of resources for the personnel, space, equipment and supplies required to make possible the attempt to handle collections without creating new preservation problems or exacerbating problems which already may exist. Such techniques will remain primary elements in efforts to get the most use out of library materials.

All six of these elements name staff or assume personnel as a primary active agent. Personnel is expensive and will remain so. Almost every aspect of preservation is labor-intensive. The continued dependence upon sheet-by-sheet techniques of paper preservation makes this basic activity so expensive that it is common practice to put it off as long as possible. Furthermore, library conservators are in such small supply that each would possibly be responsible for a group of libraries if we had a truly comprehensive program of preservation. A stated objective of computerization has been to permit the shifting of personnel from purely recordkeeping activities to activity needing human interaction and skill. While it may be hoped that some staff in libraries may be transferred to preservation work as computerization proceeds, the continued pressures of inadequate funding and inflation are such that this may be achieved, if ever, only with great difficulty.

Equipment for preservation work can range from the relatively simple and not especially costly to the rather elaborate and relatively more expensive depending upon the level of operation reached in a given library. While beginnings can be made with relatively simple equipment, a facility capable of a full range of activities and of efficient operation requires a major commitment of resources; and, if a photographic facility capable of providing quality products is included, the amount needed is still greater.

One of the marks of preservation work is that it retains old techniques which continue to meet its evolving criteria, together with the equipment needed to utilize them, as it adopts scientific ways and adapts both the equipment and the techniques of modern science to its purposes. Thus, leaves of a seventeenth-century volume may be hand cleaned using a traditional technique; deacidified in a plexiglass tank designed in the 1970s using a deacidification solution also recently developed; repaired with a handmade paper, the maker of which still uses methods predating the industrial era; sewn by hand on a sewing frame identical to those used in the fourteenth century; covered with African tanned goatskin using almost prehistoric tanning methods, stamped using binder's tools one to three centuries of age; and stored in stacks with twentieth-century protection and environmental control systems. In some libraries, such a volume may be used on an eighteenth-century table or desk beneath a portrait of the author painted from life. Thus it is that a preservation workshop may resemble both a contemporary science laboratory and a workshop in which a seventeenth- or eighteenth-century book binder would feel quite at home. A library moving into preservation may find that it already owns a considerable portion of the requisite equipment and that it is but necessary to reorganize its activities and add particular items needed to bring a preservation facility up to present-day expectations.

Supplies are continually required to keep an active program stocked with materials necessary for the full range of services to be rendered. Those doing the work are continually making inquiries of their suppliers for particular materials while the suppliers are continually adding to the range of items listed for sale. Also, these vendors will frequently fabricate items in sizes and shapes required for particular projects which permits a library to complete the work without having to adapt folders, envelopes, binders or other materials to the needs of the project. In recent years the escalation in the provision of convenience materials has proved most helpful to those faced with projects of considerable size and limited staff time to get the job done. Paper of all kinds has become increasingly expensive and the acid-free papers needed by conservators, together with other preservation products have not been exceptions. However, while prices have been increasing, the selection of materials as a whole has been improving. Production and availability of acid-free paper have increased in just the last few years. While the need for supplies is a continuing one, the needs of a particular conservation program will vary as the tasks vary, and institutions must be able to afford these materials if preservation programs are to continue.

Space as it relates to preservation is to be thought of in several different ways: space for the collections; space for the users of the collections; and space for working with the collections. Each should be adequate for its function. Storage space, or space for the collections, in particular, is a primary preservation element, and storage areas should conform to the criteria of temperature, humidity, light control, cleanliness, etc., which have been spelled out in the preservation literature. The same criteria apply also to reader space and to staff work space. In addition, the latter may also be subject to additional criteria for there is need for controlled ventilation to provide safe work areas for those using solvents and other chemicals required for some paper treatments. Space, like staff, is expensive, and must be used carefully.

Binding is, and will remain, basic to a well-conceived preservation program. It is not unusual to find incomplete and unbound periodical issues on library shelves in relatively poor condition while adjacent to them are similar issues of the same age which were bound while relatively new and which have survived in far better condition. Coupling binding and deacidification is a logical step once mass deacidification is available. If this is done, even on a selective basis, a longer usefulness is rather quickly assured for significant parts of research collections. Coupling the two operations has the advantage of achieving two major preservation operations with one handling, thereby helping to control labor costs.

With this brief consideration of linking deacidification with binding, I have slipped into the future, and it is there that I wish to continue. A second future development which seems to be more or less assured is an increased dependence on microforms as a preservation device. While microforms are not new, and while preservation is not a new use for them, there is growing emphasis on using microforms to preserve intellectual content when it is impossible or impractical to preserve original documents. The growth of cooperative programs to spread the burden of filming and to prevent needless duplication of effort in making microforms is both logical and desirable.

Other developments looming in the future are some consideration of nonprint and nonpaper media. While preservation-minded individuals have been learning how to preserve paper, libraries have broadened their missions to incorporate other newer media each of which has its own preservation needs and requirements; and still newer media continue to appear. The degree to which individual libraries will be called upon to preserve these materials has yet to be determined. Several of the newer media, in contrast with printed materials, would seem to be comparatively easily reproduced from master copies held by the issuing agencies or in a central depository so that availability may not become the problem it is with printed items. Major problems will likely be found in relation to collections of unique media materials such as sound transcriptions of local radio productions or recordings of important but noncommercial musical productions in university concert halls and similar facilities. Similarly, unique television and film materials from local stations and production facilities may also present problems to conservators and curators in widely scattered sites. All of these will require decisions and may generate preservation programs of their own as, indeed, some of them are already doing.

This completes my list of the three basic epistemological questions: (1) "Should a library preserve or conserve materials?"; (2) "What should be preserved?"; and (3) "How will they be preserved?" These are broad questions which involve all kinds of libraries, all levels of library staff, many library users and others involved in the affairs of the larger institutions to which many libraries are attached. Each of these three questions has numerous subsidiary questions a number of which have been considered here.

Technical Questions or Decisions

As we move now to the technical or physical questions as Boorstin termed them, the emphasis will change somewhat. These matters relate more directly to the materials themselves and to what is to be done to them or with them than was true for the epistemological questions. Many of us are probably more comfortable and more at home in this area; however, if this discussion centers too much on particular problems and techniques for dealing with them, there is a danger that it may become too specific. Therefore detailed consideration of specific problems will be avoided as much as possible.

The basic problem area here is that of deciding to preserve the artifact itself, to preserve its intellectual content, or to attempt both. While technically almost any paper document in almost any condition, short of its being ash or dust, may be saved, the value of the document and the expense of preservation may be such that it is so impractical as to be impossible. Since we all must deal with practicalities, we must decide when the point of impracticality or impossibility is reached. In the working world of preservation the decision is frequently to preserve the intellectual content simply because the preservation of the original document is so expensive and the need for it so marginal that retention of the document becomes too great a luxury. Preserving the intellectual content of a document may be done in any one of several ways depending upon the particular situation. Alternatives include the following:

1. Procurement of a replacement copy if available;
2. Procurement of a copy of another or a later edition, if available and if suitable for the needs of the library;
3. Procurement of an electrostatic copy made from the worn original or from another copy in better physical condition;
4. Procurement of a microcopy or some other technologically more advanced reproduction.

Each of these ways of replacing materials presents its own set of problems. Buying either a new copy or a copy of a new edition requires that the title be in print or available on the used book market. Since the majority of titles stay in print for limited periods and relatively few titles ever appear in other than the original edition, the use of new copies to replace worn-out volumes becomes problematic for all save the most basic or most popular materials. The used book market, while helpful, requires time for searches which are often expensive and not always successful. Serials tend to become unavailable even more rapidly in many cases than do monographs, and the time and expense of acquiring a sizable backfile on the used book market can become quite large very quickly.

Electrostatic copies also are not without their difficulties. Free and easy copying within libraries of materials under copyright and available for sale is controlled by the copyright law, so care in reproduction is needed. Old faded or stained materials tend not to copy well, and there are problems of size and extra bulk in some cases.[4] Despite these problems and despite their cost, electrostatic copies are useful in many situations.

Preserving intellectual content by use of microforms is a recognized preservation technique and preservation microfilming is a term which has become commonplace in our vocabularies for a number of years. The use of film assumes that the materials which are to be so preserved are appropriate in the new format, that is, the material is largely textual and can be useful in other than paper form. Filming within a library, purchasing a film from another library, or purchasing a film from a commercial vendor are all common and accepted means of reducing brittle and bulky originals to film. If filming is done within a library, a master negative should be made, registered in the *National Register of Microform Masters*,[5] and stored under appropriate conditions to serve as the basis of future copies. If film is acquired elsewhere, it should be safe to assume that a master negative exists in the vault of the vendor. There are two advantages in addition to the purely preservation aspect of preservation microfilming. First, film reduces bulk and helps libraries free space for more recent and presumably more heavily used volumes; and second, it provides the basis for the ready preparation of additional copies. In late 1979, as part of the work of the Task Force on the Preservation of the Association of Research Libraries (ARL) Collection Analysis Project in the Library of the University of Illinois at Urbana-Champaign, a very limited survey comparing costs of filming and binding periodicals was undertaken. This survey revealed that microfilm copies available from commercial sources compared favorably in cost with binding, but that those requiring original filming were two to five or more times more costly than binding.[6] If libraries can organize preservation microfilming so as to divide the work of filming and making master negatives and then sell or trade service copies, the cost of the initial filming can be spread over many institutions and copies of useful and valuable resource materials can be made available much more economically than would be possible if libraries attempt to work independently. In this area bibliographical control becomes crucial as we have already been reminded several times in this conference.

Microfiche also has promise in preservation and dissemination of deteriorating and scarce materials. Like film, microfiche, once a master negative is made, are easily and inexpensively copied. As institutions become increasingly interdependent and the lending of materials from institution to institution increases, microfiche would seem to be an excellent medium to permit dissemination of monographic materials, in particular, without subjecting aging and fragile originals to cross country transfer. This would simultaneously fill the needs of library users; provide master negatives of old and fragile materials, thereby lifting from them much of the wear and tear of use; and lighten the load on delivery systems since microfiche could be mailed as letter mail at much less cost than is involved in transporting the originals.

There are many instances when it is desirable both to prepare a microform and to retain the original. This is a practical way to make the content of rare books, manuscripts and other scarce, unique, or valuable materials available to users while taking the pressure of the use off the originals. This technique has been used widely both library to library and on a commercial scale. All of these reasons lie behind the inclusion of increasingly comprehensive photographic services as a major part of preservation programs.

Because everything can be expected to wear out, preservation is actually an attempt to make materials last as long as possible. Doing this is the general province of librarians as preservation policy is shaped and as particular approaches are adopted within libraries to achieve particular preservation objectives. As these techniques have tended to become more specialized and as the special techniques have required particular skills, preservation specialists and conservators have taken their places on library staffs. At some risk of leaving out or slighting some aspect of the preservation task, but in an effort to keep this presentation within necessary space limits, the following broad categories of preservation activity are indicated and described briefly:

1. *Preventive Measures:*

These measures are those things a library does or can do to reduce or halt certain kinds of wear and tear such as the training of staff to handle books and other library materials to prevent damage while shelving, transporting them on book trucks, packaging them for mailing, etc. Also included are good housekeeping to prevent infestations of insects, rodents, mildew and other problems in storage areas. Also to be considered here are the design and use of book returns which minimize wear and tear and the institution of safe storage conditions characterized initially as canons of the gospel of preservation having to do with temperature, humidity, light control and other environmental control measures.

2. *Binding:*

Binding is a basic preservation measure which provides essential physical protection and organization. Binding and rebinding are essential considerations in any preservation program.

3. *Storage Techniques:*

These techniques may be either temporary or permanent in their application to particular items or collections. They include tying volumes or groups of related items with tapes; wrapping and tying materials; tying materials between boards; inserting volumes into boxes; putting fragile materials into folders within boxes, portfolios, or boards, as well as many variations on these basic techniques which exclude light, dust, dirt, and polluted air. Such techniques provide physical protection and make it possible to shelve or otherwise store materials for extended periods of time. They may be used as interim measures to buy time while decisions regarding ultimate preservation are made, or they may be more or less permanent in and of themselves as in the case of rare books, collections of art prints, archives, and other similar materials. The use of acid-free wrappings, board, folders and other protective materials is mandatory if storage techniques are to be safely applied over long periods of time.

4. *Paper Preservation:*

Under this heading are a group of procedures the purpose of which is to increase strength and lengthen the period of usefulness of paper. Paper can be cleaned, washed, mended, recast, mounted, split, deacidified, re-sized, strengthened, laminated, and encapsulated, to name some, but not all, possible treatments. At their best, these processes can seemingly achieve miraculous results. Old, worn, dirty, stained, dog-eared and deteriorated papers may be restored to much of their original appearance and to some of their original durability. At their worst, attempts at these processes can become almost hideous parodies of the best applications and can be more destructive than leaving materials untreated. Paper preservation intended to be long-lasting should be done by those with skill, training, and experience in the work. The essential difficulty with paper preservation techniques is that they are very labor-intensive and, therefore, inherently expensive. There are, however, no real substitutes for them, though new techniques and materials continue to be developed which increase the efficiency with which these techniques may be applied.

5. *Book Repairs:*

Repairs range from relatively simple processes to more elaborate operations all designed to keep books in use. They are effective both in reducing binding costs by extending the usefulness of existing bindings and in permitting the retention of old bindings, thereby retaining the original structure and keeping appearance relatively unchanged. Such repairs include tightening and repairing hinges, rehanging volumes in existing cases, repairing cases and reattaching them to the contents, and restoring worn bindings. All such operations are applicable to volumes made of paper, cloth and board. Volumes with leather or part leather bindings can be similarly repaired, restored, refurbished and returned to use, but they require particular attention to the leather, and, when repairs become more elaborate than simple cleaning and leather treatment, increasing levels of training and experience are needed. Book repairs, like paper preservation, are comparatively expensive because they require piece-by-piece application. They can be almost miraculous in their result when done by those with skill, training and experience. Similarly, when done by the unskilled or untrained, they can be ruinous and more destructive than leaving the book untreated.

6. *Disaster Control:*

What to do when fire, water, windstorm or other calamity strikes or threatens the collections of an institution is included here because of its importance in preserving collections. Planning for disaster requires participation of staff at all levels and in all parts of a library, and implementing plans when disaster strikes may involve not only library staff, but emergency service personnel, administration from outside the library, volunteers and others as well. At the heart of this planning and of its application should be those who know what to do—the conservator and conservation staff. These persons cannot be expected to deal with all that must be done when whole collections are involved, but they can provide the nucleus of knowledge needed to inform and coordinate the efforts of others in salvaging materials successfully.

This is a listing of basic areas of decision making related to preservation of materials in libraries. Time and space constraints prevent delving more deeply into details of particular problems or processes. As with the treatment of epistemological questions, the consideration of technical questions was reduced to a consideration of a small number of basic areas, first, the preservation of intellectual content; and second, the preservation of the physical object. There are major decision areas involved in both of these, several of which have been indicated.

Boorstin's two-part characterization[7] of library preservation has been found to be a practical device for organizing this presentation, permitting the pulling together, in a particular order, of five basic questions or problem areas without consideration of administrative, operational, or other factors which might tend to relate to a particular kind of library or institution. These five broad areas are interrelated and their presentation includes the repetition of some elements under both major divisions. Such repetition was necessary as these questions were conceived, because it is necessary that those making decisions affecting preservation but not particularly involved in day-to-day preservation activity have some knowledge of what is possible at the technical level and because the technical and operational staff must have some knowledge of the constraints and considerations affecting administrative decisions. Both the development of preservation policy and actually doing the work require contributions from all parts of the library. Users, administrators, curatorial or collection servicing staff, and preservation staff all must be involved for any part of it to work. Policy determination also requires ongoing cooperation in order that the policies be kept up to date reflecting and responding to the realities being experienced by all these groups. While preservation staff may have the words *preservation* or *conservation* in their titles, all those connected with a library are involved in preservation by virtue of their own titles, because all those connected with a library are involved in preservation in some way and to some degree; and all should have a voice in the development of preservation policy together with an understanding of that policy and their own part in its implementation. In addition, several levels of understanding of preservation processes and techniques are needed. The knowledge and proficiency of those involved in doing preservation work of a highly technical nature need not be shared by all other staff in order that the others may make appropriate and valuable contributions to the preservation policy and preservation program of an institution. Boorstin's characterization permits the making of these distinctions and this is one of its strengths. It is hoped that others will find it helpful and useful.

This presentation was introduced by the recounting of an experience in which a single old pamphlet was rescued from oblivion and a usable service copy prepared as its replacement on the shelves of a library. The major point of that account was the involvement of a number of people in the preservation process. I wish to close the presentation with an account of another preservation process. Like the introductory story this one, too, includes a number of people working at various points within a large library. It also includes several individuals from outside the library, and it is a preliminary report on the use of an industrial fungicide, orthophenylphenol, to combat a mildew infestation in a large and valuable collection.

In the autumn and early winter of 1980, mildew was found on the bindings of a limited number of volumes in one portion of the rare book collection of the library of the University of Illinois at Urbana-Champaign. Some of the first mildew found was removed with a dustcloth, and some found later was removed using a solution of thymol in alcohol. Subsequent infestation was found scattered over volumes on a single range of shelving; and, while attempts were underway to treat it with thymol vapor under a polyethylene tent, further infestations were found throughout several parts of the stack area occupied by the rare book collections. These early evidences were on spines of bindings and other exposed edges of volumes. Some, growing on upper edges, seemed in some instances to be confined to incidental soil and dust which had accumulated on seldom used volumes. Ironically, the Rare Book stack is one of two storage areas in the library system which have, for approximately a decade, had controlled environmental conditions at least approximating those generally recognized as desirable or ideal. With the finding of the later rather widespread infestations, it was realized that without some more adequate means of control than spot treatment with thymol, the infestation would become worse and damage to the collections would be severe.

Contact was made with those responsible for the operation of the air handling system and their aid in controlling humidity sought. A campus mycologist sampled and identified the particular mold involved as a typical penicillium-type storage mold, and a phone call asking for help was placed to the Preservation Department of the Library of Congress. The call was referred to Dr. Robert E. McComb, a physical scientist on the staff of the department, who listened to my description of our problem and outlined a program of control. He recommended the use of orthophenyl-phenol (o-phenylphenol) as a control agent. This compound is much less expensive than thymol, vaporizes at room temperature at a rate sufficient to control infestations of the type we were fighting, and is not toxic to humans at the concentrations created by such vaporization. This compound is marketed in the United States by the Dow Chemical Company under the trade name Dowicide 1. In Britain it is marketed under the trade name Topane.[8]

Dr. McComb described the industrial uses of o-phenylphenol and outlined a mildew control program based on its use which included the following points. This initial oral recommendation was subsequently confirmed by letter[9] and is summarized as follows:

1. Distribute o-phenylphenol throughout the area placing one or more small containers on each bookshelf.
2. Distribute o-phenylphenol in the air supply system by placing two or three small containers of it in each air supply vent.
3. Refill the containers at intervals of approximately three weeks, or more frequently as needed.
4. Cease any routine dusting, sweeping or similar cleaning in the area.
5. During the initial three months of treatment, clean floors, furniture, and other equipment, if at all, with a solution of one cup Lysol per gallon of water or one-half cup borax per gallon of water. Workers must wear rubber gloves and protect skin from either solution to prevent chemical burns.

6. After three months, mildew should be killed and may be removed from bindings using a 10 percent solution of orthophenylphenol in denatured ethyl alcohol. Workers must wear rubber gloves and protect skin from the solution to prevent burning. Cloths used in cleaning should be turned and changed frequently to prevent spreading dirt and stain from volume to volume.

7. After six months, vacuum cleaning may be resumed, and it may be used to clean books if desired if a wet/dry vacuum cleaner charged with a solution of one-half cup Lysol in one-half gallon of water is used. The filter of the vacuum should be thoroughly soaked with the fungicide solution to impregnate it thoroughly with fungicide.

This program was discussed within the library and checked out with the campus Division of Environmental Health and Safety which approved the use of o-phenylphenol in the fashion indicated. With the arrival of the first drum of 100 pounds of o-phenylphenol, the initial distribution of crystals was begun using three-ounce paper cups and surplus cardboard microfilm containers. The initial distribution was made by the staff of the Binding and Preservation Division in work sessions of about forty-five minutes to one hour each. All together nearly ten thousand small containers were employed to achieve distribution to all the shelves in the stack area dedicated to rare book collections. The initial order of fungicide provided coverage for about 60 percent of the shelves. A second drum of similar size was needed to permit us to complete the shelf-by-shelf distribution, as well as providing a reserve to permit refilling of cups and providing a supply for the ventilation system.

With completion of the shelf-by-shelf coverage, placing o-phenylphenol in the air ducts was initiated. A sample of the crystals was provided for the manager of the campus Operations and Maintenance Division unit responsible for operation of central air-conditioning equipment together with an outline of the mildew control program recommended by Dr. McComb. The air-conditioning manager indicated that it would require several days to check the compound in the technical laboratory maintained in his division and to determine its possible effects upon the air-handling equipment. While this check was in progress, he would review the design of the equipment involved to determine whether or not it might be possible to introduce the compound at a central point more easily and efficiently than at the individual vents.

At this time the project entered a new phase, as concern about possible risks of o-phenylphenol in the atmosphere reached a peak. A few members of the Rare Book Room staff became alarmed at the introduction of the chemical into the rare book storage area, fearing it would be a hazard to those working there; and the matter was reported to a Labor Education

Program group operating in the University's Institute of Labor and Industrial Relations. A staff member from this group investigated the project and consulted with an industrial hygienist on the staff of the institute who provided data on phenol and its compounds, including both o-phenylphenol and thymol, found in chemical handbooks and similar information sources. In working with these individuals we began to gain a somewhat broader view of the limits of knowledge of the effects of these chemicals. We had known for some years that certain individuals on our staff were somewhat more subject to nose and throat irritation by thymol vapor than were others; and Dr. McComb had indicated in our initial phone conversation that typically one person in ten thousand experiences some degree of allergic reactions to o-phenylphenol. As a consequence we had cautioned all those working with either compound to be aware of the possibility of irritation and to get out of contact with either should they experience any difficulty. Combining what we have learned about both thymol and o-phenylphenol from all sources, Environmental Health and Safety, the Industrial Hygienist, Dr. McComb, and our own experience, we have concluded that both compounds if used with care should ordinarily not prove hazardous. Direct contact with solutions of either should be avoided by use of rubber gloves and other protective clothing. Individuals who experience any discomfort when in contact with the vapors should get into fresh air. Persons with existing upper respiratory irritation are subject to increased irritation by either compound and should not subject themselves to either any more than necessary. Normal working periods in contact with either are usually limited to no more than an hour without a break taken in fresh air. Finally, all who will come into contact with the vapor are informed of its nature and possible effects and are instructed to leave the area if they become uncomfortable. No one is required to work with either compound.

As the problems of exposure to o-phenylphenol were still being discussed, the air-conditioning manager reported negatively to the request to place the compound in the ductwork, indicating that his conclusion was based upon two reasons: first, it was feared that o-phenylphenol might cause damage to the ductwork or other components of the air-handling system should any of it come into direct contact with the equipment; and secondly, it was feared that vaporizing the compound within the air system might increase its concentration in the atmosphere of the stack area too much to assure a safe environment for those working there. This development came as the school year was ending and as our student staff was dispersing for the summer. Labor for routine refilling of cups was scarce throughout most of the summer, though some effort was made to use occasionally available student help to refill cups from time to time.

By the time school resumed in late summer, it was apparent that our efforts had been insufficient to hold the mildew in abeyance. The staff of the Rare Book Room began to note increasing signs of mildew, some of it on front and back covers of volumes where they had been shelved snugly together, whereas most evidences found earlier had been on spines, upper edges and other similarly exposed surfaces. Some cups were empty or nearly so; and, in many which still contained what appeared to be sufficient o-phenylphenol to generate effective quantities of vapor, crystals were found to be sticking together or coalescing to form large chunks which apparently no longer vaporized fast enough to release sufficient vapor to be effective. Clearance was obtained to hire a student to devote ten hours per week to refilling cups, stirring those in which crystals were sticking together, and to begin routine cleaning of volumes using a wet/dry vacuum charged with Lysol solution. In addition, immediately after the student began work on a regular basis, small cheesecloth bags of o-phenylphenol were made up and suspended in front of the air supply vents with priority being given to those parts of the area in which mildew had been observed to be most prevalent. This program brought to an apparent halt further spread, and the initiation of the vacuuming program began to remove not only evidences of mildew but much accumulated soil and dust which had been providing germination sites for at least some of the mildew. In addition to these efforts, thymol solution and rubber gloves were provided for use by Rare Book Room staff in cleaning individual volumes found in need of it in the normal course of the operation of the Rare Book Room. Also, with the beginning of the 1981/82 heating season, the humidity level was operated at no more than 40 percent relative humidity rather than 50 percent which had been the objective for several years. The result of these efforts has been that no further outbreaks of mildew have been observed in the collections.

Many discussions attempting to identify the cause or causes of this outbreak of mildew have taken place, but no single factor or event has emerged as the culprit. By reconstructing the history of the operation of the air-handling system as best as it can be done from the memories of the staff of the Rare Book Room and some of the Operation and Maintenance staff who have serviced the system and by including in the consideration a number of other factors relating to mildew in general and to this library in particular, a general conclusion has been drawn that the area was inadvertently over-humidified for a sufficient period to permit mildew to begin to grow. A series of malfunctions of the air-handling system, which resulted in excessive humidification; consistent attempts through several winter seasons to maintain 50 percent relative humidity; and the design of the system as part of a larger air-conditioning system operated primarily to provide comfort air conditioning in the non-stack portions of the University Library building which cause it to maintain summer humidity no lower than 60 percent and to operate with untreated air for extended periods in spring and fall, all seem to have combined to provide the environment needed to cause the problem.

O-phenylphenol has proved to be an effective part of the mildew control program when the library staff has been able to keep an adequate supply of the chemical in the affected areas. Its use, coupled with humidity control and a continuing cleaning program, serves both to inhibit spread of mildew and to prevent the start of new infestations.

The foregoing narrative is quite condensed and does not clearly indicate the parts played by all who have been involved. Mildew was first seen and reported by a student assistant retrieving a volume for patron use. Professional and support staff in the Rare Book Room have been involved in every phase of the struggle. Library administrators cleared the way to acquire o-phenylphenol, suggested calling in a mycologist, and approved the hiring of extra student staff. Library business office staff and campus Purchasing Division staff expedited orders for fungicide and related supplies. The entire staff of the Binding and Preservation Division helped with the initial distribution of fungicide. Janitorial and maintenance staff altered work routines and schedules. Operation and Maintenance Division staff provided information about and service on the air-handling system. The Labor Education Program and Environmental Health and Safety staffs provided information and counsel. And, perhaps most important, Dr. McComb shared with the library information at his disposal concerning a new technique for using o-phenylphenol in a library situation. This experience is continuing, and the final word recounting it will not be written for some time, but this progress report illustrates again the need for involvement of people at many levels, with many skills and with many points of view to provide for the preservation and protection of library materials.

NOTES

1. Boorstin, Daniel J. "Welcoming Remarks." In *A National Preservation Program; Proceedings of the Planning Conference.* Washington, D.C.: Library of Congress, 1980, p. 12.

2. Webster's Third New International Dictionary, unabridged, s.v. "epistemology."

3. Boorstin, "Welcoming Remarks."

4. Bork, Helga. "Microforms." In *Preservation of Library Materials,* edited by Joyce R. Russell, pp. 71-76. New York: Special Libraries Association, 1980.

5. *National Register of Microform Masters.* Washington, D.C.: Library of Congress, 1976- .

6. Austin, Mardell, and Henderson, William T. "A Comparison of the Costs of Binding and Microfilming Periodicals." In *Report of the Task Force on Preservation.* University of Illinois at Urbana-Champaign: Collection Analysis Project, 1980, p. 169.

7. Boorstin, "Welcoming Remarks."

8. Horton, Carolyn. "Saving the Libraries of Florence." *Wilson Library Bulletin* 41(June 1967):1043.

9. McComb to Henderson, personal communication, 17 April 1981.

ADDITIONAL NOTES

Baynes-Cope, A.D. *Caring for Books and Documents*. London: British Museum Publications, 1981.

Clapp, Verner W. *The Story of Permanent/Durable Book-Paper, 1115-1970* (Restaurator Suppl. No. 3). Copenhagen: Restaurator Press, 1972.

Council on Library Resources. Committee on Production Guidelines for Book Longevity. "Interim Report on Book Paper." Washington, D.C.: CLR, 1981.

Mucci, Paul. *Paper and Leather Conservation; A Manual*, edited by Mary Boccaccio. Mid-Atlantic Regional Archive Conference, 1978.

Swartzburg, Susan G. *Preserving Library Materials; A Manual*. Metuchen, N.J.: Scarecrow Press, 1980.

DISCUSSION

Douglas DeLong (Library, Illinois State University, Bloomington): You made reference to, in the future, combining regular commercial binding and deacidification. Do you feel there will be any problems with the typical oversewing methods used by most commercial binders—e.g., the threads that are used in this deacidification process? In other words, twenty years down the road, will the threads be falling out and the papers be fine? What are your thoughts on this?

William T Henderson: We all know what happens with existing papers and sewing. If we can slow down or halt the degradation of paper we can perhaps lengthen its life and the sewing technique won't be so all-important as it has tended to be with some materials in the past. Another thing I'm heartened by is the fact that we are getting away from the very heavy use of oversewing as it has been used for many years. A broader array of kinds of sewing and other techniques are available than was previously the case, and the use of adhesive bindings seems to hold promise for future usefulness as well as giving us volumes that open easily now.

Gerald Gibson (Library of Congress, Washingtion, D.C.): Would you talk about fumigation, and, secondly, about ink and the effect that ink has itself and in combination with other materials?

Henderson: I'm not all that knowledgeable about either ink or fumigation. On the latter, I can't say much except to say that we've been fortunate here and in my experience in not having too much difficulty with the kinds of problems that call for massive amounts of fumigation. Available information about the UIUC Library, some of which predates me by a long while, indicates that the Library has had small mildew problems from time to time. For some reason we seem not to have been bothered by insects and we also have reasonably tight buildings and have not had too much of a problem with rodents. For mildew control in the recent past we have depended primarily upon thymol. At one time we used mercuric chloride which we gave up very quickly when we found out what it did to paper if too much was used. I'm becoming more interested in the use of Dowicide because I think the problem in our Rare Book Room stack is going to be with us as long as we have our present ventilation system. I'll have to beg off regarding inks because I simply don't know.

Gibson: Is ink, then, not particularly a problem with paper materials? It certainly is a problem with nonpaper materials with the combination of dyes and inks that are fixed to, as I mentioned in my session, a paper label on a sound recording. There is a major complication.

Henderson: Some inks, as I have had a chance to think a little more, particularly the old iron gall inks that were widely used in manuscript materials, can give rise to problems if they were not properly made in the first place. They can, in such cases, become quite acid and over a long period cause browning and embrittlement and, finally, destruction of the paper. Printer's ink, as it has typically been put together and as I understand it, is basically carbon which essentially lays on the paper more or less indefinitely. Some writers have mentioned problems stemming from other particular types of inks. As for phonograph record labels and other materials of similar nature, I suspect that the colored dyes used are probably the cause of the problems, or at least a part of the cause. I think these are some of the things that you probably would find would vary almost from one printer's lot to another. I doubt if any record producer ever tried to fix a particular standard or recipe for dyes used in making their labels. Don [Krummel], can you lend some aid here?

D.W. Krummel (Graduate School of Library and Information Science, University of Illinois at Urbana-Champaign): Let me add a note on this, and then an appeal. As far as I know nobody is very much bothered about ink. I'm not sure why. Somehow I think we should be but I don't think any of us are. The one area where I think it is a problem is with photographs, and there, of course, it's not ink as used by printers. But the printing material is a problem when it comes to deteriorating photographic copies.

Henderson: Louise Kuflick has just told me that she will be mentioning ink this afternoon in her presentation. She and those she works with have found that it sometimes presents some problems in doing some of the deacidification processes.

Gibson: May I talk some more about ink? One problem, particularly with manuscripts (which is completely out of my area of work)—but I would caution people in deacidifying, especially manuscripts—is to make sure that the ink you're treating is not going to be soluble with whatever you're using. The manuscript of Berg's opera *Wozzeck* in the Library of Congress has some beautiful comments in the composer's hand in the manuscript and in the margin of the manuscript in red ink. The paper was tested. The ink which he had used to write the manuscript and the pencil marks he used have been tested, but the red ink wasn't tested. In the deacidification process a number of the pages of this manuscript are a beautiful baby pink. The comments are no longer in existence. There was a microfilm made of it before it was deacidified but the original simply does not carry the information anymore. So be particularly careful in deacidifying.

LOUISE KUFLIK

Associate
Carolyn Horton and Associates
New York, New York

Decisions in Conservation and Preservation in the Conservation Laboratory

The decision to conserve has already been made when a book is brought to a conservation studio. It means that the material has been found to have some intrinsic or artifactual value. What to conserve is the decision of the librarian, the archivist, or the bibliophile. How to conserve it is fundamentally the decision of the conservator, often made in conjunction with the custodian of the material or at least with his/her consent. All decisions are made after a careful examination and testing of the material and a thoughtful assessment of the techniques available. Unfortunately, the question of cost must enter into the discussion because book and paper conservation is a craft almost entirely executed by hand. Conservators employ time-honored techniques, sometimes supplemented by modern technological advances, but always guided by the principle of reversibility in deference to the historical, cultural or aesthetic importance of the materials with which they deal and with an awareness of the possibility that some better technique or material may come along later in this developing field.

Conservators generally find librarians to be far more understanding of the nature and needs of the materials than some kinds of clients, who may want things completed yesterday and whose ethics are often of a questionable nature—not caring to see things in the long term but merely wanting a book "held together" so that it can be sold quickly or repaired inexpensively. We can hold it together, reattaching boards quickly, but that book will not be able to stand on the shelf very long nor have its covers opened too many times. And what about the state of the paper inside? In fact, perhaps the book or document even looks more venerable and valuable with the dirt and grime. How ethical are requests to make repairs "invisible," to remove plates or bookplates or change flyleaves or separate parts of

135

a manuscript? The clearly unethical nature of some requests make them easy to turn down, but requests to execute partial repairs, where more extensive work is required, is often a problem to conservators, who see the book as a functional object and are committed to the "restoration of function" as well as to producing a harmonious repair or restoration.[1] I speak, too, of the book lover who cannot afford the proper type of repair or rebinding and for this reason selects historically or aethetically unsuitable materials.

Let us examine the types of decisions that are made in a conservation studio by following a book through the steps it undergoes in the conservation/restoration process.

First, the monetary value of an item, or to use the proper phrase, the "limit of liability" must be established by the custodian. The conservator should express no opinion in the matter and the value of the material should in no way affect the quality of the work rendered by the conservator nor should it influence the cost of the repair.[2] How realistic this principle is raises an issue of concern to conservators because the cost of the conservation work can often far exceed the worth of the item. On the other hand, an item of sentimental or personal value, but of no monetary value, is often irreplaceable.

The book is now given a preliminary physical examination and the usual bibliographic information is noted along with the type of binding. Of special significance, when it comes time to estimate the cost, will be the size and number of leaves. Then the pH of the paper is taken. Under the heading "Condition When Received" everything of significance that can be observed is described, e.g., the state of the paper, especially its tensile strength as revealed by folding a corner. Other aspects, too, are noted such as water or dirt stained or discolored paper; trimming; printing on the right grain; the presence of mold, foxing, worm holes, or tape, and the condition of the sewing. If there are inks, they must be tested. The presence of protective sheets and their condition are cited. The condition of the binding is also recorded, noting such things as staining, discoloring, abrading; detached boards or spine; cracked hinges; bent, broken, or worn corners and torn or missing headcaps. The conservator also tries to determine if the binding is original. For documentation purposes, a photograph of the materials should be taken.

Based on these observations, the conservator makes suggestions about the nature of the proposed treatment. Often there is more than one proposal; then the custodian will have a choice.

From his or her experience, the conservator must make an educated guess as to how long it will take to execute the proposed treatments. The cost estimate is based on a calculation of the time required to complete the work. Sometimes, after work begins, there are unpleasant surprises that can throw the estimate off and call for reappraisals of the proposed treatment. Such surprises include stubborn adhesives, inks that suddenly feather or even disappear, colors that strike through, and paper more embrittled than first thought.

Here, then, are some of the decisions the conservator faces, in the order in which they are made: based on the pH, should the paper be deacidified and can it be done safely. If it can be deacidified, how should it be done? (Sometimes there is no choice.) Manuscript inks that run in water but not in alcohol can be deacidified nonaqueously, but some inks are soluble in both. What about books papers? If the binding and sewing are sound and the paper is very acid, the book could be deacidified nonaqueously by brushing on methyl magnesium carbonate in a fume hood. Nonaqueous deacidification is not always the perfect answer. There are some printers' inks that can run in it and some papers discolor slightly. If the binding is at all weak, the slight swelling that results from nonaqueous deacidification can cause the outer hinges to crack. Nonaqueous deacidification for books with sound bindings and sewing may soon be replaced by a mass deacidification process. If the binding is to be replaced but the sewing is sound, what type of deacidification should be used? If the paper is very discolored it will greatly benefit from the washing that always precedes aqueous deacidification. Conservators prefer to wash discolored and embrittled paper if possible because it refreshes the paper. Stains and discolorations are removed or reduced and deteriorated size and soluble acids are washed away. The paper always feels better after it has been washed. However, washing and aqueous deacidification is a much longer process necessitating disbinding and the consequent mending of folds and resewing results in a more costly procedure. The decision, therefore, must always be made as to whether a book with sound sewing should be washed.

The type of paper mending is another consideration which must be based on suitability and economic realities. Heatset tissue allows for faster mending and makes sense when extensive mending is required. The more traditional Japanese tissue and paste mends and fills, though the process takes somewhat longer, permits a more harmonious matching of color values and paper texture. An alternative treatment, not usually available in the small conservation studio, involves the leaf casting machine.

If nonaqueous deacidification of the bound volume is selected for embrittled paper, then nothing much can be done for the paper other than to repair tears. If there are a few mold-deteriorated leaves they can be brushed sized. Only if the book is not to be heavily used should badly embrittled paper be nonaqueously deacidified. Deacidification will not restore paper to its original state or even improve it, but deacidification will slow down further deterioration.

For paper that is being aqueously deacidified and is embrittled, the options are more numerous. Sometimes washing will remove enough excess sizing that contributed to the embrittlement, so that paper can be revitalized and allow normal sewing and binding. But if the paper remains very fragile even after washing and deacidification, each leaf can be supported on either or both sides with heatset tissue. The book can then be rehinged, sewn and bound; or as an alternative, after mending, the leaves can be encapsulated in a polyester envelope and housed in a postbinding.

Water stains and tide lines can usually be removed or, at least, reduced by washing. In some cases, mold stains and damage can be reduced by washing with the damaged paper responding well to resizing. Tapes and tape stains usually must be removed with solvents; for this reason, fume hoods are a necessary piece of equipment because of the toxic nature of most solvents. Though the tapes can almost always be removed, the remaining stains often cannot be eliminated entirely. When treating manuscripts, conservators are sometimes faced with the dilemma of some reduction in legibility or some feathering of inks or type in order to rid the paper of the adhesive which, if permitted to remain, would continue to degrade the paper. When this problem arises, the final decision is often left to the custodian of the material.

Foxing and other stains on a piece of art work on paper may be bleached out if they interfere aesthetically, but on book paper, we almost never bleach. As long as all the adhesive is removed and can cause no further damage, we can live with the blemish, especially if it does not obscure legibility. Bleaching residues, which are difficult to remove entirely from paper, can cause damage later on.

Discolored protective sheets should be removed. They were inserted to protect against offset of the freshly printed plates. The ink has long since dried and the acid from these sheets can migrate.

The next series of decisions, dealing with the nature of the binding structure, is usually up to the conservator alone. How should the paper and signatures be prepared for sewing and how should the boards be attached? All these are determined by the style of the binding, the size of the book, the condition of the paper and the intended use. Will the book be merely cased (a technique we usually restrict to cloth bindings) or will the boards be attached to the book block before the book is covered? How heavy should the boards be? How many cords or tapes should the book be sewn on? The usual practice in conservation binding is to follow the original sewing structure if it is possible and appropriate.[3] What type of headbands should be used, and in what color? Color choices for headband and covering cloths, papers and leathers should be in keeping with the prevalent colors of the period. Should the book be a tightback or should it have a hollow tube? A tightback might be historically accurate but the condition of the paper or the narrowness of the inner margins might make a hollow tube more appropriate from a conservation perspective. If the paper is in a poor state or the inner margins are not very generous or for some reason it is necessary for the book to be exceptionally flexible in its opening, the conservator might consider sewing the book on a concertina so that when the book is glued up no adhesive will touch the signature folds. Another solution to the flexibility problem, especially in a book of plates, would be to have each leaf or signature thrown out on guards.

If the binding on a book is original, the questions arise as to whether the binding can be restored; whether the client wants it restored; whether the book warrants restoration because of bibliographic, historic or aesthetic significance.[4] To help in identifying original bindings, a good reference library, especially of exhibition catalogs, is most helpful. It is amazing what can be done to restore a deteriorated binding. It is possible to use original parts over new flexible materials which harmonize with or are dyed to match the original. Books can be rebacked when the boards are detached or the spine is missing. Corners can be rebuilt and recovered and worn heads and tails can be repaired. In finishing restorations, tools that duplicate or closely resemble those used on the original binding are sometimes used. A large collection of old tools can prove indispensable for this process. However, the question of whether or not to complete areas where the original gold has worn away is a sensitive issue among conservators, both due to the higher costs incurred for a purely cosmetic effect and, more importantly, because the process might be seen as an attempt to disguise or alter the original state of the binding.

If the existing binding is beyond repair or is not original, there are several possibilities to be considered concerning rebinding. A replica binding, whereby the conservator will try to find papers and other materials that duplicate as closely as possible the original, is one option. Decorated and other old papers from discarded bindings are saved for just such an occasion. There are also modern decorated papers made to replicate many of the historic patterns. Another possibility, use of a period binding, is one that will capture the spirit of the binding style of an earlier time. Or one could opt for a modest conservation binding so that more time and expense can be devoted to the inside work on the paper and the binding made just functional and conservationally sound.

A postbinding is yet another choice. Having decided that the condition of the material requires polyester encapsulation, it is also necessary to consider the nature and value of the material because its bibliographical integrity will be destroyed when the gatherings and folds are separated to accommodate encapsulation. Postbindings are a fine housing for manuscript and scrapbook collections and are currently being recommended for holdings of permanent archival or research value because of the complete reversibility and the protection offered by postbindings against temperature and humidity fluctuations, environmental pollutants and physical and mechanical abuse.[5] If possible, materials should be deacidified before encapsulation.

An alternative in conservation is to box the item. If a suitable binding or restoration cannot be executed for economic or technical reasons, yet something must be done to prevent further deterioration especially in a case where boards are no longer attached or the covering materials are in a very fragile state, the decision to box the materials, as is, might be made. Boxes are a conservation holding action, keeping the materials together, protecting them from dirt, dust and, to some degree, from environmental fluctuations and pollutants. They can be constructed with a lip for books with boards that warp, and they can be made for a newly rebound book, especially if it is desirable to keep the original binding or binding remnants housed with the book. Boxes are particularly suitable for pamphlets, permitting them to be shelved along with books.

After restoration a ticket outlining the treatments and materials used should be attached to the back inside cover to be kept as a permanent record with the book.

Whatever treatment is finally decided upon must be based on considerations of use and stability of materials. No technique or materials must be used, however attractive to the eye, which may deteriorate and cause irreversible damage.

NOTES

1. Horton, Carolyn. "The Ethics of Book Restoration." (Paper presented at the Hunt Seminar, Pittsburgh, Pa., 13 Nov. 1979).

2. American Institute for Conservation of Historic and Artistic Works. *Code of Ethics and Standards of Practice.* Washington, D.C.: AICHAW, 1979.

3. Cains, Anthony. "Techniques of Preservation Based on Early Binding Methods and Materials." *Paper Conservator* 1(1976):2-8.

4. Morrow, Carolyn C. *A Conservation Policy Statement for Research Libraries* (Occasional Papers No. 139). Urbana-Champaign: University of Illinois Graduate School of Library Science, 1979.

5. Waters, Peter. "Archival Methods of Treatment for Library Documents." In *Preservation of Paper and Textiles of Historic and Artistic Value* (Advances in Chemistry Series, no. 193), edited by John C. Williams, pp. 13-23. Washington, D.C.: American Chemical Society, 1981.

DISCUSSION

Anthony Amodeo (Newberry Library, Chicago, Illinois): When you deal with a binding that is fairly old and maybe not typical, especially of some commercial production, and when you decide to rebind it, do you save not only the covers but perhaps photograph the sewing as it existed and the top edge as well? Do you save pieces of the sewing thread for documentation of binding history?

Louise Kuflik: Normally we don't document. In a laboratory, it's probably done automatically. In a studio, we don't, but we certainly retain all parts of the original binding until the client has picked it up, so, if they want any remains of the binding, it's certainly theirs. If they expressed an interest in having this documentation, we would do it.

Amodeo: If your customers are libraries, do they usually request such a saving?

Kuflik: Not really. No.

Kathryn Luther Henderson (Graduate School of Library and Information Science, University of Illinois at Urbana-Champaign): I have a three-pronged question. In these days librarians are sometimes seeking alternative careers related to librarianship. Could you comment on the following since you hold library degrees? First of all, do you really consider this an alternative career to librarianship? Second, how does your library degree and your library work experience relate to your conservation experience? And third, what advice can you offer to students who might be interested in pursuing a career using their library degree in the way that you are using yours?

Kuflik: I suppose it might be viewed as an alternate career for a librarian although I think I slipped into it somewhat accidentally. It all hinged on my interest in books and materials so in a sense it is related. How does my experience help me? It is helpful especially when it comes to a bibliographic concern, usually toward the end of the process. One of our problems is in finding out from the owners of the materials how they want the book titled. What should the title be? Should we follow the title on the bindings as it came to us? We often have to research or suggest to the client what should be put on the finished binding. I suppose my familiarity with the reference tools has been helpful. As I said before, I was particularly lucky—I came along at just the right moment. Even though there is a great need for people in the field, the opportunities still seem somewhat limited for training. Pam [Darling] mentioned earlier the program at Columbia and, if that's successful, we can hope there will be more programs in the future. I think if you're interested in this field you just have to be persistent. If you want to do something, you can do it.

Heinke Pensky-Adams (Monastery Hill Bindery, Chicago, Illinois): I might be able to fill in on this a little bit, because I would like to say that any librarian who is interested in the field, should be persistent, as Louise said, in trying to learn as much as possible. It is very difficult to find apprenticeships in this country. It is, therefore, very frustrating. A long period is involved in order to learn everything. But be persistent because we need every hand possible to do the job that needs to be done. There's so much material that has to be treated and should be treated more or less immediately.

Nancy Gwinn (Research Libraries Group): The Library of Congress has, at times, been quoted as saying that it could cost up to $300 a volume to restore a book. I wonder if you could state a range of average figures?

Kuflik: There is *such* a range of possibilities! When you say an average book does that mean resewing or does it not? What type of binding is it? Is it a cloth binding; is it a leather binding? How big is it? How many leaves? It's impossible to give a figure without knowing specifics.

Gwinn: Let's say that it's an average 300-page monograph with a cloth binding requiring deacifidication but doesn't have any unusual restoration properties.

Kuflik: But how is it being deacidified? Is it being aqueously or nonaqueously deacidified? Is it being resewed?

Gwinn: Realizing all this, I wondered if you could give a range. Is it $100 to $500; or is it $200 to $300; or $50 to $100?

Kuflik: It's really almost impossible without having the material in hand. Perhaps the backbone of the whole field is the ability to estimate accurately. We keep very detailed time records for all different types of treatments based upon size. Mrs. Horton has graphs—e.g., of a 6½-inch leaf and an 8-inch leaf and the time it takes to mend. Somehow you have to come up with an estimate by looking at the book and deciding what it is you're going to do. I think one of the things that we've been doing more often is citing alternative treatments. Rather than just saying "This is what should be done," we say "If you can't afford to have this done maybe you will want to have a box made." Or we give the alternative between a cloth binding and a leather binding. So, there is some range there from which the client can select. It's expensive work. It will certainly cost more than $100. After that, there isn't much I can say.

D.W. Krummel (Graduate School of Library and Information Science, University of Illinois at Urbana-Champaign): The antiquarian book sellers say they are selling more and more to private sellers and less and less to institutional collections today. Would you care to comment on this? Is it your experience that you are doing less work for institutional collections and more for collectors now? Or is this something that Carolyn Horton herself handles?

Kuflik: It would be more up Mrs. Horton's alley but I haven't noticed any particular change in recent years.

Krummel: A related question that comes out of this that I wish might be considered here today is how many libraries are considering reinstating their own on-the-premises binding and conservation units? What are the considerations that might be involved in such efforts?

Pensky-Adams: I think I would like to say something on this. Listening to you librarians and to your problems during the last few days, I have a feeling that the private conservator gets only a little drop of what the problem really is and what you're trying to do in your libraries. Therefore, I would like to suggest that we have a closer relationship with each other to work out the problems and to cut out little processes in having things done. For example, I think libraries can have an inside shop which does minor repairs and cleaning, but the major work should be done by conservators because they have the bench experience and the training and they know how to approach the problem.

Alan Calmes (National Archives): In regard to Mylar encapsulation, there's a debate whether or not to seal up the page entirely or ventilate at a corner. What are your thoughts about that?

Kuflik: There are pros and cons. I assume that since the Library of Congress currently has two of these sealing machines, two different varieties, that they have come to the conclusion that it's okay to completely seal the envelopes although with these machines you could also, I'm sure, leave a slight gap to permit some passage of air. Of course, this is one of the reasons why it should be deacidified prior to encapsulation. If you're not deacidifying the material, you're not talking about the same thing. Material should be deacidified and certainly should be completely dry at the time of encapsulation. I would leave to the scientists the question as to whether there should be a complete sealing or not.

Walter C. Allen (Graduate School of Library and Information Science, University of Illinois at Urbana-Champaign) to Calmes: You raised the question; what's the difficulty? I think there are those among us who are not aware of the problem.

Calmes: You trap in the products of degradation if you do seal it up entirely. If it is deacidified, then, probably you can seal it up entirely, but it is good to caution people that if you do not deacidify, you probably should not encapsulate and if you do encapsulate, then you should leave some ventilation. Maybe you should take it out and air it out from time to time.

Kuflik: That's redoing the whole process.

Keith Dowden (Purdue University Libraries, West Lafayette, Indiana): I'd like to hear something more about reversiblity. Some processes, I assume, would be only partially reversible. To what degree are they reversible? And what is the great need for this in your work?

Kuflik: The feeling is that, since we are dealing with materials of some intrinsic value, should the materials that we're using at the current time not be as stable as we are assuming they are, we can reverse what we've done. We can remove what we've added if we find that there's a more suitable material that comes along in the future. In other words, we can change whatever we've done to the item if necessary. Most of the processes are completely reversible. The heatset tissue, which might be the material that would be most called into question, is reversible only if the item can be treated with water or alcohol and so you've got to determine whether the item that you're lining or mending with this can be subjected either to water or alcohol. It's sort of one of the time honored principles in the field of conservation and probably harks back more to paper supported works of art where it is even of greater concern than with books. But this is one of the principles: what you can do to the material you can undo to the material and it will be in the same condition as it was before.

Dowden: I was thinking about binding, and possibly, rebinding.

Kuflik: The binding itself is usually fairly easy to remove. The adhesives that we're using are generally reversible. After all, in the process of rebinding, in any case, we have to clean off the spine before we start rebinding. We can remove the binding every easily. We will probably destroy it, but it can be removed.

Amodeo: This is a sort of hypothetical question. Say that you have someone coming in saying, "I'm going to give this particular book that has been in the family for so many generations to my grandchildren." Assume it's an early nineteenth-century or late eighteenth-century Germantown Bible, or something similar and they would like a nice brand new leather cover all gussied up with ornaments, etc. Would you try to dissuade them from destroying the book as it is other than perhaps doing a little needed structural correction, and perhaps try to preserve the book by putting it in a box rather than just rebinding the whole thing as they had asked? Or lacking that, would you photograph it and send a copy of the binding to a local research library? Do you have any sort of contingency plan if the person insists on rebinding it?

Kuflik: No. But if they wanted it rebound in full leather and they heard what the cost would be, that might discourage them. There are so many factors. People all love their family Bibles and usually, of course, they are very large books, as you all know.

Amodeo: I'm talking about something unusual of binding interest, something extraordinary, in fact. If you ran across something extraordinary would you ask the patron if you could photograph the item because it was very different from anything you had ever seen? Or, maybe, I'm suggesting that if there is a research library of some sort that you might be in contact with, that you might establish a file of photographs of this sort of thing before they get covered up again with new leather especially if there is something unusual or of particular historic binding interest that you have run across.

Kuflik: We don't maintain any contact as you're suggesting. An instance of that really has not arisen. I'm sure the owner of the material would probably have no reason not to permit it to be photographed. I can't possibly see why. If it's possible to restore the binding especially if the binding has some intrinsic value, we prefer to restore or refurbish it, but if it's no longer protecting the book and the book is no longer usable with the boards, then in that case, we might suggest either rebinding, or, possibly rebacking. We do try to encourage that. I think most people who value this type of material, value the nature of their material, too; otherwise they would not bring it to us. So, I think they would favor that solution if at all possible.

Robert J. Adelsperger (University of Illinois at Chicago Circle): It's generally believed that conservators should tell us how to do things, what might be done, and as you say, give us alternatives, but that curators (and Paul Banks has said this frequently) must decide what the priorities are—what things should be conserved and preserved, what are important bibliographically, and so forth. To follow up with Tony's [Amodeo] point, though, are conservators ready and able to advise curators (many of whom will not be experts in the history of binding styles, etc.), as to the proper type of treatment if rebinding is necessary—e.g., shall it be a binding relating to the period? Can curators expect that sort of service from conservators?

Kuflik: Yes, I think we would make every effort. As I said, we have a fairly extensive reference collection. And we would do so, especially if the curator expressed an interest. It's up to the curator to inform the conservator what he or she would like; the conservator can then respond to those needs.

Peter Chang (Florida State University, Tallahassee): I would just like a few words from personal experience. Last year we sent fifty rare books to a company, which sent its representative to us. He told us how much it would cost to do each process. We added it together and figured that we could afford such treatment. Then, they sent us a shipment. I think they averaged about $150 each. We found this too much to spend. Then we found out about another binder who said he could do hand binding. We thought this, too, would be too expensive but he gave us a list—e.g., leather is $16; if you keep the spine, it is $12. He tells us this is hand binding. Why the price difference?

Kuflik: What was the quality of the materials he used?

Chang: With the first binder, we were happy. He restored quite well. It's quite a good job but that cost us $150 a volume. As to the second one, the first shipment is just on the way back.

Pensky-Adams: How can he do a leather binding for $12 when a foot of leather on the market is already between $12 and $15?

Kuflik: As a rule they're talking about commercial binding as opposed to hand and conservation binding. I don't think they treated the inside of the book either. The quality of materials must be considered. I think it's up to the curator to question the binder as to the quality of the material being used on the books. Are the end papers acid-free? Are they using good-quality cloths? Have the leathers been subjected or approved? There's a test called the PIRA test that most conservation binders use. If the curators express an interest I don't think the conservators would mind at all answering these questions.

JAMES ORR

President
Hertzberg-New Method, Inc.
Jacksonville, Illinois

Role of Commercial Services in Conservation and Preservation

ROLE OF THE LIBRARY BINDER IN CONSERVATION AND PRESERVATION

I am here to represent library binders, a business that I have been in for over thirty-five years. Our industry is a small industry as industries go. It is about a 50-million-dollar industry which means that there are probably about 12 million or so volumes bound yearly and there are roughly twenty-five to thirty binders throughout the country.

Basically, our job is to handle current materials such as magazines, books, theses, and more recently, paperbacks. In this group there is quite a conglomeration of material. Here the concern is durability. We also handle semi-rare materials where the need is for mending, folding, hinging, laminating, and encapsulating. Recently, we have made a concerted effort to look at deacidification, but my hopes were somewhat dampened yesterday when I asked how many of you would be willing to move ahead with it and sign a release for responsibility of the results. I didn't get much enthusiastic response from that request. As a complete library binder, our firm must be ready to take care of all of these categories of material and engage in all these processes.

We are well aware of the money crunch that libraries face. Libraries, on one hand, have to pay salaries and operating costs, while on the other hand, they have to pay for acquisitions and binding costs. Because the binding business is so labor-intensive (there are about forty-two individual operations that go into binding each book and magazine), we're trying to become more standardized in order to bring more economy into the picture. Up to now, the oversewing process, which sewed tight bindings, has

147

been an accepted standard and we have not been able to compensate for the problems of oversewing—problems which have been complained about by archivists, conservationists, and bibliophiles for a long time. Of late, we are doing much more with adhesive binding which promises to be a dramatic new development and to compensate for some of the difficulties of oversewing. At the conservation fair this evening, we will have on display some volumes to which the new adhesive has been applied. What we like about the volumes which have been bound in this way is that the volume will lie perfectly flat without stress on the hinge when the volume is placed on a photocopying machine.

Briefly and basically, this is what a commercial library binder does. We have been at this work for nearly 100 years or so. There are many new developments on the scene and we are trying to adjust to them and to use them as fast as possible to serve you better.

WILLIAM ANTHONY

Partner
Kner and Anthony, Bookbinders
Chicago, Illinois

ROLE OF THE HAND BINDER IN
CONSERVATION AND PRESERVATION

My business is the preservation of books and documents. I have a small studio in Chicago which employs two people in the bindery, David Brock and Mark Esser. David is in the fifth year of his apprenticeship and Mark has been with me for about nine months. My wife, Bernie, comes in to help in the office.

In addition to preservation work we bind fine bindings and limited editions from private presses. For the purpose of this talk, I will stay with preservation work.

Our customers are custodians of special collections in university libraries and other institutions, private collectors, and people who have books that are very special to them.

Private collectors and people with special books usually come to the studio where I examine their books, recommend treatment and explain what is involved, answer any questions they might have and quote them a price. Because of the small number of books usually involved, it is no problem for them to bring the books to the studio.

In dealing with library special collections, there are more books involved and many more people. There may be as many as six people working in a special collections department, all of whom are interested in the preservation of their collection. Because so many books and people are involved, I like to go to the library and pick up books in need of preservation treatment and deliver books on which I've worked.

The books to be worked on have been chosen before I get there. We take each book separately and discuss what has to be done. We then examine the books that I have brought back and discuss thoroughly the work that has been done. This way the people in the library gain some understanding of what is involved in book preservation.

Generally speaking, books in need of preservation treatment fall into two categories: books with brittle paper and books with flexible paper. Books with brittle paper are mostly from the eighteenth, nineteenth and twentieth centuries. Books with flexible paper are from the fifteenth, sixteenth and seventeenth centuries.

A thorough examination of the book reveals the condition of the paper, the condition of the cover and the condition of the construction. With this information, the curator or owner with the binder decide on the best way to preserve the book.

I would like to describe for you a couple of fairly common preservation problems that are encountered in the studio and how we deal with them.

Conservation means preserving the artifact in its present condition, in which case a drop spine box may be the answer; however, the book is an object which has to function in order to be useful so that, in most cases, anything from minor repair to complete rebinding is necessary.

A fairly common case for preservation might be a nineteenth-century book with brittle paper. Examination reveals that the leather has deteriorated due to red rot. Both boards are broken at the hinges and the paper is brittle and has a pH of 4. In addition to the slips being broken the sewing is weak and broken and the spine has been glued up with acidic animal glue. If the book is very valuable to the collection and a better copy cannot be obtained, an extremely conservative binding may be possible. This binding is designed to do as little damage as possible to the book block and to function with as little strain as possible on the paper.

The book, then, is carefully disbound by pulling the sections from the sewing. Because of the acidic glue on the spine, the outer sheets of each section may break; possibly more than the outer sheet may break. After pulling, the sections are washed in warm water. When the folds of the sections are weak and possibly held together by glue that has penetrated the sewing holes, I wash the book in sections rather than in single sheets. I do this by folding polyester film called "Remey" and placing a folded piece somewhat larger than the sheets of the book into the center of each section and then place the sections in the water. When the sections have been thoroughly washed and rehydrated, I remove them from the water and allow them to drain before placing them into the deacidifying solution. For this purpose we use magnesium bicarbonate or calcium hydroxide. I find calcium hydroxide easier to use and it gives a higher pH than magnesium bicarbonate. If the sheets being deacidified have colored inks, then magnesium bicarbondate is the better solution.

After soaking thoroughly in the solution, the sections are removed by the supporting Remey and air dried. They are then collated and lightly pressed. The successful collation of the sheets at this stage may depend on how well loose sheets and unnumbered sheets at the beginning and end of the book were marked before the book was pulled.

The sheets are examined for tears and mended with Japanese paper and acid free wheat paste. Torn folds are mended and reinforced with wet-torn Japanese paper.

When dry, the book is ready for sewing. The original binding may have been sewn flexible on raised cords or it may have been sewn on recessed cords. Neither method may now be considered suitable because flexible sewing imposes too great a strain on the weak paper and recessed sewing is destructive to the paper. The sewing which is most compatible with the weak paper may be sewing on linen tapes or frayed out hemp cords. This method of sewing is flush with the spine and allows the spine to open and close with a minimum of strain.

The "gluing up" of the spine is done with a mixture of wheat paste and methyl cellulose. The methyl cellulose tends to add flexibility to the paste. Flexible polyvinyl acetate (PVA) is the modern glue designed for this purpose. I don't use it directly on the spine because it is not water soluable and would, therefore, make reversing the binding extremely difficult, if not impossible. Either of these adhesives are stronger than paste on this most vulnerable part of the binding but, on balance, the book block will last longer by using a reversible adhesive.

The sewing of endbands on this delicate paper would further damage the paper and add no strength to the binding. In this case, I favor head-bands made by rolling natural linen around hemp or linen to form the end bands and then adhere them to the spine.

A spine lining of Japanese paper is pasted directly to the spine, again using a mixture of paste and methyl cellulose. When dry, a coat of diluted PVA is applied to the Japanese paper. This helps to keep the spine flexible. A hollow or tube is then made and attached to the spine. The book block is now forwarded and ready for covering. This may be done by lacing on the boards and covering or by making a case.

I favor natural linen and handmade paper for this purpose because they are strong and durable. If the paper is decorated with colored paste and used with linen it can be harmonious with paper from any period.

With this book we have recognized that the book block is brittle and weak and we have designed a binding that has been as conservative and harmonious as possible. I consider it advisable to protect such a binding further in a drop spine box.

Another common problem is the book that is in need of rebacking. The most vulnerable part of the book is the spine, and particularly the hinge area. If the boards have become detached, this means that the covering material has broken, the inner hinge of paper, cloth or leather has broken, and the slips that have been laced into the boards have broken. Probably damage has been done to the first and last sections of the book. These sections are removed and carefully marked so that their sequence will not be lost. They may be washed and deacidified and mended with Japanese paper.

Next, we remove the spine. This is easy to do on a hollow back or tube spine but not so easy when the leather has been directly adhered to the spine. If the leather is weak and crumbling, then, we brush a liquid called Pliantex on the leather. This consolidates the fibers and enables us to pry the leather off with scalpels and folders. When the leather has been removed, the spine is paste washed and cleaned. All of this work on the spine is done with the utmost care for the sewing.

The sewing structure is examined and breaks and weaknesses repaired. New slips are added by oversewing new hemp cords to the old ones.

The damaged first and last sections have now been repaired and are sewn to the new slips. New linen endbands are sewn on and the spine is lined. We are now ready to attach the new leather spine.

The boards are prepared by lifting the leather from the back edges and by lifting the paste down from the inside back edges of the boards. The boards are put in place on the book and then held in a press. The leather is pared and pasted and carefully attached to the spine and inserted under the lifted leather on each board.

The ends are turned in and the headcaps are set. When dry, the boards are opened and a linen hinge, which has been wrapped around the repaired sections, is pasted down under the lifted paste down. Then the lifted paste down is pasted on the new hinge and the lifted leather is put down on the new leather. The old spine is attached to the new spine and the rebacking is finished.

I have described to you two of the most common book preservation techniques we use. In order to become familiar with these and many other preservation techniques I advise you to communicate with your binder and even take lessons from him/her if possible.

In addition to the many preservation techniques needed for the conservation and restoration of the variety of books that come to the studio, I would like to mention that we also preserve documents. We do this by washing, deacidifying and encapsulating in Mylar. A method I particularly like, especially with letters, is to lay the letter on an acid free board under a Mylar flap.

LEEDOM KETTELL

President and Chief Operating Officer
Gaylord Bros., Inc.
Syracuse, New York

ROLE OF THE LIBRARY SUPPLY HOUSE IN CONSERVATION AND PRESERVATION

Gaylord Bros., Inc. has existed for eighty-five years. However, I haven't. I've been with Gaylord only two years, coming from two other corporate experiences, eleven years with Xerox (a great portion of that time with University Microfilms) and, then, with Brodart. One of the things that Gaylord has had to do as a relatively older company, that is now caught up in the tremendous change in the technological processes that librarians are using, and at the same time lack of growing budgets, is to go through a planning process, the same kind of planning process that many of you wrestle with every year. Especially, we have had to do this a great deal over the last six months, in an attempt to redescribe to ourselves who we are, what we are, and what we would like to be. Eighty-five years ago, the two Gaylord brothers would go out to talk with librarians in an attempt to understand their needs for supply-type items. They would then go back to their place of business, take a largely paper product and twist it around into a different shape, print something on it, and they had a new product for librarians. Unfortunately today we're dealing with plastics, metals, microprocessers, the need for acid free paper, and a whole host of technologies for which our small company and the library market cannot afford original R&D. So we are defining ourselves as a vendor, a distributor of products, in the same way that Sears might be described as a vendor of products. We like to be a very credible company, concentrating on the library marketplace. Because we are a credible company we have very good relationships with a number of very large companies, including IBM, Xerox, Kodak, 3M, etc. These companies, of course, have substantial research and development budgets. So, we are increasingly trying to define our company as an interpreter of technology. We try to understand what some of these larger companies are doing and, then, use their new technologies to help librarians.

Today I'd like to talk about one such technology which, I think, will be an interesting one for you. First of all, I would mention that there have been a number of companies that sell products such as pamphlet binders and boxes of all shapes made from acid free paper used to store the documents you have in the library. While companies such as Gaylord, University Products, and Hollinger make a good-quality product for these purposes, we, at Gaylord, believe that some things happen in the paper industry that are real problems. First of all, simply defining what is acid free paper is somewhat of a controversial issue. How have you buffered it? Are you talking about the liner? Are you talking about the board itself? Do you have some form of glue or joining device in it which can ruin the neutrality of the materials? Also, paper is absorbent; over the years it might absorb the water vapor and the acids that are in the air itself. So we believe that there is a problem with products that any vendor sells as acid free. We know that paper prices have gone up greatly in the past ten years and, by the very nature of our society, and by the nature of the paper and pulp industry, we believe prices for paper are going to accelerate very rapidly in the next few years. At Gaylord, we have explored making storage boxes out of a different material. We believe a plastic that is called polypropolene will be of great interest to you. This plastic product is made from a natural gas and talc which are both raw materials quite available here in the United States; therefore, we do not have to be worried about importing oil and getting cut off in the event of war.

Polypropolene has very interesting properties. First of all, it is totally inert, therefore acidity is simply not relevant. It is neither acidic nor alkaline and never can be. It has very high temperature resistance. You can actually sterilize this material at 250 degrees and you will not damage it. It has great resistance to absorption of water vapor—about as great as any material that we are able to find—so we think that will be of great use in library preservation work. The material can also be configured in virtually any shape that you might want to have. By indenting the material as it is formed, you can change the strength and flexibility of the material. You can also add different additives to make it more or less flexible. You can color it in almost any way that you might possibly want, and it has the feature called a living hinge. When this material is compressed, it actually changes the molecular configuration so that this hinge can be flexed thousands and thousands of times. You are not going to have the problem of the lid of the box coming off in your hand—it will last as long as the material itself. The material can also be textured so that if you want it slick, we can make that; if you want it to have a woodgrained type of pattern, we can do that. We can print on it. By ourselves, we could not afford to develop this technology because it is a multimillion-dollar investment, not only investing in the plastic production itself, but also in the extrusion devices that are used to melt it and form sheets and to vacuum form it into useful products that you would want to buy; therefore we are in the process of making arrangements with other companies to work with us to make the product available. After working with the product for two years, we believe that we will have this material on the market, thoroughly tested, within six months.

Other fields such as the medical field are increasingly substituting polypropolene for materials such as glass, paper, and metal. In medicine, operating room trays, packages, kits, and so forth, are made of polypropolene because of its inherent high resistance to chemicals, solvents, and bacterial development. Polypropolene containerization of pharmaceuticals is common now due to high temperature resistance combined with unusually low water absorption and moisture vapor permeability. These are vital characteristics to effective storage of pills, powders, capsules, and medicines. This is material that has passed the stringent requirements of the medical profession.

In another difficult area, food packaging demands are met more favorably with polypropolene than with any other plastic resin. It meets the requirements of the U.S. Food and Drug Administration as specified in the Code of Federal Regulations, no. 21, for the safe use of articles intended for repeated use applications. Again, the inherent inertness of the material makes it resistant to oils, acids, alkalines, and practically all chemicals. Food products successfully contained in polypropolene include dairy products, fruit juices, vegetables, toppings, and syrups.

We believe that the use of polypropolene is more cost-effective than any other polymer, and competes economically with all traditionally used materials. Physical properties of polypropolene can be readily changed by varying amounts of additives to obtain precise properties of impact resistance, tensile strength, and flexual modules. Tailoring polypropolene to specific products and uses is relatively simple. For example, it is possible to achieve optimized balances of stiffness, impact resistance, or resistance to heat aging, plus resistance to solvents, chemicals and environmental stress cracking. This is accomplished by well-known, proven procedural methods. When you look at some samples this evening you will notice that we have used a sonic welding to put in an adhesive strip. This will be used for pamphlet binders. Sonic welding is a very permanent method of adhering two products together. Before we bring the product out, we will do careful testing of the adhesive to make sure that it is non-damaging to paper.

In summary, we believe this material, polypropolene, will have a significant impact on libraries because it is totally intert. It can be shipped flat so it will save cost in transportation. We believe that it will be priced competitively with the paper products as we know them today. The living hinge will last as long as the product. We can use sonic welding techniques to reduce the labor involved when we make the product, and to improve its strength. The product is extremely heat resistant and can be actually sterilized at temperatures of up to 250 degrees. It is moisture resistant and very long-lasting. It can be attractively produced, and its raw materials are readily available. There is, however, one problem whenever you deal with this technology. Set-up costs are somewhat high, making it prohibitively expensive to produce only a few of any one particular product. We have to participate with some of the consumer industries and add our demands to part of their run. Therefore, one difficulty with this product is that we will not be able to offer the great range of sizes and shapes that we might be able to offer in a paper product. We will probably pick the most popular sizes and shapes, make those out of this particular product, and work our way through this as best we can. We believe that will be the only disadvantage of this product and we will have it available for marketing to you in 1982.

ANITA WERLING

Manager, Collection Development
University Microfilms International
Ann Arbor, Michigan

ROLE OF THE MICROPUBLISHER IN CONSERVATION AND PRESERVATION

I must say that after listening to my colleagues from the commercial end I feel somewhat in a "bind," especially since I represent a company concerned with microfilming which is frequently touted as an alternative to binding of current serial materials and as an alternative method of preserving information as opposed to restoring the object itself. While microfilming has been around for a long time, commercial application of microfilming for libraries really dates back only to the 1930s. This also marks the beginning of the use of microforms for preservation of library materials. Newspapers were one of the first items that went under the camera, so to speak, the reasons being primarily because the paper is highly acidic and becomes brittle, and because newspapers are very difficult to bind under any circumstances.

It was also late in the decade of the thirties that commercial micropublishers made their appearance. University Microfilms International (UMI), the company that I represent, is the oldest of the commercial micropublishers, having been founded in 1938; Readex Microprint was founded late in the next decade. These companies, and others which came on the scene later, are involved in the commercial *publishing* of materials on microfilm, or in many cases, the republishing of materials that have previously been published, and offering them in a different medium. The objective is not primarily that of preservation—micropublishing has a profit motive behind it—but the by-products of the filming of large retrospective sets of materials such as the Early American Imprints Project offered by Readex, or the Early English Books projects offered by University Microfilms, have in fact resulted in the preservation of information and the preservation of the cultural heritage of virtually all early British and American imprints. So preservation is an added benefit of micropublishing. The medium of microfilm has made proliferation and dissemination of the materials economically feasible in a format that can be purchased readily by libraries and which also enables users to handle the materials without risk of damage to the originals.

Today, there are literally hundreds of commercial micropublishers. In addition there are several hundred other commercial microfilming companies. The distinction here is similar to the difference between a printing shop and a publisher. That is basically what a commercial microfilming service is in comparison to a commercial micropublisher. The publishing involves adding value. The added value might be the editorial selection of the materials that are going to be filmed, or a unique arrangement of the materials. It may be added access to the materials that the publisher provides through indexes or guides to the product. The commercial microfilming firm, like the printshop or commercial printer, makes its profit from the filming itself. The commercial micropublisher, on the other hand, is also interested in disseminating and marketing the materials, so the economic motive is somewhat different—dissemination and distribution is the aim of the publisher—which means that there must be some added value to the product. Sometimes both services are offered under the same roof. A micropublishing company may provide some commercial filming operations, or may handle some jobs on a custom basis where the intent is not to market the product but simply to film and preserve it. We have one such project at University Microfilms which has been under way for several decades and which is one of the preservation microfilming projects which has received widespread attention. This involves the filming of monastic manuscripts under the auspices of St. John's University in Collegeville, Minnesota. Thousands of medieval manuscripts, many of them illuminated, have been filmed in both color and black and white from a number of monasteries throughout Europe and North Africa. University Microfilms provides technical training and assistance for this project, inspecting and storing all of the master microfilms. We also produce distribution copies for this project upon directives from St. John's. We do not market the materials ourselves but do provide storage for all of their masters in our vaults.

The micropublisher and the commercial microfilmer are in business to make money. For the micropublisher the only way to do that is to publish those projects which have the greatest potential for success. That is, the projects for which there is market need. Once filmed, the materials are preserved as long as the master negative is preserved and kept in archival conditions. Unfortunately we have found, in many cases, that once we have filmed projects and offered them for sale, there is no longer an immediate need for the customer to buy them since the materials are now preserved, and the microfilm is going to be around for a long time. You can buy it today; you can buy it tomorrow; you can buy it five or ten years from now! Therefore, one of the great added benefits of microfilm can also become, in some cases, a detriment to the micropublisher. A publisher, then, has to be concerned about raising the priority of purchase for the issued products.

In fact, I think we have seen in recent years that the micropublishing industry, as a whole, has become more concerned with doing as much as possible to produce products which have more immediate impact for libraries and institutions. One way, of course, of doing this is to provide additional value—that of improved access to the materials themselves. Bibliographic control has become a major issue for the micropublishing industry and, of course, for libraries. One way to enhance the value of the product is to make sure that as much access as can possibly be afforded has been provided. That means cataloging monographic and serial collections and making that cataloging data as widely available as possible. And it means indexing at a fairly specific level the nonmonographic or serial projects (archival collections, for example). It means selecting a format that is going to be the most usable format for a particular application. What it all boils down to is trying to make the product match the end users' needs and trying to make sure that once on film, the materials can be retrieved quickly and easily.

In recent years at University Microfilms we have spent a great deal of time and effort in providing bibliographic control for our products. And, to give you some ideas as to how costly this actually is, we have frequently found that in our operations the access is anywhere from 4 to 5 times more costly than the actual filming of materials. Providing access is critical, nonetheless, because if the customer doesn't know what we have filmed, obviously, the customer can't purchase our microfilm. In addition, bibliographic control reduces the amount of duplicated effort among micropublishers and private institutions in filming of the same item more than once. The *National Register of Microfilm Masters,* and other tools of this sort which identify microfilmed titles, have gone a long way to cut down on the duplication of filming activity.

What materials are ripe for preservation filming, or microfilming in general? Basically, any materials that have an image content can be considered for microfilming. This includes books, printed materials, manuscript materials, archival collections of documents and letters, etc., or visual collections, such as photographs, prints, maps. The decision on whether to preserve by microfilming or by conserving is never an easy one, because the value of the original as an object has to be assessed as well as the informational value of the material. For materials which cannot be restored, the choice may become one of whether to preserve the information or to conserve or preserve the object. If an item has deteriorated to the point where filming might completely destroy it, do you save the object or do you save the information? This difficult decision usually rests in the hands of librarians trained to assess these various issues. Fortunately, the alternatives are usually not that drastic, and the decision is one of whether the original can be saved by rebinding, preserving the original through deacidification, or replacing the deteriorated binding, while at the same time perhaps microfilming the item to provide a use copy which will prevent further unnecessary handling of the original. Frequently, microfilming can also be used to make a complete edition of a work from several imperfect copies that are in institutions scattered over wide distances. So there are a number of applications for microfilming that make the value of microfilming in preservation something to consider.

How do you decide whether to microfilm locally or whether to go to a commercial microfilmer, or to a micropublisher? Under what circumstances is one more desirable than another? This is a very complex issue and one that we could discuss at great length. It's very expensive to set up a local preservation microfilming operation, as many of you can attest, but frequently this is the best means of perserving the materials that are not likely to be picked up by a commercial micropublisher. If there are widespread applications in your institution for microfilming of rare or other materials that are not widely available elsewhere, then setting up your own in-house operation might be the best way to go. Or, perhaps a commercial microfilming company is the answer for materials which cannot be marketed or for which dissemination is really not a factor. Where there is an interest in making material available to other institutions, and in preserving or rearranging materials on microfilm, then it is a good idea to talk to one or more micropublishers to explore the idea of publishing a particular collection of materials.

To give you an idea of the variety of collections that University Microfilms is considering or is publishing this year and in the year ahead, I would first mention the filming and indexing of the Archives of the United Negro College Fund (UNCF), which will result in the availability of a unique collection which has resided, until this point in time, only at the headquarters of the UNCF. We are also releasing a very large collection of nursing materials—the History of Nursing and the Nursing Education Archives of Teachers College, Columbia University. This past year we filmed and introduced the Photographic Views of New York City—a collection of 54,000 photographs taken over the last century representing the growth and development of the city, fully indexed and with the images now preserved. One of the major interests of the New York Public Library in having that collection filmed by University Microfilms was in providing a use copy so that patrons could consult a microfiche edition that serves as a visual index to the photograph collection . The users are able to select prints that they want the Library to reproduce without actually handling the original prints.

These, then, are some of UMI's recent applications of microfilming for preservation and for dissemination. Those of you who are in charge of collections or trying to decide which part of that collection should be preserved by microfilming certainly have quite a challenge ahead. If there are potential applications that University Microfilms can help you with, we would be happy to discuss them.

DISCUSSION

William T Henderson (Library, University of Illinois at Urbana-Champaign): It occurs to me that these four people have just proven one of my points in my presentation of this morning—i.e., in preservation, we keep the old and bring the new along with us.

Kenneth Lavendar (North Texas State University, Denton): The title of this institute is "Conserving and Preserving Library Materials." The title of the panel discussion is the role of commercial services in conservation and preservation. Mr. Anthony, in his talk, defined conservation as the preservation of material in its present state. Could you talk to the distinction between preservation and conservation?

Henderson: A couple of us who have written papers for this conference talked about this earlier today. We concluded that we tend to use preservation and conservation interchangeably—one term relieves the other if it seemed like we were getting a bit monotonous in the use of it in our manuscripts. I think you can make some subtle distinctions; if we had a dictionary here we could probably do it. Conservation is literally saving what you have in the way it is. There's a difference between conservation and preservation but the difference is a subtle one, and we're literally doing both. I see that Pam Darling is going to the microphone and she probably is the one who can define these terms.

Pamela Darling (Association of Research Libraries): This is, as everyone knows, a perennial question and I think we're coming closer to an answer than we have been up until now. It seems to me that if you look through the literature and in what has come to be more common usage now, preservation is the broader term. Conservation, it seems to me, relates chiefly to those activities dealing with the care and treatment of the artifact. Preservation encompasses that as well as all of the other programs for care, handling, and replacement, brittle books programs, as well as the administra-tion of all of the activities within a library that bear upon the condition of the collections. Now, you will sometimes find the terms defined in the literature in a reverse way. That is, there are some who say conservation is the broader term. However, it seems the preponderance of evidence is moving toward preservation as being the broader term. The fact that we use the term *conservator* to mean the person who deals in a hands-on way with the artifact, helps, I think, to confirm that. It will probably be another couple of years before we have really settled on that, but it seems to me that it is definitely going in that direction.

James Orr (Hertzberg-New Method, Inc., Jacksonville, Illinois): I am going to turn it around a little bit. Maybe I could ask a question of you folks. When you send your work to a commercial bindery, do you send it to preserve it or do you send it to conserve it? Which of those two do you put the emphasis on, or do you?

Unidentified: To restore it.

Orr: What's your definition of restoration? *(Editors' note:* No response came.)

Philip Metzger (School of Medicine, Southern Illinois University at Carbondale): I have a question for Mr. Orr about oversewing. We haven't heard too many kind words about oversewing lately, as you hinted, and, I think most of us would agree that oversewing is great for materials that will never be used once they are put on the shelf, but the process of using an oversewn book contributes to its destruction. Would you care to comment on that and say something about the future of oversewing?

Orr: Yes, I would. First of all, I hope that when you think of a commercial binder you don't automatically think of oversewing because there are a number of other ways to bind a book. There is hand oversewing, or through sewing to tape, through sewing the core, and, of late, adhesive binding. When the oversewing method was invented, binders, and probably people in the libraries, thought it was the greatest thing since sliced bread, because it was extremely strong. It *is* strong binding but to oversew you must perforate each section from the top and the needles come up from the bottom, sewing section to section, so in essence what you have is a perforated section. Granted, if that paper becomes weak and acidic throughout its lifetime, the book isn't going to be all that strong. Now, of late, there are a lot of improvements in adhesives. When I'm talking about adhesives, I'm not talking about a hot melt (used by a lot of publishers and some binders). Hot melt has a memory and you can't round it and back it for a scoring action. We have been using a polyvinyl that is put on in a fanning method. It is put on much as in the European process where they use an Ehlermann machine. Of course, we have a certain combination of how we make the mixture. Of late we've been using it on very coated stocks, something unheard of before—and it works very well. So, to answer your question precisely, I can see the industry leaning to adhesive binding, and of late, I've been through other binderies and I have seen the same indications in those plants where they are starting to get in adhesive equipment and rely more on adhesive binding. We've been doing it for a long time now for books that have extremely narrow margins where there's no place to go regardless of whether you sew it by hand or hand oversew it, or whatever. There, the only thing that you can do is use an adhesive binding. There was some skepticism when adhesive bindings came out and I know they refer to adhesive binding as "perfect" binding. "Perfect" binding is a carry-over from the old days and has a bad connotation. So I like to call it adhesive binding and we, personally, put a guarantee on it—an unconditional guarantee—that this book is going to stand up just like any other book that we put out. That's how sure we are of it.

Heinke Pensky-Adams (Monastery Hill Bindery, Chicago, Illinois): I have a question for Mr. Orr. What took you so long to get this message to this country? I know this adhesive has been used in Europe for about twenty years.

Orr: Binders are very slow to move. Our association has been very slow to move and adopt any new changes. You're right! Before we adopted it, it was being used in Europe for five years prior to the time that we had it. Now that we're moving, we hope we can keep the ball rolling and the momentum up and that is where we intend to go.

D.W. Krummel (Graduate School of Library and Information Science, University of Illinois at Urbana-Champaign): In all fairness, you had a legendary freeze in New York State to worry about, didn't you? In the late fifties wasn't there a scandal—perfect bound books rendered useless because the freeze had destroyed the binding substance?

Orr: We didn't start to use this until 1961 when we used it on our paperback books. And, as everybody knows, the paperback was much smaller in format and the results were extremely good so we began to branch out into other books, and then into magazines. We didn't really start on magazines until maybe the late sixties. The only thing I can tell you about a freeze in the adhesive is that, when it is shipped, we can't ship it in the winter. We won't take it in the wintertime. It has to be very carefully guarded and not allowed to freeze.

John Thompson (Billy Graham Center Library, Wheaton College, Wheaton, Illinois): Most library bindings that I've been experienced with come back in buckram. Recently our binder has started to supply us with a synthetic book cloth. I believe it's produced by 3M. I was wondering if anyone is familiar with any tests performed on this.

Orr: I have similar material right here. It's a type two material. We've tested it in the Universal Book Tester and the only thing that I can tell you is that the results have been extremely favorable and have compared equally well to buckram.

Henderson: On my office shelves, I have some samples of both this material and buckram that have been through his book tester. If any of you want to see them, you may do so. They wear a little bit differently but they wear about equally on either material.

Anthony Amodeo (Newberry Library, Chicago, Illinois): This is for Ms. Werling. We tried to do a project at the Newberry Library filming pre-1500 manuscripts, and, because of the tight bindings, we were restricted in the number that we were able to do. I'm wondering how you handle bindings that are tight. Do you have a cradle of some sort that takes 90-degree exposures, and if so, would your company be willing to rent it?

Anita Werling (University Microfilms International): We do have a cradle camera that was designed for the filming of just the type of book that you described. We do have a number of those holders. Certainly I'd be happy to talk with you afterward about whether such arrangements could be made. But the camera bed itself is designed to hold the book at an opening that is slightly greater than ninety degrees, and pivots the volume in such a way that it is then raised up against a flat glass plate and held there with just enough pressure to keep the page flat against the glass surface. We used this particular camera very successfully in the filming of dime novels at the University of Minnesota. And, as many of you are aware, the typical condition of dime novel collections, from the 1860s and 1870s, is that the paper was very high in acid. It was newsprint, basically. The materials are, in most cases, extremely brittle. If you touch them to read them, you've got crumbs all over the floor. We were able to film quite successfully with very little additional damage to these materials and that's an extreme case.

Amodeo: You don't manufacture this yourself, though?

Werling: We did manufacture it ourselves, but we have made only two or three beds for specific applications. It may be possible to arrange for use of them elsewhere.

D.W. KRUMMEL

Professor
Graduate School of Library and Information Science
University of Illinois at Urbana-Champaign

Kepler and His Custody; Scholarship and Conservation Policy

Johannes Kepler ends the preface to his *Harmonice mundi* of 1619 with these sentiments: "The die is cast; my book is written, to be read either now or posterity, I don't care. It may wait a century for a reader, much as God has waited six thousand years for an audience."[1] This moving statement of faith epitomizes the conservator's cause before the world of scholarship. Its sentiments are worth remembering; for if our libraries are to survive, their cause will need to be supported by the modern Keplers who use them, and who expect them to keep their work around for readers a century from now.[2]

What really can be expected from our scholarly researchers, thousands of them strong, spread across a Babel of disciplines and inquiries around the world, each of them preoccupied with the importance of their efforts and their centrality to learning and to the human condition? The researcher's first contribution is to the dialogue on policy; and it is problematical insofar as it is ideological and political. The second involves practices of handling library materials; and it is basically so self-obvious as to be insulting. The third involves the prospect of better control over access and use; and it is painful to consider. All three involve commitments by scholars that are essential to the survival of our libraries; and each involves deeply felt attitudes, ingrained as part of the practice of their art, science, or craft. The 1976 Association of Research Libraries (ARL) *Detailed Specifications* are right in affirming "the fundamental requirement that preservation...be seen as an inseparable part of the broader objective of extending access to recorded information...."[3] The problem is merely one of reconciling diachronous access and synchronous access: in order for Kepler to be accessible tomorrow, what must we do, and ask readers to do, today?

It should be obvious, at the outset, that the aim of conservation is *not* to provide more materials for future generations to continue to conserve. Use of library materials has to be the aim: consulting, reading, experiencing and handling books. This fourth verb is the problem. Readers, no matter how fastidious their habits, will inevitably weaken the physical item in the act of handling it. Our growing awareness of the implications of the fact has been overshadowed by the very circumstance to which we attribute great libraries in our day, namely our pragmatic philosophy of library service. Serve our readers; the more our books are used, the better we achieve our objectives; and knowing what books are used, the more we can devote our attention to similar books so as to make our efforts and institutions the more useful; and the more we should concentrate our limited funds on immediate needs, such as will enhance this year's readership and next year's appropriations. Work for the definable objective, and, for the rest, dream and pray. The prevalent philosophy of librarianship, however praiseworthy in its own right, can obviously work against the objectives of library conservation, and of Kepler's vision. The fact remains that even Kepler tells us that his book is waiting for a reader. Ranganathan had it right in his first law: books are for use, the only questions being when and how.

When we get around to writing the history of the modern library conservation movement, two events will probably stand out. One was a disaster—namely, the Florence flood of 1966. The other was the recognition of a handling problem, specifically, the discovery that the card catalog at the New York Public Library, as it was documenting the fact that a great institution had fulfilled its mission gloriously, was also suggesting that the institution as well as its catalog was working its way out of existence. The awareness of our handling problems goes back even further, of course. When William Blades included bigots, servants, and children among his enemies of books,[4] he did so in an "Upstairs-Downstairs" context that already suggests the recurring questions of "elitism." Randolph Adams's addition of librarians to the hit-list,[5] in retrospect, now seems intended for the purpose mostly of delivering a Calvinist sermon to the damned, thereby lining up the service-minded library profession against the cause of rare books and, with Blades in mind, of conservation as well. The list of enemies, of course, is much larger. The fullest catalog, to my knowledge, is one proposed some twenty-five years ago by Robert Land, who sees it as ranging "from religious zealots to unconscionable forgers, from brilliant scholars to ignorant housemaids, from collectors with delicate sensibilities to second-hand furniture dealers with indelicate sensibilities, from efficiency experts to inefficient file clerks, from royalty and the families of Presidents to butchers, bakers, and candlestick makers, and from censors to grangerizers."[6]

The greatness of modern libraries has clearly been our reward for a profound concern for service to all of these; and to question its ideal would be both impolitic and wrong. But some basic distinctions do need to be kept in mind. There is a mighty important difference, for instance, between the library that stocks paperbacks to be worn out and discarded, and the librarian who condones theft and mutilation on grounds that the books are "at least getting used." Failure to be sensitive to the difference makes ours an uphill battle. Unless and until our cause can be understood, conservators will end up facing a mighty formidable, if fuzzy, array of ideological opponents. In that they may appear to withhold books from an enlightened populace, they line up against Thomas Jefferson, John Stuart Mill, and even Karl Marx. In their concern and affection for historical materials, they find themselves attacked by the old guard of social Darwinism and the new elite of the "paperless society." Finally (the crowning insult), to the heirs of Sigmund Freud, conservators will be seen as displaying psychopathological symptoms that will be labeled as "anal-retentive."

Under the circumstances, Kepler needs to come over to our side; we need his help. God can take the longer view of human destiny; but if Kepler's book is to be around a hundred years from now, Kepler will have to see himself not as part of the problem but as part of the solution. Back in the 1780s, soon after modern copyright was first established and as its impact was just coming to be sorted out, William Blackstone made a landmark analogy: the rights of an author to the rewards for personal creative efforts need to be counterbalanced by the rights of society to access to those ideas. So today's access needs to be counterbalanced by the rights of tomorrow's researchers. In devising our programs we need Kepler's support, and his insight as well. It may be impossible and even dangerous to presume who among today's Keplers will be rediscovered in, say, A.D. 2050, 2250, and 2550; who will rediscover them; for what reasons; and with what effects.[7] The best we can do is talk to the Keplers of today, and learn how they are consulting the present record. There are, indeed, different kinds of research use, determined in great part by our different kinds of scholars, and with different conceptions of library conservation appropriate to each. Adapting another classic notion of Randolph Adams,[8] for instance, we might distinguish (1) general admirers from (2) readers interested mostly in the intellectual content and (3) bibliographers working with the physical items.

With significant—and inevitably, highly significant—exceptions, the "high spots" in our collections are there mostly to be gazed at in the exhibition cases (or, as Adams grumbled, to be pawed over by the local Boy

Scouts). When last, as library administrators have been heard to muse, did anyone sit down and actually *read* a Shakespeare folio? Some books are like religious relics in a baroque monastery, more the *verum corpus* than the *sanctus spiritus* of our civilization; and for much of the public we serve, the act of worship is of profound significance. This situation will be particularly maddening to the zealous ascetics among us who come to be narrowly preoccupied with the intellectual content of our collections.

Admittedly, even the robust hedonists among us still able to confess our love for books will be bothered to see how conservation funds become available for the spectacular but unused treasure, rather than for the tired but loyal reference book. Faith, not necessarily supported by any questioning spirit at all, has nourished and probably will continue to nourish our collections and our conservation programs more than we care to admit.

In contrast, there is library use that is commonly seen as involving the text exclusively: the ideas and their incorporation into a verbal (or mathematical, or musical; in any event, a formal) message. When the text can be shown to be the only thing that matters, the conservation options are different, as cheap and as numerous as they are obvious. Convert to another medium, be it film, reprints of widely consulted work, or digital storage; discard the original; and then worry about preserving the surrogate medium. We have long done this with newspapers, and no doubt the practice will come to be extended to more and more library materials.

Preservation of a sort can be accomplished through a transformation of the medium. In the history of civilization we have seen our intellectual diasporas; and in folk legend we have heard about Tarnhelms in the service of Valhalla. (One hopes for happier outcome.) The very principle of transformation of medium is profoundly disturbing insofar as it assumes a necessarily simplistic answer to the question of what constitutes the text itself. What is "original evidence"? The text, for instance, consists of both symbols and contexts. The latter must not be forgotten now if use of documents rather than mere preservation is the ultimate goal. Reading the *New York Times* on a rush-hour subway is simply not the same as reading it in front of a microfilm reader. (Part of the difference, as others have observed, is that you can't wrap fish in a microfilm.) Abrams art books simply do not look the same on coated paper and on screen projections. The images do not read in the same way: the very content is different, in ways that make the word *aesthetic* at once highly appropriate, much too broad, and very fuzzy.[9] Scholars working on the 1930s can gather some very meaningful impressions by comparing English paper and presswork with their German counterparts; but detailing the exact differences confounds the imagination. Even so, more library materials will surely need to be converted to nonprint media, and even conceived in terms of these media.

At this point, we must introduce our third group of readers, whose concern is "not the life-blood of a master spirit but a collection of pieces of paper with printing on them."[10] Our bibliographers will clearly understand the Platonic distinction between the physical and the intellectual book.[11] They might then also appear to be the conservator's true soul mates. Alas, not necessarily so. Eventually they usually will want to dig into the gutters and bend back the headcaps in search of a cancel stub, or perform irreparable minor surgery with a penknife or even a ball-point pen. They have been known to dangle large folios by a single leaf as they hold the sheet up to the light in search for the chain lines or watermark. And asked what to do with a book that is falling apart, they will consider and reply, "nothing at all." Meanwhile, our crystal balls threaten us with the prospect that these readers will consist of more and more of our visitors. The reasoning behind such a prospect, admittedly, is probably too obvious to be trustworthy. Even so, the justification of our conservation efforts for bibliographical study is a particularly compelling one, especially insofar as our bibliographers serve to epitomize the scrupulous scholar's passionate search for and commitment to what lawyers call "best evidence."

Familiarity with the practices and intentions in creating library materials should qualify our bibliographers to help us in addressing the question of context just mentioned. The thought of playing God, consigning some originals to oblivion but not others, is acceptable and flattering enough for any scholar; but finding authoritative grounds on which to do so is another matter. What *exactly* is there about reading John Dryden in an original folio that is different from reading him in a new paperback? To turn to timely examples, should any library really wish to bind the latest copies of *Harper's*, or the *Times Literary Supplement*, or *AB/Bookman's Weekly* or even *College & Research Libraries* (let alone *CRL News*)? Specificially, is there really enough—or anything—lost in content through consulting a film or photocopy, so as to justify the expense in binding and maintaining the originals? The bibliographer might perhaps be excused for begging off the decision on whether *Playboy* demands color film rather than black-and-white; but for expertise based on the practices of printing, the aesthetics of the graphic arts, and the likely dangers of "best evidence" being lost, the bibliographer is very much needed.

Ultimately, however, each of our three "special interest lobbies" has to be seen as contributing part, but not all, of the solution to our problems. Admittedly, the reasoning for this pluralism may not look all that good: our best defense is to confuse the issue through the bold, romantic plea that "the medium is the message." We must fall back on that sentimental and libertarian notion of the "unity of learning." In specific instances, one of our three prototypical readers may emerge as the likely objective in guiding a conservation decision; but for conservation policy in general, all three must be recognized.

No less problematic, meanwhile, is the question of who we talk to as the representative of our readership. The topic is filled with ironies. For instance, in an age of specialization, the more eminent the scholars, the more limited their perspective and the more unreasonable their demands are likely to be. Given an opportunity to help, they will typically devise exciting, new, and very expensive "state-of-the-art" models rather than address present predicaments. The doctoral students who rewrite their professors' dissertations are no great problem. Those who rewrite history and who realign our disciplines are the ones who ruin our programs, louse up our classification schemes, and prove to us that we have been preserving the wrong materials.

But can we expect much more by turning to that fashionable world of library user studies? The consensus to date, naturally, suggests that more work needs to be done.[12] And the notion of dynamic scholarship by its very nature implies that today's findings may be inappropriate tomorrow. Even so, a good deal of damage has already been done. The simplistic patterns have so far suggested that new books are consulted more often than older ones, and thus that books are most likely to be consulted within the first few years after their appearance. Besides infuriating our historians, the immediate implications have naturally been to work against the cause of conservation in general: why preserve what so few will ever use? More precisely, the enlightened but politically sensitive administrator will inevitably ask why so much of a budget should be given over to materials that stand the lesser chance of being consulted.

The standard advice for librarians, however, has long been to go to those who have most benefited from the collection for advice and support. The instincts of a seasoned scholar—preferably, of course, one of wide experience and long involvement—are likely to be able to tell us whether the new bibliography will allow us to discard the superseded one, or retire it to the stacks, or restore it to stand next to the new one on the reference shelf, or refurbish it for the rare book room. Our user studies mostly are still too stochastic to tell us even whether our Kepler editions are being used by students or professors who are unable to get their call numbers right, or by admirers on their pilgrimages, or by students needing simply to verify citations, or by astronomers about to discover a relationship that has been neglected for 350 years.

Related to these aspects of our dialogue with scholars, of course, is the sheer burgeoning complexity of learning today. The one big feuding family may be what keeps the library fairly neutral and honest; it is also the source of the best advice and the worst advice we will ever get. The conservation dialogue is comparable in some ways to the acquisitions dialogue. The point is worth making, although there are some basic differences, the obvious one being a comparison of the fifteenth- and the nineteenth-century historian. In acquisitions, we can usually dismiss the former with travel money while we build a collection for the latter; in conservation, on the other hand, we can usually take the former quite seriously in his concern for working on our local holdings, whereas for the nineteenth-century specialist we need to mumble assurances about mass deacidification being just around the corner. But pursuing this matter in any productive detail would quickly get into deep waters of another kind; let us instead briefly turn to a second major topic, the question of getting our Keplers to handle materials properly.

The basic problem is that proper handling is so much a matter of mere thoughtfulness. Outright malice does indeed take place—scribbling, articles razored from a periodical, defacement. Mark Twain once announced his preferences for a thin book because it would steady a table, a leather volume because it would strop a razor, and a heavy book because it could be thrown at a cat;[13] and as we chuckle, perhaps we should make sure that his books be kept in an area apart from that keeping our Keplers. In fact, thoughtless mistreatment is much more common than mischievous. And it is most likely to occur in the moment of use, which is also likely to be the moment of discovery. The flash of insight too easily blinds the reader to that essential quality of content and form, of intellectual book and physical book. It probably follows that the more inspired the reader, the greater the danger.

The ensuing mischief, unfortunately, is also likely to resemble the great moments of Harold Lloyd, Buster Keaton, or Laurel and Hardy. The key ingredient is preoccupation. And no rational instruction or admonition can anticipate its forms, except to observe after the event that the worthiest of intentions are customarily undermined by glorious spectacles of human fallibility. For this reason, as others have remarked, the Universal Book Tester may fail us for being too rational.

The cause is almost always undermined by an honest and direct appeal to reason. This very point, I sense, was well recognized in that admirable slide show developed by the Yale conservation program last spring. Some of its scenes are simply too delicious to be true—except that we have all seen similar circumstances, and all too often. One more of Blades's enemies, alas, has to be identified under the heading of sheer slapstick.

Thus while we should defer to his great experience, it may be hard to agree with Edwin Williams's recent lament that the mishandling of books is increased through administrative patterns requiring the senior staff to delegate the day-to-day work in the collections to less respectful juniors.[14] It is standard etiquette for old-timers to regret publicly their inability to work with the books any longer; and bless them all for expressing these regrets. In fact, handling is probably best done by the most alert and least preoccupied members of the staff; inculcating respect is much of the problem. As for the library readership, mass-printed instructional reminders, as brief as possible—such as are found at the reader's desk in major research libraries, but which might also be inserted today at a circulation desk—are probably well worth the effort.[15]

Digressing from the topic for the moment, let me propose that there is one simple resolve among all others that needs to be forced through, with as much noise, solidarity, and urgency as possible. Too much of our photocopying equipment calls for the most unnatural act that a book can be subjected to. Flipping a book over facedown on a copying plate too clearly shows an utter disregard for the physical construction on cords and covers, all the more so in that it requires lifting off, turning right-side up, and then flipping over for each page-turn. The only possible benefit could be an exposure of the basic danger in oversewing, admittedly; but this price is much too high to pay. Much like the Luddites 150 years ago who broke up the looms in the English Midlands, so perhaps we need our sledge-hammer—wielding Xerites (or Savites) today—the "Carrie Nations of Conservation" brigade, perhaps—at least until such times as the ALA, SLA, ARL, and NCLIS can demand copying machines that photograph from above, in the manner of a hospital X-ray. Such observations are not meant to disparage the photocopy as an aid to scholarship. On the contrary, the camera has been a vast and unsung benefit to learning, saving time, insuring an accurate transcript of a text, and making possible the comparison of distant copies side by side. Along the way it has no doubt saved wear and tear on books as well. Rather, the price we have been paying is too high insofar as it was, and really continues to be, so *unnecessarily* destructive.

The third contribution Kepler can make to his cause would appear to be the most painful and counterproductive of all: the library can be used under diminished and restricted circumstances. The mere suggestion has, of course, more than once evoked a classic response: fire the librarian! The topic is one that still needs to be addressed. Selling it to our researchers—in effect, asking them (as B.F. Skinner might have it) to forgo their freedom and dignity—could be less of a problem than determining what exactly they might appropriately be asked to forgo.

Indeed, there is a wide range of precedents involving readers working under circumstances more restricted than we generally know today. The idea that libraries should provide for circulating collections at all, in fact, is mostly a product of the eighteenth-century Enlightenment. Even through the nineteenth-century, great "reference" libraries continued to be established, this term set up in contradistinction to the "circulating" collections. Among research libraries in Europe today, the so-called *Präzensbibliothek* is the rule more than the exception.[16] Special dispensations over the years, and the pressure to attract greater readership, have inevitably tended to relax our policies. This liberalization took place, of course, in those innocent days before our conservation predicament was even recognized.

The inconvenience of reading on the premises as opposed to taking the books to the study or home is in many ways analogous to taking the trouble to go to a play or concert instead of watching the play on television, or hearing the music at home. Those who go to the effort swear by their practices to the point of exhilaration if not of boredom: one sees, learns, understands more by consulting a book in its proper library context, even if it means, along the way, eating German food or arguing with Paris merchants or coping with Italian plumbing or freezing in February in the Bodleian. Furthermore, at the library one meets kindred spirits, becomes part of the gossip circles, and is stimulated to explore unsuspected fields.

Do readers actually learn more from reading under restricted conditions? And are noncirculating copies really likely to be handled any better than circulating ones? Both ideas seem plausible; but testing either would be quite impossible. What is almost certain is that restrictive policies that are conspicuously wise are also impossible. The best of intentions usually produces another fine range of ironies, conundrums, anomalies, Catch-22s, exposed flanks, and vicious circles. Calling on our Keplers for help in setting up intelligent programs, and asking their indulgence in forgoing access—these are likely to be lesser problems than those we will face later on as we ask them for help and sympathy when things go wrong. Let me identify some of the likely problems that will arise.

First, what should be restricted? The decision has actually already been addressed fairly extensively and quite intelligently. Curiously, the basic criteria for "what makes a rare book" identify the targets for conservation, but for somewhat different and strange reasons. Scarcity, for instance, justifies attention in that it reminds us of our precarious ties with the past; the dealer's market value rises with a conservator's anxiety. As for market value, it offers conservators their most convincing cases in arguing with business-minded administrators. Date of publication can also be a handy expedient insofar as it enables us to devote attention first to those easy problems from the age of handmade paper, deferring to later the acid

problems of the nineteenth and twentieth centuries. Add to this the fact
that our bibliophiles are the readers most likely to be attentive and sympathetic to the condition and handling of physical books, and the rare-book
context of conservation becomes clearly understood.

Paul Banks is among the first to specify a different criterion called
"permanent research value."[17] His term is characteristically sensible and
his case typically persuasive; alas, the more closely we look at the idea, the
less happy it becomes. The basic problem is the dynamic nature of research
itself. If we accept a Baconian definition of science, we can proceed in
comfort. We are now accommodating the doctoral students who rewrite
their professors' dissertations; and eventually we will be maintaining
libraries to be worshiped as much as fought over. But for better or worse,
Baconian science is now past us. Researchers now think of "paradigms,"
arising, changing, and disappearing with later "scientific revolutions."
Even our historians enjoy evoking the concept of "revisionism," whether
noisily or implicitly. This search for new perspectives, of course, is precisely what produces what Gordon Ray once identified as the "fertile
chaos" of scholarship. Rather than proposing that there is any such thing
as "permanent research value," we might better remember that most
anything—and therefore everything—has potential value. If Bernard
Bailyn is justified in advising us to preserve "latent" as well as "manifest"
history,[18] how can we ever wish to save anything less than the totality of the
record of civilization? Thomas Tanselle, for instance, argues effectively for
preserving book jackets[19] and for collecting other than first editions.[20] Such
visions are what keep our research librarians young in spirit as they
continue to scramble for the document they just threw away.[21]

One genre in particular, meanwhile, may deserve special isolated
treatment. Periodicals are an endless and limitless nuisance to librarians,
but they are also the very lifeblood of scholars; and while no drastic action
seems appropriate just now, for several reasons we may need to consider
extensive and arbitrary restrictions very soon. However hopelessly ill-
defined the genre itself, whatever it is, is eating up more and more of our
budgets. Its internal content is under weak bibliographical control
through conventional cataloging, and thus readers will want to browse.
This last factor, and the relatively predictable short-term growth patterns,
probably argue against compact storage at the same time. The contents, in
their customary brevity, are particularly vulnerable to the devastation of
the copying machine, all the more's the pity since these are books that so
often have been oversewn. If any one area needs attention more than others
in the stacks, this is probably the one.

In discussing specific materials, that flamboyant notion of an "endangered titles list"[22] may yet be worth scholarly consideration. The problem
lies not with the sentiment behind the ecological analogy but with the

extravagant implications of the idea. Of the (wildly guessing) 30 million titles issued since Gutenberg's day, an amazing and disturbing proportion exist in single recorded copies. (Of the early Low German titles in Borchling and Classen for instance, Taylor Starck tells us that 60 percent exist in single copies, and only 14 percent in three copies or more.[23] Modern titles—Wright American fiction, for instance—survive better; but when— to paraphrase Huxley on Pope—do we have enough copies to be out of danger?) Furthermore, bibliographers stand in justified awe at what Falconer Madan called the "duplicity of duplicates." Even so, there is good work to be done in developing conservation programs with the bibliographical record in mind.

We should also remember that today's most conspicuous, and sometimes the most successful, restriction programs approach the problem from the opposite direction, controlling readers rather than materials. To handle the Dead Sea Scrolls in Jerusalem, or the Book of Kells in Dublin, or the Washington or Adams papers in Boston, one must present established credentials. Restrictions like these, of course, have obvious analogies in the scientific community: it is very difficult, I suspect, to go in off the street in Los Alamos and be allowed to smash a few atoms, or to use "state-of-the-art" machinery in our great research labs. What is called for are credentials, and a "need to know."

Restricting readers is a treacherous business, as public librarians in particular can assure us. My own experience at the Newberry in the early 1960s suggests that the choice is between the arbitrary and ridiculous, and the flexible and ridiculous. Admit only card-carrying members of professional societies? Exclude high school students (thereby allowing high school dropouts to be admitted)? Admit only those over eighteen (thereby excluding the precocious)? Exclude those who demonstrably haven't bathed in six months? Such are among the considerations that always have made and always will make library work essentially labor-intensive, and more to the point, learning-intensive and sensitivity-intensive. As for that frightening phrase, "need to know," it can only evoke the most negative impressions of Big Brother, officially sanctioned research, and intellectual suppression. It is very hard to justify on any grounds, except perhaps in dealing with sleight-of-hand artists or those Christian Scientists[24] with known kleptomaniac tendencies.

Furthermore, the natural—at least, the desirable—outgrowth of greater control is an enlargement (or redefinition) of our rare book facilities. Can we afford this? Even if we should look for a model in such operations, it is well to remember that so many of them are more impressive than functional. The carpets may be thick and the tables big, but usually the paging is inadequate, the room badly controlled (either from the external entry or from the bookstack entry if not from both), the space extravagant, and the noise level high; and the changing needs of readers—for typing, spreading out papers, storing many books, conversation, using the telephone—badly accommodated. Meanwhile, our instincts for control through closed-circuit television do battle with our faith in civil liberties. (I could accept the former; many of my more conservative colleagues could not.) Do we really want *all* of our Keplers around under such circumstances—further remembering their propensities for distracting the staff with idle chatter and endless complaints? Furthermore, in time our Keplers have more than once ended up thinking they own the place.

One sensible-sounding alternative may be seen, mostly in European libraries. One is expected to use a photocopy first, turning to an original only as a "last resort." The practice is beset by two fallacies, the one almost but not quite facetious, the other very real. On the facetious side: how can one expect to see anything at all after one has been blinded by badly designed microform reading equipment? More real: what can one expect to find in the photocopy if one is not alerted by idiosyncrasies not picked up from the original? Occasionally a very well done photofacsimile will suggest differences in paper, such as might point to different printing conditions. But the recently returned holograph music manuscripts in East Berlin clearly show different darkness in the ink on various pages, distinguishing composers' first thoughts from their afterthoughts, such as were not noticeable on the luxurious facsimiles prepared before the War. As for the laboratory documentation in a scientific experiment, it is well to remember that falsification with an eraser will hardly ever be detectable, and never provable, on a photocopy.[25] A scholar needs "best evidence," and for all their great and monumental advantages the problem with photocopies of any kind is that you can't tell what you can't tell. The problem is not one of graphic resolution, of definition being lost; rather, what is lost—the ultimate irreversibility—is the evidence itself. On much published matter there is likely to be no problem, other than the fundamental problem of when to know that you may have a problem.

One step beyond the library-backup to photocopy consultation, in which one has final recourse to the original, is the library set up exclusively for preservation, accessible only through photocopies. This is the library set up by Gordon Williams at the North Pole and moved by Edwin Williams to the Greenland Icecap.[26] By way of contributing to this particular dialogue, let me introduce the possibility of refrigerated bookmobiles, traveling through our Western states disguised as portable silos. Besides confusing the Russians, such a plan would stimulate the national economy (especially the manufacturers of refrigerated bookmobiles), and it would make library statistics in these states all the more impressive. More seriously, we do have an interesting model for restricted access in the *National Register of Microform Masters*. As stated in the introduction to the volumes of the *Register,* the principle is that "no film is listed...which, to the knowledge of the editors, is available for patrons or clients of an institution to use as a reading copy." The principle is well delimited, even if the enforcement is less than trustworthy; and above all, the appropriateness as part of the overall plan for conserving library materials, while very useful, is still secondary.

In 1749 Lord Chesterfield announced to his son: "Due attention to the inside of books, and due contempt for the outside, is the proper relation between a man of sense and his books."[27] His sentiments, miguided as they are, do hold wide favor in our scholarly communities, even in our own community of librarianship as well. At times, considering the vastness and the complexity of the problem, we can understandably sympathize. But for better or worse, the classic distinction between physical form and intellectual content will not go away. No matter how illustrious or preoccupied the scholar, the medium is necessary, with all of its limitations and peculiarities. Our scholars' access is through that medium. And their rights to access extend into the future as much as they exist today. If their own contributions are to be available a hundred years hence, they must be asked to be sensitive to the problem, and sympathetic to the need for policy and to the inevitable shortcomings of our programs. Kepler could be part of that scientific tradition that plotted and thus predicted the courses of the planets. The course of the use of books and libraries through history, on the other hand, if it will or should ever be predictable at all, is a matter to be understood some distance in the future. Conservation and civilization have to depend on one another.

NOTES

1. *See* Kepler, Johannes. "Prooemium." In *Gesammelte Werke,* edited by Max von Caspar, lines 181-84. Munich: C.H. Beck, 1940. (Si ignoscitis, gaudebo; si succensetis, feram; jacio en aleam, librumque scribo, seu praesentibus, seu posteris legendum, nihil interest: expectet ille suum lectorem per annos centum; si Deus ipse per annorum sena millia contemplatorem praestoatus est.)

2. In this discussion it can rather simplistically be assumed that (a) any reader who reads a lot is a scholar, (b) any scholar who stops reading a lot is no longer a scholar, and (c) any further attempt at differentiation would be presumptuous. On such naïve and hopeful assumptions the work of the conservator, necessarily, must be based. This approach would not of course be appropriate to many other discussions of the scholarly use of libraries.

3. Haas, Warren J. "Author's Abstract." In *Preparation of Detailed Specifications for a National System for the Preservation of Library Materials,* compiled by the Association of Research Libraries, p. ii. Washington, D.C.: HEW, 1976.

4. Blades, William. *The Enemies of Books.* London: Elliot Stock, 1888.

5. Adams, Randolph G. "Librarians as Enemies of Books." *Library Quarterly* 7(July 1937):317-31.

6. Land, Robert H. "Defense of Archives Against Human Foes." *American Archivist* 19(1956):122.

7. I say this in respectful deference, of course, to Isaac Asimov's "Foundation and Empire" books.

8. I must confess to having failed to find the best source. Adams's general idea is that he really needed three copies of a given rare book (sometimes specified as the Nuremberg chronicle): one for readers to read, one for exhibition (or, as sometimes cited, for the local Boy Scouts to examine), and one to be preserved for posterity. Other classic differentiations between the kinds of reading would probably be no less usefully applied to the matter of conservation, i.e., Coleridges's sponges, sand-glasses, strain-bags, and mogul diamonds; Richard Heber's show, use, and borrowing (perhaps Adams's model); Sir John Denham's wisdom, piety, delight, and use; and above all Bacon's ants, spiders, and bees analogy, also the essay on studies.

9. Among the few writings on the subject, *see* Jackson, William A. "Some Limitations on Microfilm." *Papers of the Bibliographical Society of America* 35(1941):282-88; and Cummings, Lawrence A. "Pitfalls of Photocopy Research." *Bulletin of the New York Public Library* 65(1961):97-101.

10. Wilson, F.P. "Shakespeare and the 'New Bibliography.'" In *The Bibliographical Society, 1892-1942: Studies in Retrospect.* London: The Bibliographical Society, 1945, p. 95.

11. The distinction is well developed *in* Tanselle, G. Thomas. "Bibliographers and the Library." *Library Trends* 25(April 1977):745-62. *See also,* Brynolfson, Gaylord. "Book as Object." In *Preservation of Library Materials,* edited by Joyce R. Russell, pp. 45-49. New York: Special Libraries Association, 1980.

12. The literature has been well surveyed recently *in* Gapen, D. Kaye, and Milner, Sigrid P. "Obsolescence." *Library Trends* 30(Summer 1981):107-24.

13. Quoted in Starrett, Vincent. "'High Spots' and Other Mysteries." in his *Books Alive,* p. 348. New York: Random House, 1940. Other relevant impressions are suggested *in* Bamberger, Fritz. *Books are the Best Things: An Anthology from Old Hebrew Writings.* Philadelphia: Maurice Jacobs, 1962, p. 14. ("A teacher should not strike his pupil with a book, and the student should not ward off a blow with a book....Do not use a book to protect yourself against sun or smoke. Do not keep books together with food lest mice be lured by the food to nibble at the books. If a book does not close easily, do not force it together with your knees.")

14 Quoted in *LJ Hotline* 10(26 Oct. 1981):1.

15. Collections and analysis of the handling statements distributed by libraries to their readers could be a very useful effort. Notable among these is the one used in the North Library at the British Library (copies of which were kindly supplied by Mr. David Paisey). Some statements involve particular library settings ("Do not put books on the floor"), but others would seem to be more widely applicable ("Do not lean on books while reading," or "Do not write on paper resting on a book, open or closed"). Above all, the tone of Nicolas Barker's statement strikes a happy balance between talking down and talking up to the readers. For an alternative that captures the element of slapstick, see the 24-page pamphlet prepared by the Public Archives of Canada in 1977, entitled, *A Guide to the Preservation of Archival Materials.* Bibliographic instruction, meanwhile, should not be overlooked as a forum for introducing to readers the concern for proper handling.

16. The basic points are well explored *in* Press, Richard L. "The Non-Circulating Academic Research Library: A Paradigm for Change." *Library Journal* 98(1973):2821-23.

17. Banks, Paul N. "Some Problems in Book Conservation." *Library Resources & Technical Services* 12(1968):332ff.

18. Paraphrased and summarized in *LJ Hotline* 10(26 Oct. 1981):1.

19. Tanselle, G. Thomas. "Book-Jackets, Blurbs, and Bibliographers." *The Library,* 5th series, 26(1971):91-134.

20. _____ . "Non-Firsts." In *Collectible Books: Some New Paths,* edited by Jean Peters, pp. 1-31. New York: Bowker, 1979.

21. Under the circumstances, particularly relevant to this discussion is Asheim, Lester. "Not Censorship but Selection." *Wilson Library Bulletin* 53(1953):63-67.

22. The basic statement, to my knowledge, is the brief presentation in the second paragraph under the rubric 4.4.2.1 *in* Association of Research Libraries. *Preparation of Detailed Specifications for a National System for the Preservation of Library Materials.* Washington, D.C.: HEW, 1976, p. 20.

23. Starck, Taylor. "The Fate of Old Low German Printings: A Preliminary Report." In *Humaniora; Essays in Literature, Folklore, Bibliography Honoring Archer Taylor....* Locust Valley, N.Y.: J.J. Augustin, 1960, pp. 69-77.

24. The legend, whether in fact true or not, is described, for instance, *in* Braden, Charles S. *Christian Science Today.* Dallas: Southern Methodist University Press, 1969, pp. 187-89.

25. Scientific experiments, to be accepted by the scientific community, must be replicable; but meanwhile, the precise evidence on which the inferences were based, or even the exact conditions necessary for the replication cannot always be uncontrovertably specified in the published description. It is not always so much that the limitations of the publication format will exclude the detailed peripheral information that specifies exactly what evidence was recorded and what delimitations were accepted, but rather that the delimitations are themselves likely to be the subject of subsequent concern. Archival preservation of raw data and other primary records is likely to be ultimately crucial, commensurate of course with the protection of such confidence as may be appropriate in work with human subjects. The importance of primary evidence should haunt the reader of such major writings on scientific frauds as Zuckerman, Harriet. "Deviant Behavior and Social Control in Science." In *Deviance and Social Change,* edited by Edward Sagarin, pp. 87-138. Beverly Hills, Calif. and London: Sage Publications, 1977; also for some of the discussions of specific instances, *see* Willmott, Peter. "Integrity in Social Science—the Upshot of Scandal." *International Social Science Journal* 29(1977):333-36; or Hunt, Morton. "A Fraud that Shook the World of Science." *New York Times Magazine,* 1 Nov. 1981, pp. 42-75 *passim.* In this field, the work of the Joint Committee on the Archives of Science and Technology (involving the Society of American Archivists, the History of Science Society, the Society for the History of Technology, and the Association of Records Managers and Administrators) is particularly important; and a key document is their "Premilinary Report" on *The Documentation of Science and Technology in America: Needs and Opportunities,* May 1980, see especially pp. 19-21. An important related perspective is provided *in* Lide, David R., Jr. "Critical Data for Critical Needs." *Science* 212(19 June 1981):1343-49.

26. Williams, Edwin E. "Deterioration of Library Collections Today." *Library Quarterly* 40(1970):16.

27. Lord Chesterfield to his son, letter 174, 10 Jan. 1749, as quoted *in* his *Works.* New York: Harper, 1855, p. 239.

E. DALE CLUFF

Director of Library Services
Morris Library
Southern Illinois University at Carbondale

The Role and Responsibility
of the Library in
Preservation and Conservation

INTRODUCTION

This institute has been a fine learning experience for me. It has offered a valuable mix of preservation topics. It is an important link in the chain of relatively recent meetings about a subject receiving increasing attention. Admittedly, no program can expect to be all things to all people, but this one has offered much to many. In two and a half days we have briefly dipped into the past, spent considerable time on the present and tried to focus on the future. Many questions have been asked, some have been answered and some directions have been established. It is to be hoped that each person will leave this institute with some valuable information, a greater awareness of the magnitude of the problem, a renewed determination to find answers to his/her library's preservation needs, or at least a desire to contribute to the resolution of the problems still facing us in this multifaceted and challenging field.

Those preceding me have shared valuable insights into this complex and important matter. These insights come from pioneers as well as from recent entrants in the field. Preservation of library materials literature dates back several years but becomes substantial during the 1970s and is proliferating now. The field is so new that terminology is still being defined, a philosophy is still emerging, a rationale is still developing, approaches are still being sought, and library administrators are still seeking ways to fund library preservation programs. In fact, this library administrator is still wondering why he was even invited to participate in this program with such notables. Perhaps my contribution stems from experience in research libraries generally, and from almost two years of involvement with a rapidly developing conservation program at Southern Illinois University at Carbondale (SIUC) specifically, neither of which qualifies me as an expert no matter how you define the word. However, with excellent help from some of those who have spoken earlier and from my own conservation colleagues, especially Carolyn Morrow, I shall launch into what I see as the role and responsibility of the library in preservation and conservation.

While reading a 1977 article by Terry Belanger,[1] who is involved in conservation from a rare books point of view, I was struck by the question he seemed to be asking: "Why do we acquire for our libraries that for which we cannot care?" A simple question, but one for which there is no simple answer. On the one hand, we weakly argue that we don't intend to keep for long periods of time much of what is acquired for our libraries. On the other hand, we boast that we acquire research materials to support long-standing academic programs knowing that they will exist for many years. We proudly point out that we acquire materials for new and developing fields of knowledge. No matter how you look at it, we *are* building library collections for the future. Though we discard some material along the way, we purposefully keep, for as long as possible, the majority of our material because it contains information which supports the research and curricular needs of our institution.

We spend thousands of dollars to install security systems and pay people to sit at library exits to "insure" that materials are properly charged so they will be returned for future use. We also identify many of our resources as noncirculating because of their value. Now the obvious paradox: we acquire for the future, and build in elaborate and extremely expensive tracking (circulation control) and security systems, yet pay little attention to the quality of the vehicle in which the information is carried (paper, film, etc.), the manner in which it is handled, and the environment in which it is stored. We will subject the information carrier to adverse humidity, light, temperature and pollutant levels in its storage place; rough handling by unconcerned or untrained staff; book returns which could double as trash compactors; stressful shelving positions; and environments vulnerable to water, fire, insect, and rodent damage. A comprehensive library preservation program would address all of these issues as well as disaster preparedness and appropriate binding, repair, and restoration practices.

To do the job right would be too costly, right? I would argue that to do the job poorly is even more costly. This statement may be an oversimplification, but let's take a closer look. Basically, we have two challenges. The first is how to cope with the resources and facilities we presently have or, to state it another way, how to cure the ailments caused by so many past mistakes. The second challenge is to insure that steps are taken to prevent the same mistakes from happening again. In other words, we are faced with impeding the deterioration of our present collections on one hand and with preventing deterioration of future collections on the other. The first challenge is probably the most expensive and overwhelming. The second is more manageable. I dare say that every library could begin today, at little or no cost, to apply preventive measures which would save considerable future "cure" money.

WHERE TO BEGIN

To begin with, before progress can be made, those who are responsible for the decision making and policy setting in the library must become aware of the need for a comprehensive conservation program. This awareness is increasing in the profession as a result of the relatively recent literature blitz, programs such as this which have been held over the past decade, the emphasis placed on it in the American Library Association (ALA), the Association of Research Libraries (ARL) project, and many other state and nationally funded activities.

Once administration is convinced of the need, the next step is to establish the need in the minds of library staff at all levels. Robert H. Patterson suggests the use of a well-chosen committee to insure a broad-based approach. I agree with Patterson that:

> It is vital that conservation be viewed from a systems approach involving the entire library context in which materials are selected, processed, housed, utilized, and cared for. To concentrate upon only one of these elements is to lose sight of many important factors in the life-cycle of materials and the ways in which they are used.[2]

The committee approach has several advantages. Patterson continues:

> if the committee membership is broadly and thoughtfully constituted, conservation education is disseminated widely through the library, into areas where this heightened awareness is most useful and applicable. This approach also insures a broad base of support for conservation programs, creating a general interest rather than a narrow-based concern coming from only one department or division. It is important...that all areas within the library with real or potential conservation responsibilities be involved in the committee.[3]

It is so important to have broad staff interest and support early on that I'd like to spend a few moments on this. Preservation and conservation are generally viewed by staff as costly add-ons to existing demands on their time and budget, instead of as valuable processes which, if interspersed through all aspects of their jobs, will result in better service to the library user as well as in dollar savings. Like most changes, if conservation and preservation are viewed as being imposed from the top or as being the concern of only a small number in the organization, the program is in for a rocky future. Conversely, problems will appear if the preservation program is too heavily dependent upon committee efforts. Strong support from the top is also needed for a successful preservation program.

To strike a balance, then, between a top- and grassroots-implemented program is the goal. This balance will insure strong support and commitment at all levels for the program. Leadership at the top is needed to train, direct, listen, design, set resource support parameters and evaluate, while staff is needed to engender enthusiasm, carry out the plans, give initial feedback, educate the library user, and make program modification suggestions. A program, especially a new one, will function much more smoothly and will have a greater chance of success if this kind of teamwork is evident.

Let me illustrate. A smoothly functioning organization might be visualized as a sphere rolling along at a comfortable pace. All parts of the organization are interacting with a single purpose. Then one day, someone suggests an idea which necessitates change in the organization. This change causes stress because it requires adjustments in schedules, relocation of parts of the organization, additional training, and changes in thought patterns, routines, and working partners. The change (in this case, the addition of a conservation program) requires additional funds, people, supplies, and equipment, or a reallocation of such. The stress becomes more severe in those parts of the organization from which resources are being siphoned. As this siphoning occurs, stress increases and the organization takes on the shape of a sphere with a bulge on its surface. The

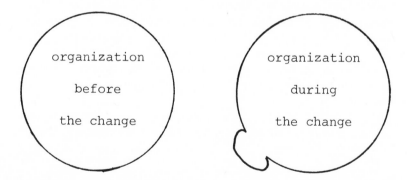

organization
before
the change

organization
during
the change

bulge represents the part of the organization into which the dollar and human resources, including considerable human energies, are being directed. We all know how difficult it is to handle a ball containing a bulge. This is the period in the life of the organization which is most crucial. The goal is to round out the sphere and to get all parts of the organization readjusted and working smoothly together again. This can be done more quickly when leadership and staff are together at the genesis of the change. When they are together, stress is minimal, resistance to the change low, commitment high, and the program successful. The organizational sphere adjusts, the bulge deflates and it is rolling smoothly once again. An organization, like a human body, has a way of either severing or incorporating an appendage. If the appendage (bulge) is seen as unnecessary, it is rejected. Conversely, if the appendage is seen as helpful, it will be accepted and willingly incorporated. A comprehensive preservation program, if handled well, will be accepted by most staff and become not only a valuable, but essential, part of the operation of the library.

Let's return to the topic of where to begin. Once a committee has been selected, the next task is to assess the conservation needs in some detail. Some outside help may be necessary at this stage unless the organization presently has a knowledgeable person in this area. This process is the critical one. This is the stage at which broad understanding and realization throughout the organization is necessary. The more people involved in identifying and agreeing upon the needs at the outset, the more cooperation will be realized at time of implementation. During the needs assessment time, the following will be evaluated:

1. the physical plant in which the materials are stored, including lights, temperature, humidity, cleanliness, filtration systems, potential water leakage and fire hazards, and building security;
2. the manner in which books are presently handled, including number packed on the shelf, how they are placed on the shelf, manner in which they are bound, style of book returns and drop boxes, manner in which books are handled during photocopying of pages, how books are transported, adequate shelf size for varying book sizes, manner in which materials are packed for shipping and mailing, and even what types of materials are best suited for circulating as against those which ought not circulate;
3. the physical condition of the books presently on the library shelves, paying particular attention to dirt, brittleness, disrepair, evidence of fungal growth, insect or rodent damage, fading, etc.

After the needs have been firmly established, priorities must be set. The needs assessment study will likely leave the staff feeling overwhelmed. The universe must now be broken into manageable units and then placed in order of approach. Unfortunately, items needing the most attention may not be affordable for some time. List them, however, and see that they begin to appear in future planning statements. I speak of items such as changing the environment in the building, securing the building, changing or modifying lighting systems, and conservation treatment of valuable books, maps, and manuscripts. Placing these items in planning statements will likely influence allocation of supporting funds from the parent institution. It is important to express these needs in such a manner as to influence the parent institution to include these same items as institutional needs. Institutional needs are carefully reviewed by governing bodies such as boards of trustees. The ultimate goal is to have these needs reach legislative bodies which allocate funds. While seeking funding for long-term programs, short-term goals can be accomplished.

As priorities and order of approach begin to sort out, the framework for a conservation policy will evolve and procedures will begin to take shape. Both of these should be codified to be used to implement the program. Carolyn Morrow has created a "mock" policy statement "designed to provide logical guidelines and outline optimum conditions for the conservation of a research library collection."[4]

ADMINISTRATIVE STRUCTURE

If a committee is used in the beginning stages for assessing needs, establishing priorities and drafting policy statements, at some point a determination must be made as to what the eventual organizational structure for the conservation program will be. Size of budget, collection, and staff as well as complexity and degree of need are all factors important to this matter.

Under some circumstances such as during dire financial times, a committee might be the appropriate long-term approach for operating a conservation program. The best approach, however, is to hire a trained conservation person and to provide staff support to carry out the program. Perhaps a combination of these two approaches might work.

Regardless of the approach, some important factors should be considered. The reporting relationship is critical. Ideally, the committee chairperson or the conservation librarian should be responsible to the individual in the organization who has stewardship over all the areas which will be touched by the conservation program. This is important for a number of reasons.

1. Budget allocation should be administered to include the entire program. It would be unfortunate if more than one fiscal officer were involved since there is a potential for competition for money and an imbalance in the program.

2. When conflicts arise, judgment must be exercised which reflects the entire program, not just a portion.
3. It is usually preferable for policy to be enforced by the person overseeing the entire program.
4. The higher up the administrative ladder the person responsible for the program is, the more clout that can be exerted.
5. Staff perception of the value of the conservation program is always influenced by the level of administrative support.
6. A unified conservation program will most likely develop when a single administrator is responsible for it.
7. It eliminates the possibility of conservation being perceived by staff as a stepchild to other programs.

The placement of the conservation program in the organization has another dimension: the functions it should incorporate. Some candidates for inclusion under the conservation umbrella include materials preparation; in-house repair and maintenance, and protective encasement; preparation of items for contract binding; stack maintenance (shelving, shelf-reading, cleaning, etc.); and perhaps a full-scale conservation treatment laboratory. Again, the specific needs of individual libraries will help answer this question.

Another aspect of administrative structure is whether the conservation librarian should be in a staff or line position. Acting in a staff relationship to an administrator provides mobility about the organization but does not allow authority to be exercised by the conservation librarian. Lack of clout can slow progress. In this configuration, the administrator would, of necessity, need to be more directly involved in conservation matters. I believe it preferable to place the conservation person in a line position so that authority and responsibility can be fixed. The position also ought to be at a high enough level so the person can comfortably interact and carry weight with others also holding responsible positions. Darling and Ogden point out that actual organizational patterns varied considerably among some of the libraries which were pioneers in establishing preservation programs, and in every case but one, "the person charged with responsibility for the program was placed in a line rather than staff position and given specific authority to develop and implement programs."[5]

PLANNING

With the needs assessment completed, priorities established and administrative structure determined, it is time to forge ahead, to lay plans for implementation. It is hardly necessary to remind ourselves how important it is to plan any program carefully. Conservation is no exception. It is vital to involve all people in the early stages of planning whose areas of responsibility are going to be affected by the conservation program. Change will be more readily accepted and more strongly supported if these individuals have an opportunity to influence the program at the outset.

Planning will involve several facets. The literature contains some helpful suggestions on ways to approach planning. Darling states it succinctly:

> The concrete steps to be taken to turn priorities from paper plans into concrete programs should be set forth in specific terms, with realistic target dates. This may involve further analysis of existing resources (staff, space, equipment, and money), and should lead directly into the organizational modifications that will, usually, be the first step of plan implementation.[6]

FINANCIAL BACKING

In terms of financial support, as far as I can tell, Patterson's observation in 1979 still stands: "Conservation is so new a subject of national concern that no one has addressed in the literature the question of funding sources. Each library must simply strive to identify agencies, organizations, and individuals potentially offering support."[7] Start-up funds provided by granting agencies are helpful but in the final analysis, those institutions which provide their own funds will be the most successful.

By and large, those libraries which have forged ahead have done so out of dogged determination and have made inroads into this massive problem. They have ususally reallocated funds in addition to the normal binding budget to begin in a small way to make an impact on the beginnings of a more comprehensive conservation program.

The size of a library's commitment to conservation can best be measured by the percentage of its budget allocated to conservation. How much is enough for an adequate conservation program? I am told that Newberry spends 10 percent of its total budget on conservation. At a recent conference, it was reported that Jim Haas asked, "Why doesn't every research library take ten percent of its money for new acquisitions and put it into preservation?"[8] At the same meeting Rudy Rogers reported that Yale puts "$800,000 a year into conservation as against a $3,000,000 acquisitions expenditure."[9] This represents 26.6 percent of the acquisition budget. SIUC put 12.6 percent of its acquisitions budget into the conservation program last year. At the University of Utah where Paul Foulger is the conservation officer, 10 percent of the library's acquisitions budget is committed to this effort.

Deciding how much of the budget should go into conservation is difficult. But the decision must be made. Ironically, the decision to support binding of library materials was made years ago. Today it is a given. Binding costs are considered an integral part of a library's acquisitions budget. Somehow, we have to broaden our thinking. The responsibility of the library is to decide where conservation fits in its program and service priorities, then to support it with dollars and administrative clout. Frankly, I am not prepared to recommend a percentage-of-budget figure that a library should put toward conservation; however, I would recommend that this would be an appropriate topic for discussion in individual libraries and also at the state and national levels within ALA's Preservation of Library Materials Section, Association of Research Libraries, and other forums. Perhaps the Northeast Document Conservation Center or the Western States Conservation Congress have considered this and could share their thinking about it.

We have a responsibility to provide funding to support conservation beyond the library binding level. The following are positive steps which can be taken by library administrators to help the situation:

1. Encourage and participate in preparing proposals to outside funding agencies for assistance.
2. Work with other library administrators in the state and region to raise the awareness of conservation needs on the part of legislators.
3. Seek special funding from the administrative person(s) to whom the library administrator reports, e.g., the vice-president for academic affairs.
4. Reallocate funds internally to support the program. One idea is to watch student wage expenditures during the year and shift unused wages to specific preplanned conservation or preservation projects. End-of-year wage money could be used in any number of ways, e.g., leather book treatment, encapsulation, etc.
5. Change existing policies, procedures, and staffing to allow for immediate implementation of low-cost procedures.
6. Identify environmental and building matters which need modification and bring these to the attention of those on campus who have responsibility for these concerns.

Most of these steps require time; however, something can be done on each almost immediately. If a start on each of these steps was accomplished today, a decided difference would be recognized a year from now, considerable change would be evident three years away, and great strides would be made in five years. I firmly believe that there are very few institutions which couldn't find the money to begin a conservation program. With a firm commitment and resolve to begin a program, it can be done over time.

The two conservation programs of which I am most aware, those of University of Utah (UU) and Southern Illinois University at Carbondale, had different beginnings. At Utah, Kem Newby, a biology professor emeritus who worked as a volunteer in the library for several years, can be given partial credit for the conservation program currently underway. Part of this professor's voluntary work was done in the special collections area where he helped protect and treat rare or brittle manuscripts. The importance of this professor's self-initiated work came to the attention of the library administration. Seeds for a comprehensive conservation program had thus been planted. After plans had been laid to launch an expanded conservation program, the administration reallocated internal positions and funding. The money from an appropriate vacant position was used to hire Paul Foulger as conservator and support costs were gathered over a period of time from other areas by consolidating procedures, reducing or eliminating some services, and by maintaining flat budgets in some lines in order to use small budget increases for conservation. As the emerging conservation program took shape, the University of Utah became aware of the availability of the equipment which had been a part of the conservation laboratory of Colton and Nancy Storm, formerly of the Newberry Library. Further reallocation of funds made it possible for the Marriott Library at UU to acquire the equipment.

At SIUC, an idea conceived by the Special Collections Librarian of an expanded conservation program generated a National Endowment for the Humanities (NEH) challenge grant. This paid off by realizing funds from four sources. These combined dollars were used to hire Carolyn Clark Morrow, create a modest laboratory, and treat the John Dewey Papers. Three years later the program was shifted to state funds by receiving a base budget increase to pay the conservator's salary, and some internal reallocation of funds to support the rest of the operation. Some CETA positions were also successfully sought and became part of the program for about a year.

These two approaches were considerably different but both were workable and certainly successful. Both started about the same time, both have had some funding challenge over the years and both had their genesis in special collections departments. Both programs are strong and will continue. They have proven their worth. Both programs deserve more financial backing because there is so much to do. But, again, other programs must also be supported.

ENVIRONMENTAL CONTROL

The control of the library environment is the responsibility of the library administration and is the single, most important aspect of materials' preservation. If a library could be designed to address the environmental needs of library collections it might contain at the minimum the following facilities and features.

—The building materials used and the construction would be as earthquake and fire resistant as possible.

—It would be built on ground which would not be easily flooded or would be designed so that collections would not be endangered by heavy rains, flash floods, etc.

—The roof would be pitched and designed to insure against pooling of water.

—The insulation would be of such quality that temperature and humidity could be maintained at consistent levels and at levels conducive to storing the type of materials housed in the library.

—The heating, cooling and humidity controls would allow for differences to be established in various parts of the building, thus tailoring the air for the requirements of special materials.

—Filtering systems would be installed to eliminate, as far as possible, such gases as sulfur dioxide, hydrogen sulfide, nitrogen dioxide, ozone, and just plain dirt and dust.

—Building systems, including water pipes, would be located well away from stack areas and would not be on the roof directly above library storage areas.

—The building would be constructed in such a way to insure against encroachment by rodents and insects. If rooms are to be used for eating or food preparation, they would be far removed from areas where collections were to be housed.

—Windows would be screened to filter out ultraviolet rays in sunlight.

—Lights installed would be incandescent or, if fluorescent, would be screened to filter out ultraviolet energy.

—Fire extinguishing systems would operate specific to the area of the fire.

—Stacks installed would be of heavy construction and would accommodate shelves of sufficient size to hold adquately different-sized books without their hanging over the edge. Shelves would be tied together by braces across the top to reduce the possibility of tipping and would not contain rough or sharp edges or surfaces which could cut or snag books.

—Book return systems would be designed to lessen the distance that books must drop, reduce the amount of rough jamming together, and mitigate deep stacking of books.

—An adequate fire and burglar alarm system would be installed as an early warning system.

COLLECTION DEVELOPMENT

I would like to close by emphasizing an important element of the library conservation program which was touched on earlier by Mr. Patterson and others but which warrants repeating: preservation through collection development.

A significant part of a library budget (second only to salaries and wages) is allocated for the acquisition of materials for the collection. These large sums of money are being expended for books and other materials which, if they are not subjected to some form of disaster during their lifetime, are destined to deteriorate in a relatively few years. We enhance our collections by the addition of appropriate information which is wrapped in different packages or is carried on different vehicles. We can often acquire the intellectual content at different prices based upon the information carrier. (Parenthetically, I recognize that we do acquire some information because of the package in which it is wrapped.) Of prime importance when considering the acquisition of material is user convenience. Quick access to the information is an important consideration which relates directly to the format in which the information is packaged. I believe that we should add another dimension to our acquisitions consideration. This dimension is longevity. This is not to suggest that we should acquire everything on acid-free paper or on silver halide microform. It *is* to suggest, however, that we project our thinking to include the dimension of access in 100 or more years from the time of acquisition. When this dimension is added to the acquisition decision process, a more usable collection will result.

Some factors to be considered, once it has been determined that the information should be acquired for the collection, are:

1. whether the information is printed on acid-free paper;
2. whether it is in a hard- or soft-bound cover;
3. if it is in paperback, whether it ought to be bound before it is put into the hands of the user;
4. if is to be bound, whether it should be bound in-house using less expensive materials or be sent to a library bindery;
5. whether or not it is available in a format other than paper, such as microform (if it available in microform, whether it would be more desirable to acquire in that format);
6. if microform is selected, whether it is of a type, such as silver halide, for which longevity standards exist (it is important to remember, however, that film is only archival if it is processed and stored in archival conditions);

7. whether or not the item will circulate, be used in the library, or be used only under supervision;
8. the condition of retrospective materials. If possible, it should be determined before purchase whether the material contains mold or insects, or whether it is in disrepair.

Considering these matters before acquisition can realize long-term benefits in both user convenience and dollar savings.

Ongoing development of a library collection includes adding, withdrawing, relocating, reformatting, and replacing materials. Among the materials added to the collection are periodicals. Most of these arrive in paper cover format. These single issues are generally placed on the shelves for public use and at the end of the year are gathered and bound together to form a new physical volume to add to the continuing run. Based on the collection development policy and user needs, careful consideration should be given to whether retrospective volumes of some of the titles would be more suitable in microfilm or microfiche. There are several advantages to receiving the current issues in paper and the annual output in microform, not the least of which are: (1) space savings; (2) elimination of the need to seek replacement copies before being bound; (3) elimination of the need to retrieve, sort, process and package for binding; (4) the ability to use some of the money earmarked for binding for the purchase of microform periodicals; and (5) being able to keep the film longer than the paper if it is maintained properly.

When an item is determined to be in a condition where it is physically no longer usable, the following options are open: withdraw it from the collection and discard it; replace it with the exact edition, a reprint edition, or a book with similar content; replace it by reformatting, e.g., microform; or place it where it can't be used except on rare occasions.

Factors such as those mentioned above are generally not considered part of the collection development program of a library. Under a comprehensive preservation program, however, they are an important part of collection development. Administrators should take steps to educate staff responsible for strengthening library collections to make preservation through collection development an integral part of the overall collection development program.

CONCLUSION

Now that we know where to begin, what the administrative structure should be, how to support financially the beginnings of a preservation program, and what constitutes the components of a comprehensive preservation program, let's go back to our libraries and either start or improve the program.

NOTES

1. Belanger, Terry. "The Price of Preservation." *Times Literary Supplement* 3947 (18 Nov. 1977):1358-59.

2. Patterson, Robert H. "Organizing for Conservation." *Library Journal* 104(15 May 1979):1116.

3. Ibid., p. 1117.

4. Morrow, Carolyn C. *A Conservation Policy Statement for Research Libraries* (Occasional Papers No. 139). Urbana-Champaign: University of Illinois Graduate School of Library Science, 1979, p. 2.

5. Darling, Pamela W., and Ogden, Sherelyn. "From Problems Perceived to Programs in Practice: The Preservation of Library Resources in the U.S.A., 1956-1980." *Library Resources & Technical Services* 25(Jan./March 1981):9-29.

6. Darling, Pamela W. "A Local Preservation Program: Where to Start." *Library Journal* 101(15 Nov. 1976):2347.

7. Patterson, "Organizing," p. 1119.

8. *LJ/SLJ Hotline* 10(26 Oct. 1981):3.

9. Ibid., p. 3.

DISCUSSION

Richard H. Kaige (Illinois State Library, Normal): Do you have a person on your staff who does retrospective bibliography?

Dale Cluff: I see that encompassed under our present program in the brittle books program (e.g., looking at the disrepair of volumes on the shelf). There is a systematic program of going to the shelf by those individuals in conservation to identify the brittle books. That was the area that I talked about in the presentation which is causing us a little anxiety. Once that is done, then, the subject librarian or the subject bibliographer is asked whether it is important to retain that item in the collection. If so, then the conservation staff determines in which way it would be best to replace it.

Andrew L. Makuch (University of Arizona Library, Tucson): Are there separate funds for the replacement of books administered by the preservation people? Do you know of any situation where funds are in existence for replacement?

Cluff: Yes. But it's not at our institution and that is one of the areas, I think, we could look at. Let's see, who of those here with conservation programs have a separate budget for the replacement of books? One—that institution is Texas A&M.

Gerald Lundeen (Graduate School of Library Science, University of Hawaii, Honolulu): I'd like to add one additional task to the list that you gave us for the preservation officer—that is, education of staff and, perhaps, patrons. Along that line I have to say I am somewhat sympathetic to the subject experts if they are not provided with some guidance in making the decisions about the proper way to go with brittle books.

Cluff: I appreciate that—that's a good comment.

Karen L. Sampson (University of Nebraska at Omaha): How did your commitment to preservation as a library administrator develop, and what suggestions do you have for us to develop awareness and commitment in administrators?

Cluff: I really can't point to a particular day or time or article or person which developed my thinking or developed the level of commitment that I have. I suppose that it was just a gradual working in various aspects of the overall library which caused that. Certainly meeting people and associating with others like people attending this conference also contributed. A lot of the credit goes to Carolyn Morrow, Paul Foulger, and other conservators who share the same commitment.

As to how to convince or help influence library administrators, I feel strongly that in those areas where library staff know the most about preservation—e.g., serials, binding, local mending and repair persons, persons who work with special collections, rare books, manuscripts and archives—these persons will be pounding on the desk of the administrator in a kind and tactful way for the cause of preservation. I think that any open administrator, trying to do a job for the overall good of the organizational operation of the library, will eventually become tuned in. In our own library, I ask for a planning statement from every area. Every year, these planning statements should have an area built into them asking for comments and rationale for a comprehensive preservation program.

Carolyn Clark Morrow (Southern Illinois University at Carbondale): I'd like to add two things to what Dale said, and that is, first, tell the administrator it's really going to save money in the long run, and, next, you say that everybody else is doing it. If we don't do it, we're going to look bad.

Gerald Gibson (Library of Congress, Washington, D.C.): How many libraries which have conservation programs are involved, in any way, with actively conserving newspaper materials? (*Editors' note*: There was a show of hands from librarians from six such libraries.) Second question, you spoke of budget in general. Is there any active thought at all in applying a portion of this budget to nonpaper conservation? Do you have any thoughts on that?

Cluff: If you are asking about our specific institution, we hope that our overall conservation program includes those materials. One of the problems that we have at Southern Illinois University at Carbondale is the level at which the conservation program reports. Conservation reports to me through the head of the serials department. However, that excludes a large portion of the overall organization, the Learning Resources Services on campus, which is housed in the same building as the library. Learning Resources Services does not report to me but to the Dean of Library Affairs.

Recognizing that there is a need for conserving nonpaper materials, the conservation individuals are aware of and sympathetic to these needs and as we meet in administrative council, they discuss those needs at that level. Here is the very thing that I brought up in my paper—the need for the conservation individuals reporting to the highest level in the overall program. My budget is not used in the Learning Resources Services area. However, we do have a lot of nonprint materials in Library Services. If we are talking about the overall environment which is monitored constantly by our conservation people and if we are talking about using nonprint materials for the replacement of brittle books, yes, we are allocating budget as part of the conservation budget to nonpaper preservation.

Gibson: Do you really consider that simply the accident of application of a portion of your budget to preservation of nonpaper materials, because they happen to be in the same building where you are keeping a basic temperature and humidity level, is an adequate justification of preservation of nonpaper any more than it is an adequate justification of preservation of paper materials?

Cluff: Let me indicate from my past experience and education that I consider myself a print and nonprint individual. I understand what you are saying; however, we are not sorting out paper and nonpaper. We are hoping to involve the whole program.

Morrow: We don't make that distinction in the Morris Library of SIUC. We have nonprint materials in Library Services, and I would remind Dale [Cluff] that we've spent hundreds and hundreds of dollars on better protective encasement for our phonograph records, for example. That was not questioned. We had a whole procedure for improving the storage of those materials and I don't think that anyone considered the bias—print/nonprint—the phonograph records were just part of the collection.

Cluff: When, about a year ago, the request for additional funds for supplies to support that program came across my desk, I did not weigh it as to whether it was paper/nonpaper. I approved it.

CONTRIBUTORS

WILLIAM ANTHONY of Anthony & Associates, Bookbinders, Inc. is a native of Ireland where he served a bookbinding apprenticeship from 1942 to 1949. From 1950 to 1962, he was a journeyman in London, England. In 1961, he was a teacher of bookbinding at the Camberwell School of Art in London and became a member of the Guild of Contemporary Bookbinders in that same year. He came to the Fine Binding Studio of Cuneo Press in 1964 serving there until 1971 when he established a partnership with Elizabeth Kner in a Chicago conservation studio.

E. DALE CLUFF is Director of Libraries, Texas Tech University, Lubbock. He was former Director of Library Services at Southern Illinois University at Carbondale. He has held positions in administration, reference, acquisitions, and media at the University of Utah Library. He has served on numerous committees at the state and national level dealing with microforms, standards and budget and has authored articles and delivered papers in these areas. He has been a member of and held offices in the ALA RTSD Reproduction of Library Materials Section and presently he is a consultant to University Microfilms International.

PAMELA W. DARLING is Special Consultant to the National Preservation Program at the Library of Congress, and Lecturer in the Columbia University School of Library Service. As Preservation Specialist at the Office of Management Studies of the Association of Research Libraries from 1980-82, she prepared technical and managerial tools for libraries seeking to expand their preservation programs. She served as the Head of the Preservation Department, Columbia University Libraries (1974-1980), Head of the Preservation Programs Office, Conservation Division, New York Public Library (1973-74) and as Executive Assistant, Processing Department, Library of Congress (1972). She is active in professional organizations, including the American Library Association and the National Conservation Advisory Council. She has authored many articles on the preservation of library materials and is a frequent speaker on the subject.

GERALD D. GIBSON is Head of the Curatorial Section of the Motion Picture, Broadcasting and Recorded Sound Division of the Library of Congress. He is responsible for the housing of 150,000 motion pictures, 1.3 million sound recordings and 50,000 video tapes thereby becoming involved in many aspects of the Library's preservation activities. This collection includes every kind of recording from wax cylinders to quadrophonic discs and audiovisual media from nitrate film to video disc. Prior to coming to this position in 1978, Mr. Gibson held other positions in music librarianship at the Library of Congress and at the Eastman School of Music. He has held numerous offices and been a member of many committees including serving currently as the chairperson of the Association for Recorded Sound Collections' Associated Audio Archives, Working Group for a Union Catalog of Sound Recordings; and as a member of the American National Standards Committee Z-39, Subcommittee K (Standards for Indexing) and of the International Copyright Commission, International Association of Sound Archives. He has become well known for his bibliographies of discography.

CAROLYN HARRIS is Head of the Preservation Department at Columbia University. She has been a manuscript cataloger, Humanities Research Center, University of Texas at Austin, where her responsibilities also included developing and coordinating the preservation program. In 1981, she assumed her present position where she is responsible for a microform production facility and its bibliographic support unit, an in-house bindery and repair laboratory, and other system-wide preservation activities. She was one of the twelve participants in the Institute on the Development and Administration of Programs for the Preservation of Library Materials. She is the author of "Mass Deacidification" in the *Library Journal* preservation series and is active in ALA, RTSD's PLMS.

KATHRYN LUTHER HENDERSON is Associate Professor of Library and Information Science, Graduate School of Library and Information Science, University of Illinois at Urbana-Champaign, where she teaches courses related to cataloging and classification, bibliographic organization and control, and technical services. Preservation and conservation concerns are a part of the technical services seminar. She was the editor of the proceedings of two previous Allerton Park Institutes: *Trends in American Publishing* and *Major Classification Systems: the Dewey Centennial*. In addition, her paper on serials cataloging is a part of the proceedings of the Allerton Institute on *Serials Publications in Large Libraries*. She edited *MARC Uses and Users* in the School's Clinic on Library Applications of Data Processing series and has authored works on the history of descriptive cataloging.

WILLIAM T HENDERSON is Binding and Preservation Librarian and Associate Professor of Library Administration at the University of Illinois at Urbana-Champaign. For over fifteen years he has worked on a system-wide basis with the binding and preservation aspects of a large university library. He has been instrumental in developing a local in-house mending and repair section into a conservation facility. He serves as chairperson of the Library's Preservation Committee. He was a consultant for the planning of the 1980 Conservation Workshop of the Illinois Association of

College and Research Libraries and shared in the leadership of the sessions devoted to Practical Library Conservation Techniques. No stranger to Allerton Park Institutes, he previously presented a paper on "Serials Binding—A Librarian's View" at the 1969 conference on Serials Publications in Large Libraries.

LEEDOM KETTELL is president and chief operating officer at Gaylord Bros., Inc. In January 1981, he was appointed to his present position with Gaylord Bros., Inc. a firm founded some eighty-five years ago which has concentrated on serving the domestic and international market for library supplies, furniture and systems. In the past five years, the firm has expanded its line of products designed for the preservation of library materials. Before coming to this position, he served in sales, marketing, administration and planning functions for Xerox Corporation, University Microfilms International, Brodart, and Gaylord. He has lectured at the Institute for Graphic Communications and has participated in the activities of the American Library Association, the National Microfilm Association, and the Information Industry Association. Recently, he has been invited to serve on the Visitor's Council for Syracuse University's School of Information Studies.

D.W. KRUMMEL is a Professor at the Graduate School of Library and Information Science at the University of Illinois at Urbana-Champaign. For over a decade, he has taught courses related to bibliography, library history and research libraries resources. Prior to his coming to the University of Illinois at Urbana-Champaign, he was Associate Librarian of the Newberry Library in Chicago where he was involved in the development and administration of its conservation program. He is the author of several studies in historical and music bibliography and in library history.

LOUISE KUFLIK is owner of her own binding studio—Sky Meadow Bindery—in Suffern, New York. She brings the perspective of both a librarian and a conservator to the decision making processes of conservation and preservation. After serving as Reference Librarian with the Young & Rubicam advertising agency in New York and studying bookbinding with Deborah Evetts, she began as an apprentice in book and document binding and restoration with Carolyn Horton & Associates where she was actively engaged in conservation and preservation activities as well as supervising the work of other employees in these activities.

GERALD LUNDEEN is Associate Professor of the Graduate School of Library Science, University of Hawaii. His background includes a Doctorate of Philosophy from the University of Minnesota in the areas of physical and organic chemistry. He has developed a course at the University of Hawaii related to the conservation of library materials. He has authored numerous publications relating to chemistry and to information storage and retrieval and served as the editor of the fall 1981 issue of *Library Trends* on the "Conservation of Library Materials."

CAROLYN CLARK MORROW is Conservation Librarian at Southern Illinois University at Carbondale. Since 1978 she has been involved in numerous workshops, presentations and lectures on library and archival conservation. In 1980, she conducted a Needs Assessment Survey for the Illinois Cooperative Conservation Program and has been active in promoting cooperative conservation. Her publications include *A Conservation Bibliography for Librarians, Archivists and Administrators* (Whitson, 1979); *A Conservation Policy Statement for Research Libraries* (University of Illinois Graduate School of Library Science *Occasional Papers* No. 139, 1979); *Conservation Treatment Procedures* (Libraries Unlimited, 1982); and *The Preservation Challenge* (Knowledge Industry Publications, 1982).

JAMES ORR is president of Hertzberg-New Method, Inc. He has been engaged in many aspects of the library binding business for over thirty-five years, starting his early training in binding craftsmanship and preservation, in the Monastery Hill Bindery (Chicago), a family business founded by his grandfather. Later he managed the Northwestern Bindery in Evanston, Illinois, and in 1954, assumed the sales and manufacturing duties in the newly formed Hertzberg-New Method bindery in Jacksonville, Illinois. Upon the death of Lawrence Hertzberg in April 1970, Mr. Orr was elected president of Hertzberg-New Method, Inc., a position he holds today. The bindery is one of the largest binderies in the United States and has pioneered some of the newest technology and methodology in binding advancements.

ROBERT H. PATTERSON is Director of Libraries, McFarlin Library at the University of Tulsa. He brings to this topic the perspective of a librarian who has worked in the administrative, collection development, special collection and organizational areas of librarianship in several different libraries. He was a participant in the Columbia University, Graduate School of Library Service, Institute on the Development and Administration of Programs for the Preservation of Library Materials. He attended the 1980 Cambridge (England) Preservation Conference. While Director of Libraries, University of Wyoming, he served as the Leader of the Wyoming Disaster Recovery Assistance Team. Currently he serves as the editor and publisher of the *Conservation Administration News* (CAN) and as a member of the American Library Association (ALA) Resources and Technical Services Division (RTSD), Preservation of Library Materials Section (PLMS).

ANITA WERLING is Manager of Collection Development of University Microfilms International. She was an Assistant Reference Librarian at Fairleigh Dickinson University before coming to University Microfilms International in 1972. Prior to assuming her present position at University Microfilms, she served first as Supervisor of Books and Series and later as Manager of Photographic and Editorial Operations. She is active in ALA organizations relating to reprography resources.

INDEX

Accident preparedness, and self-study, 22

Adams, Randolph, 166, 167

Adhesive binding. *See* Binding, Adhesive.

Administrative structure, of conservation program, 186-87

AIC. *See* American Institute for Conservation

ALA. *See* American Library Association

Alkaline paper making, 80-83

Alum, as source of acid in book paper, 76-77

Alum-rosin size, 58, 74

American Institute for Conservation, 41-42

American Library Association, Preservation of Library Materials Section, 3, 41, 47

American National Standards Institute, 30

Anthony, William, 5-6

ARL Preservation Planning Project. *See* Preservation Planning Project

Arney, Jonathan, 59

Audio materials, characteristics of, 94-96

Backup copies, for magnetic tapes, 102

Bailyn, Bernard, 174

Banks, Paul, 38, 174

Barrow morpholine process, 3, 60-63

Barrow Research Laboratory, 37, 60

Basic Archival Conservation Program, 2, 24

Battelle Columbus Laboratories, 78

Belanger, Terry, 182

Bibliographers, and conservation, 169

Bibliographic control, 32-33, 157

Binding: 119, 123, 137-40, 147; adhesive, 148, 161

Blackstone, William, 167

Blades, William, 166

Bleaching, 58, 83

Book cloth, synthetic, 162

Book Preservation Center (N.Y.), 3, 45, 49

Boorstin, Daniel, 112-13

Booz, Allen, and Hamilton, 39

Boxing, of conserved item, 140

Brittle paper, 149

Buckram, 162

Budget allocation, for conservation program, 15, 186

Buffering agents, and deacidification, 59-60

Calcium hydroxide, 150

CAP. *See* Collection Analysis Project

CAV. *See* Constant Angular Velocity

Cellulose, 73, 74, 76-77

Cellulose acetate lamination, 60

Cellulose nitrate based film, and fire, 97-98

Chemiluminescence studies, 78

Circulating collections, 173

Climate control systems, 30-31. *See also* Environmental control

Cluff, E. Dale, 6

CLV. *See* Constant Linear Velocity

Collection Analysis Project, 2, 20

Collection development, and preservation, 12, 192-93

Colorado Statewide Plan for Preservation, 3, 46-47

Columbia University: conservator training, 26, 43; establishment of preservation department, 39

Committee on Production Guidelines for Book Longevity, 30

Conservation: as alternate career for librarian, 141-42; *v.* preservation, 160

Conservation Administration News, 41

Conservation Advisory Committee (Kentucky), 47

Conservation Center for Art and Historic Artifacts (Philadelphia), 48

Conservation of Cultural Property in the United States, 39-40

Conservation studio, decisions made in, 136-40

Conservators, training of, 11, 26, 43

Constant Angular Velocity, 93, 105

Constant Linear Velocity, 93

Consultants, 50